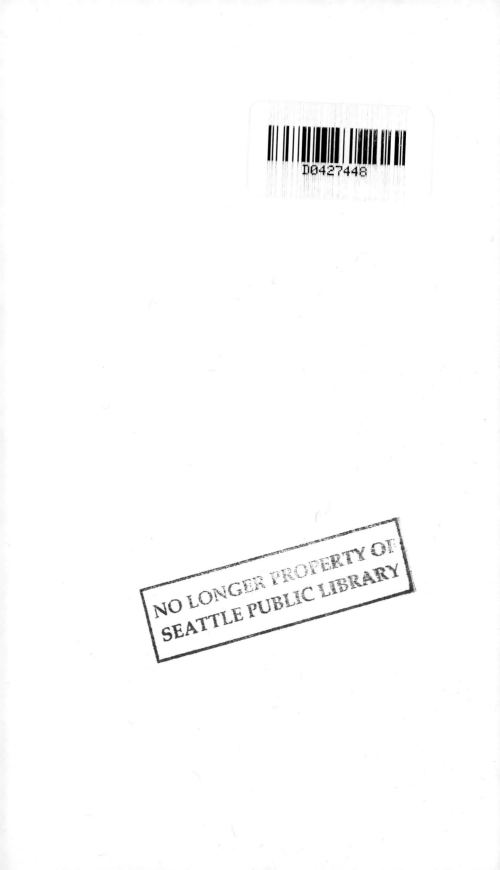

D0427448

The Five Front War

The Five Front War

The Better Way to Fight Global Jihad

Daniel Byman

John Wiley & Sons, Inc.

Published by John Wiley & Sons, Inc., Hoboken, New Jersey
Published simultaneously in Canada

For general information about our other products and services, please contact our Customer Care Department within the United States at (800) 762-2974, outside the United States at (317) 572-3993 or fax (317) 572-4002.

Wiley also publishes its books in a variety of electronic formats. Some content that appears in print may not be available in electronic books. For more information about Wiley products, visit our web site at www.wiley.com.

Library of Congress Cataloging-in-Publication Data:

Byman, Daniel, date.
    The five front war : the better way to fight global jihad / Daniel Byman.
        p. cm.
    Includes bibliographical references and index.
    ISBN 978-0-471-78834-8 (cloth)
    1. Terrorism–Prevention. 2. War on Terrorism, 2001– 3. Jihad.
4. Islam and world politics. I. Title.
    HV6431.B963 2007
    363.325'17–dc22
                                                        2007001701

Printed in the United States of America
10 9 8 7 6 5 4 3 2 1

To Beryl

Contents

Acknowledgments

Many people contributed to this work, and the brief words that follow do not do justice to their assistance and patience.

Beryl Taswell (aka Beryl Byman) painstakingly read every line of every chapter, offering her thoughts and ways to clarify my often purple prose. The result is a far more readable book; any remaining clunkyness is despite her best efforts. Several friends and colleagues read parts of the draft and offered many insights. Nora Bensahel, Michael E. Brown, Chris Connell, David Edelstein, F. Gregory Gause III, Bruce Hoffman, Pat Jones, Mara Miller, Andrew Pierre, Paul Pillar, Justine Rosenthal, Brent Sterling, Steve Ward, and Tamara Cofman Wittes all deserve many thanks. Kenneth Pollack and Bruce Riedel both carefully read an early version of the manuscript and offered many helpful suggestions. Jeremy Shapiro not only served as a helpful critic, but also allowed me to draw on the work we coauthored on U.S.-European differences in counterterrorism. Ned Moran's assistance on jihadist propaganda was particularly helpful. Sara Bjerg Moller's thoughts and research support were invaluable, and I am also grateful to Sarah Yerkes for taking the ball from Sara and helping move the manuscript to completion. Bilal Saab and Shai Gruber helped identify and compile important data on arrests for terrorism in the United States.

At Wiley, Eric Nelson has been a constant source of encouragement from start to finish.

Georgetown University's Center for Peace and Security Studies and School of Foreign Service are hospitable homes for scholars.

Particular thanks go to Robert Gallucci and Ellen McHugh for making my life at Georgetown so pleasant. Support also came from the Saban Center for Middle East Policy at the Brookings Institution. I am grateful to Martin Indyk and Kenneth Pollack for securing the Center's institutional support.

Introduction

For weeks and months following the September 11 attacks, the government issued alerts that signaled the possibility of future attacks. Chatter indicated that terrorists were plotting even more violence. Any alert was enough to send a chill through the population. People avoided crowds and stayed off airplanes when they could. Yet despite the ominous warnings, nothing happened. Al-Qa'ida has not attacked the U.S. homeland since 9/11. So in March 2006, when the Department of Homeland Security lowered the mass transit alert level to Code Yellow, Americans hardly noticed. People yawned and continued their business as usual.

But al-Qa'ida and the broader movement it leads have not been vanquished. Osama bin Ladin and his deputy Ayman al-Zawahiri remain at liberty. And their jihad rages on. The pace of terrorist attacks overseas has increased since the bloody events of 9/11. Hundreds died when a bomb exploded in a Bali nightclub. Almost two hundred died and far more were wounded when terrorists blew up trains in Madrid. Though insurgencies with links to al-Qa'ida have been set back in Uzbekistan, the Philippines, and Indonesia, the brutal wars in Chechnya and Kashmir persist. Afghanistan, Indonesia, and Pakistan have been added to the list of countries with new anti-U.S. insurgencies against the governments. Bin Ladin–inspired militants may have been bloodied, but they remain unbowed.

Even when we recognize that al-Qa'ida remains formidable, we often fail to understand that the organization has morphed from the terrorist group that struck America so brutally on 9/11. The core organization is weaker and less capable of a catastrophic attack on U.S. soil than it was six years ago. However, the cause it champions is far more popular, and the overall level of anti-U.S. and anti-Western anger is much higher. In addition, bin Ladin and his lieutenants are having some success in re-creating a haven in tribal parts of Pakistan comparable to what they enjoyed in the Taliban's Afghanistan.

Perhaps the biggest change is Iraq. The war itself led to unprecedented levels of hostility toward the United States throughout the world. Failures of planning and execution have allowed jihadists to gain a foothold in the country, and they are tapping into a lethal mix of religious inspiration and xenophobic nationalism.[1] In fighting the insurgency, the United States has managed to look both brutal and weak at the same time, a dangerous combination that encourages resistance.

Our narrow vision and blunders have exacted a heavy toll. We have produced a policy long on good intentions but short on success. Because we misjudged the nature of the threat, we failed to develop an overall strategy. We ignored al-Qa'ida's broad insurgent network. We disregarded the allure of al-Qa'ida's ideology for young Muslims. We failed to develop a comprehensive strategy against our new enemy, as we did with the containment of the Soviet Union after World War II. Because our strategic thinking has been muddled, we have uncritically pushed democracy and overly militarized our response to terrorism.

As we reconsider our approach, we must recognize that the fight against the global jihad will be a long one. Any policy, no matter how expedient, should be judged by long-term criteria. If it is not sustainable, it is usually a mistake.

Even as we recognize the long-term nature of the struggle, we must also focus our efforts more narrowly. The enemy is not a generic phenomenon called terrorism but rather a specific set of foes, in particular al-Qa'ida and its allies. We can parse this narrow group even further. The United States should try to disrupt or hinder al-Qa'ida–linked jihadists around the world, but Washington should focus its efforts on the relatively small number of groups and individuals that are capable of inflicting catastrophic harm on Americans and close allies.

We can begin to fight more effectively on five fronts.

The Five Front War

1. The Military

We should rethink the role of the military. The military plays a vital role in toppling overt sponsors of al-Qa'ida–linked terrorists such as the Taliban and deterring the emergence of new ones. In the absence of such an overt state sponsor, the primary military role is fighting the various guerrilla armies linked to al-Qa'ida—and at times conducting targeted killings of terrorist leaders. Rather than the U.S. Army fighting insurgencies, we can offer our military expertise to allied governments that will fight them directly. A more effective military will require dramatically changing procurement, recruitment, training, and doctrine.

2. The War of Ideas

Because much of the battle is fought "over there," we need to think hard about the abysmal world opinion of America. Terrorist cells and guerrilla fighters draw from a large stream of anti-U.S. sentiment that runs wider than ever before. Al-Qa'ida's claim that the United States has long subjugated Muslim lands and dishonored its people grows more popular each day. Most of our propaganda has so far been useless. Instead of trying to justify unpopular U.S. policies, we should go negative and remind people of the jihadists' unpopular deeds and theology. Make the debate about them, not about us.

3. Intelligence

Intelligence, the most important counterterrorism tool, must emphasize working effectively with local partners. Al-Qa'ida and like-minded groups easily blend in with local Muslim communities in Europe. Often they hide in remote parts of the world, such as the tribal areas of Pakistan and Yemen. Once found, however, they can be defeated. Together, counterterrorism agents and local authorities can piece together disparate pieces of information, ranging from phone numbers to family backgrounds. Cooperation is essential.

4. Homeland Defense

At home, we must use the full potential of law enforcement and focus it on realistic threats rather than on worst-case scenarios that have little to do with the jihadists' own goals. As we improve defenses, we must also recognize that defenses can go too far: they are costly, at best imperfect, and can alienate American Muslims and other important constituencies who are vital to ultimate success in the war on terrorism. Perception management and bolstering public will are often critical parts of successful defense against terrorism.

5. Democratic Reform

One of bin Ladin's most compelling claims is that the United States backs brutal and tyrannical regimes throughout the Middle East—a sorry truth. But bringing democracy to this part of the world is both difficult and risky for the fight against terrorism. In the short term, democracy might be a boon for al-Qa'ida by weakening local governments and empowering anti-U.S. voices. We should rethink—but not abandon—the goal of spreading democracy throughout the world, focusing on bolstering it where it already is occurring. We must find ways to promote democratic reform without the specter of an enemy rising up against us. When we cannot, we must recognize the limits of reform.

Every part of the war on terrorism requires close cooperation with our allies, which makes our neglect of them and the failure to aggressively recruit new ones a baffling and unconscionable part of our war on terrorism. Since 9/11, the list of key allies has shifted. New countries, particularly those in the Muslim world, emerge as essential to the war against the jihadists. But so too are allies in Western Europe and other areas that have large, disgruntled Muslim populations. Because allies are vital to the U.S. military, homeland defense, and particularly intelligence efforts, we must avoid alienating them for short-term gains. We must also consider policy initiatives that will make it easier for allies to associate themselves with the United States. Restarting a Middle East peace process will help reduce some hostility toward the United States.

Nuance is important with allies. We must recognize that not all states will cooperate fully with the United States. The real key is whether they are knowingly giving jihadists sanctuary, even by their passivity. Instead of saying, "If you're not with us, you're against us," we ought to say, "If you're not for the jihadists, you're for us."

Defeating the jihadist menace is vital for America's security and, if anything, more important for the rest of the world. Jihadist operatives seek to kill thousands of Americans at home and abroad and foment deadly insurgencies around the world. The jihadist ideology is strongly anti-American and threatens to destabilize key U.S. allies.

We can do better than we have in the past. American foreign policy can succeed in defeating al-Qa'ida and its fellow travelers. We must sort through our choices and design a strategy that will result in an effective course of action. We must weigh the available options against their costs, their risks, and their uncertainties. We must find the political courage to go forward. No longer should we stumble from challenge to challenge without a coherent policy. It will not be easy. But we can begin.

1

The Faces of the Adversary

Although Britain had bravely confronted almost thirty years of Irish Republican Army terrorism, the July 7, 2005, terrorist attacks were a challenge of a different order. On that bloody day, Shehzad Tanweer, Hasib Hussain, Jamal Lindsay, and Mohammad Sidique Khan blew themselves up in four attacks on London's subway and bus network, killing fifty-two and injuring several hundred.

The attack had all the hallmarks of an al-Qa'ida strike: they were simultaneous, bloody, and suicidal. Al-Jazeera broadcast a videotape of Khan, the apparent leader of the bombers. After his death the video declared his attack was to punish the British government for "atrocities against my people all over the world"—a speech bin Ladin could have written. One year after the attacks, al-Jazeera broadcast a message Shehzad Tanweer taped before the bombing, in which he explained his killings: "For the non-Muslims in Britain, you may wonder what you have done to deserve this. You are those who have voted in your government who in turn have and still continue to this day continue to oppress our mothers and children, brothers and sisters from the east to the west in Palestine, Afghanistan, Iraq and Chechnya." The security services had earlier identified Khan as a radical worth monitoring but did not fully investigate him because they lacked sufficient resources.

Several of the killers had gone to Pakistan and probably made contact with al-Qa'ida members there, and the perpetrators admired

7

the master terrorist and embraced his goals.[1] But despite the similarities of the attacks to previous al-Qa'ida strikes, bin Ladin and his lieutenants did not orchestrate the minutiae of this plot, as they did past spectaculars.

Perhaps even more worrisome than the attack itself were the revelations about radicalism within the British Muslim community. In contrast to 9/11, the attackers were homegrown rather than infiltrators. Three of the bombers were of Pakistani origin but born and raised in the United Kingdom; Jamal Lindsay was also a British national but had been born in Jamaica. All four of the bombers were integrated into the local community. The attempted follow-on attacks of July 21, 2005 (which failed to kill anyone), were carried out by Muslims born in Africa who had lived in the United Kingdom since they were children.

London hosts a wide range of figures associated with radical groups, exploiting Britain's freedom and tradition of tolerance to sow hatred around the world. Much of the Muslim population has little loyalty to the British government and feels no sense of being "British." A poll in the *Telegraph* of London even found that four in ten British Muslims want Islamic law implemented in the United Kingdom, and another report found that a fifth of those British Muslims surveyed felt "some sympathy" for the bombers.[2] The problem, it seems, is not just a small group of fanatics but also the broader community's support for their radical activities.

The London attacks—and similar strikes in Madrid, Bali, and Iraq, among other places—are successors to 9/11 even though bin Ladin and al-Qa'ida's direct role is more limited. The difference between reality and perception lies in defining al-Qa'ida. When the definition of al-Qa'ida is extended to include the wide range of radicals who share one or many of bin Ladin's goals, al-Qa'ida is indeed an organization of vast proportions. However, such an expanded view of the adversary must also recognize that the larger movement has many weaknesses not found among bin Ladin's core followers.

So what exactly is al-Qa'ida? Some accounts suggest al-Qa'ida includes tens or even hundreds of thousands of angry Muslims, all of whom are bent on the destruction of the United States and its way of life. Al-Qa'ida itself encourages such confusion: they link their organization to a broad range of local groups around the world, and they shamelessly take responsibility for local successes to enhance their own global standing.

Yet it is a mistake to see al-Qa'ida and those who support parts of its agenda as a monolith. Although bin Ladin successfully united a fractious set of terrorists and cast himself as the Robin Hood of the Muslim world, he does not command a unified army.

Bin Ladin created a global movement in the years before 9/11 but has not led his troops to victory in the aftermath.

Al-Qa'ida vs. America

If Americans were asked today to identify their number one enemy, most would name Osama bin Ladin. But they might be surprised to learn that the core followers loyal to bin Ladin number only in the hundreds.[3] Al-Qa'ida's ability to inflict devastating damage conjures up an image of a gargantuan organization, when it is really quite small.

The al-Qa'ida core is a daunting but also perplexing organization. It is unlike any enemy America has ever faced. In the United States, al-Qa'ida is seen as the vicious perpetrator of the 9/11 attacks and brutal assaults on civilians. But in much of the Muslim world al-Qa'ida is seen as the champion of beleaguered Chechens, Palestinians, Kashmiris, and other oppressed Muslim groups. The al-Qa'ida core is devoted to terrorism and skilled operations as well as simple participation in guerrilla war. Al-Qa'ida is an organization that promotes a sweeping agenda of revolution. It is neither nihilistic nor utopian, but its adherents neither wish to negotiate nor accommodate.

The exact nature of al-Qa'ida's objectives remains in dispute, particularly with regard to the United States. Two camps have emerged. The analytic community maintains that al-Qa'ida's objectives are bound up in U.S. Middle East policy: in particular, the U.S. security presence in Iraq and other Persian Gulf states and U.S. support for Israel. According to this view, al-Qa'ida is using terrorism to achieve concrete goals, such as driving the United States out of

Muslim lands. Politicians, on the other hand, portray an existential struggle against Western values. As President Bush noted in his address to Congress on September 21, 2001, "They hate our freedoms: our freedom of religion, our freedom of speech, our freedom to vote and assemble and disagree with each other. . . . These terrorists kill not merely to end lives, but to disrupt and end a way of life."[4]

Resolving this debate is vital for informed policy. Hatred caused by U.S. policy implies that certain changes—a withdrawal of U.S. forces from Iraq or a strong push for a Palestinian-Israeli peace— could hinder al-Qa'ida efforts to recruit new terrorists. If, however, al-Qa'ida can never be appeased, there is no incentive for the United States to change its policies. A closer look reveals that al-Qa'ida has both a long list of concrete grievances and exploits a broad social critique. The grievance list is so long as to make appeasement exceptionally difficult (and it would be a mistake, even if the list were shorter). But because the grievances are melded with other social and historic grievances, appeasement becomes effectively impossible.

Al-Qa'ida's rage is deep but not inchoate. Their complaints against the United States include the following:

- *A blasphemous military presence*. Trespassing on the heart of the holy land is the ultimate American sin. Stationing U.S. and Western forces in the Middle East, particularly in the Arabian Peninsula near Muslim holy sites, demonstrates America's desire to subjugate Islam.[5]

- *The destruction—and now enslavement—of Iraq*. In jihadists' eyes the presence of more than a hundred thousand U.S. troops in Iraq is part of an overall U.S. plot to occupy the entire Muslim world. The United States, they claim, has long sought to crush Iraq. Bin Ladin's February 23, 1998, statement claimed that the United States had long intended "to destroy Iraq, the most powerful neighboring Arab state." In the process, the United States has engaged in deliberate cruelty, allowing 1 million innocent Iraqis to die under sanctions.[6] The subsequent U.S. invasion and occupation of Iraq appeared to confirm Bin Ladin's prophecy.

- A *blinding bias toward Israel*. The United States is creating and nurturing the Jewish state as part of a modern-day colonial venture. As Fu'ad Husayn, a Jordanian expert on al-Qa'ida, argues, "Islamist jihadists believe that the state of Israel is the head of the spear that the West planted in the heart of the Islamic world."[7]
- *Support for a range of corrupt regimes in the Muslim world*. The United States props up regimes that oppress and impoverish Muslims. According to bin Ladin and other al-Qa'ida leaders, only two countries have approached proper Islamic standards: the Taliban's Afghanistan, and the Sudan, when Hassan al-Turabi held influence. Others were at best disappointing and at worst, apostates.
- *Subordination of the Muslim world*. In general, the United States seeks to undermine any effort by a Muslim nation to gain strength. In bin Ladin's words, the West seeks to "keep Muslims weak and incapable of defending themselves."[8] Thus the United States opposes Pakistan's nuclear program while endorsing India's.
- *Creation of a hegemonic international system*. Bin Ladin blames not only the United States, but also the structure it has created to ensure its dominance. Thus, even bodies like the United Nations are part of the problem. In 2004, bin Ladin offered a reward for the killing of UN secretary-general Kofi Annan: "And as for the United Nations," he said, "it is nothing but an instrument of the Zionist crusade hiding behind works of charity . . . therefore, whoever kills Kofi Annan or the president of the UN mission in Iraq or its representatives such as Lakhdar Brahimi, then he will be given a prize of ten thousand grams of gold."[9]
- A *willingness to tolerate, or even inflict, Muslim deaths* in struggles around the world. Al-Qa'ida's list would include Chechnya, Kashmir, Indonesia, Nigeria, Uzbekistan, the Philippines, and Xinjiang Province in China, among others.

A careful look at this list, exaggerated and shrill as it is, shows that it is not completely baseless. The United States is indeed a proud friend of Israel, it does occupy Iraq, and it often hesitated to intervene when Muslim lives were at risk.

Prioritizing the above grievances is difficult. Indeed, the specific order varies according to which al-Qa'ida member is telling the tale. For some, the true U.S. crime is backing Mubarak's brutality in Egypt, while for others U.S. troops in Iraq or support for Israel are the ultimate sins. It is also worth recognizing what is not on this list. Peter Bergen states that these grievances are political. Bin Ladin "does not rail against the pernicious effects of Hollywood movies, or against Madonna's midriff, or against the pornography protected by the U.S Constitution. Nor does he inveigh against the drug and alcohol culture of the West, or its tolerance for homosexuals. He leaves that kind of material to the American Christian fundamentalist Jerry Falwell."[10] Many of the issues that have risen to the fore in Europe since 9/11 are not part of al-Qa'ida's focus. Bin Ladin said nothing about the "blasphemous" film of Dutch director Theo Van Gogh, the producer of the movie that graphically criticized the treatment of women under Islam.

Instead, bin Ladin's grievances are focused on power—who possesses it; why it is used; and, in his judgment, how it is abused.

Indeed, al-Qa'ida's mix of specific grievances and cosmic injustice creates a self-fulfilling prophecy. America's numerous sins prove its inherent corruption, which, in turn, taints any U.S. gesture that might appear to be pro-Muslim. The United States is damned either way: when we delayed intervention in the Balkans, we were accused of condoning Muslim deaths; when we intervened in Somalia, we were charged with pursuing imperialist ambitions.[11] The U.S. attempt to broker a Middle East peace is similarly interpreted as an attempt to force docile Muslim regimes to legitimate Zionist imperialism rather than as a step forward in the Palestinian cause.

According to former CIA official Michael Scheuer, what al-Qa'ida seeks from America is unconditional surrender—a withdrawal of all forms of military, political, and cultural influence from the Muslim world.[12] Any concessions the United States might grant regarding Israel or Iraq would be touted as milestones on al-Qa'ida's path to victory rather than a means of negotiation. In other words, no matter what we do, al-Qa'ida will attempt more violence.

Successful attacks show the world that the movement is strong and determined. Negotiation is almost impossible because of the vast scope of al-Qa'ida's grievances and its even broader agenda of rectifying humiliation. Al-Qa'ida glorification of jihad as a solution renders appeasement as difficult in theory as it is in practice.

It is also hard to imagine any reconciliation that would satisfy al-Qa'ida because of the broad emotional issues in its agenda: namely, their strong quest for revenge. In the 1990s, this revenge was theoretical, based largely on perceived slights to the Muslim world and the jihadist movement. Now al-Qa'ida's thirst for vengeance is personal. The American response that followed 9/11 resulted in the death and arrest of thousands of jihadists, many of whom were friends and family of al-Qa'ida members. The speeches of bin Ladin and his number two, Ayman al-Zawahiri, from the 1990s suggest that their vendetta is driven by the increasing success of U.S. counterterrorism crackdowns.

A New Approach to Jihad

Though many Muslims share al-Qa'ida's grievances, their agenda is different from that of most Islamist groups, even violent ones. Radical Islamist groups sought first to overthrow the "near enemy"— secular and repressive Arab regimes. But bin Ladin and his followers turned this idea on its head. He declared instead that the "far enemy"—the United States—was the first to be confronted. Ending U.S. hegemony, he argues, will produce the collapse of pro-Western regimes in the Muslim world. As bin Ladin remarked, "If we cut off the head of America, the kingdoms in the Arab world will cease to exist."[13]

Jihad is a central concept in this struggle. Radical Islamists reject one common interpretation of jihad as an individual's spiritual struggle against his baser instincts. The radicals interpret jihad as actual warfare. In their eyes, jihad is as much a pillar of faith as the time-honored customs of fasting during Ramadan and praying five times a day. Bin Ladin claims that all Muslims must participate as best they can; it is not enough for selected members of the community to do so. Indeed, the radicals take this concept of jihad to new heights, arguing that war can be declared against Muslims who are insufficiently pious, particularly Muslim rulers.[14]

Al-Qa'ida is often cast as a *salafist* organization. The word *salaf* means predecessors or ancestors, with an implication that they were righteous. *Salafism* is a reference to the earliest generations of Islam, and its current adherents believe that only the prophet Mohammad and the following two generations of Muslims practiced Islam in the appropriate manner. Subsequent years saw the steady intrusion of practices that are not truly Islamic. Salafists stress that the Koran and established oral traditions are enough to derive law and moral behavior. They oppose anything that smacks of polytheism, superstition, or theological (not technological!) innovation. They reject Shi'ism, Sufism, the veneration of past leaders, religious pluralism, attempts to creatively interpret the Koran, and the attempt to reconcile Islam with Western values. Wahhabism, the dominant credo in Saudi Arabia, is one strand of salafism.[15]

To label al-Qa'ida as a "salafist" organization, however, simplifies complex theological and political divisions within this community. Most salafis stress religious activism. They believe in spreading God's word and focusing on education and self-purification, not engaging in politics.[16] Indeed, many salafis view the intrusion of politics as an inherently corrupting force because it leads to a focus on life outside religion and creates divisions among the faithful. This belief has led to tension between salafis and another, and much larger, bloc: the political Islamists. "Political Islam" is a vast term encompassing any political group that believes Islam should play an important role in law, society, and government. Salafists have often criticized mainstream Islamist groups such as the Muslim Brotherhood for their acceptance of Muslims who are not sufficiently pious and for engaging in the political process.[17] Zawahiri even wrote a brutal polemic, "The Bitter Harvest," in which he accuses the Muslim Brotherhood of being unbelievers because they placed man before God in their embrace of democracy.[18] There are even divisions within the salafist movement, and the jihadi element that espouses violence appears to be a minority.

Despite these doctrinal differences, the borders between the salafis and more political groups such as the Muslim Brotherhood and jihadist organizations such as al-Qa'ida are porous. Individuals often move back and forth among the various groups, depending on the stature of individual leaders and whether the various paths proffered appear to promise the hope of change.

The salafists attracted to al-Qa'ida share their belief that strikes against the United States are justified because the United States subjugated Muslim lands and dishonored their people. They see themselves as acting defensively against a country that wishes to destroy them. This distinction between the offensive and the defensive is more than just semantics. Muslim scholars argue that the defense of Islam is a duty that all individuals must fulfill. For example, bin Ladin's teacher Abdallah Azzam declared that "jihad is every man's duty" if foreigners seize Muslim lands.[19] In a video that circulated in the Middle East in the months before September 2001, bin Ladin declared, "If you don't fight you will be punished by God."[20]

Al-Qa'ida's structure is as unusual as its agenda and ideology. Unlike many radical groups that have a single purpose, al-Qa'ida cadres assume a variety of functions. Its organizational structure reflects its multipurpose nature. Bin Ladin and his senior leaders set the strategic agenda, but there is no clear rule on how the agenda will be implemented. At times bin Ladin acted as a micromanager: in 1993, for example, he reportedly pointed to a map of the U.S. embassy in Kenya and told the operative where the truck bomb should go. Yet at other times he allowed local groups tremendous freedom to plan their attacks.

Though al-Qa'ida has demonstrated a capability for lethal terrorist attacks on a global scale, terrorism is not necessarily its primary function. Al-Qa'ida sees itself as a missionary organization. It issues propaganda against the al-Saud and other Arab regimes, spreading its particular interpretation of Islam throughout the Arab world, raising the consciousness of Muslims worldwide. And it seeks to influence the agendas of other terrorist groups by making them more anti-American and less inclined to compromise with secular states.

For many years, the bulk of al-Qa'ida's violent activities went into training and supporting guerrilla fighters who fought with the

Taliban against their opponents. Similarly, al-Qa'ida has backed Islamist insurgencies and terrorist groups in Tajikistan, Kashmir, Bosnia, Dagestan, Xinjiang, Yemen, Jordan, the Philippines, Chechnya, Indonesia, former Soviet Georgia, Algeria, and elsewhere in the world, acting, according to Daniel Benjamin and Steven Simon, two former U.S. government counterterrorism officials, as the "quartermaster for jihad."[21]

Al-Qa'ida's fund-raising approach is also unusual for a terrorist group. Most successful groups rely on their local supporters for money, or they supply creature comforts such as a bed to sleep in or food for the night to members on the run. Others rob banks or traffic drugs to raise money for their cause. Although al-Qa'ida's operatives have dabbled in these methods, the organization relies primarily on sympathetic donors within the Islamist community. (Funding for the core organization has declined since 9/11.) The Muslim nongovernmental organization (NGO) network is particularly important. NGOs are a means of raising money, but they also are valuable for giving activists jobs, channeling money, and acquiring necessary documents. Al-Qa'ida has taken advantage of Western police and security forces' reluctance (particularly before September 11) to investigate any charity.[22]

Al-Qa'ida enjoys its status as the world's most dangerous terrorist group. New recruits sign up to its local affiliates every day. Its success is only partially due to its agenda and its fundraising capacity. Al-Qa'ida's ability to tap into broader resentment in the Muslim world ensures it of a steady stream of supporters, even as governments step up efforts to crush it. Yet other organizations share some of these advantages. Why then has al-Qa'ida developed into such a powerful organization?

The strongest pillar of al-Qa'ida's structure is its members. Scheuer notes, "Bin Laden's organization is larger, more ethnically diverse, more geographically dispersed, younger, richer, better educated, better led, and more military trained and combat experienced" than other terrorist groups in history.[23] Al-Qa'ida is an organization composed of elites. Those not capable of leadership are not recruited, unless they possess some other useful skill. Its membership is diverse: constituents come from many different countries. Because members blend in easily with populations on every continent, they can easily engage in global operations. Al-Qa'ida uses its elite core well by establishing committees of specialists, ranging from military operations to public relations.

A second strength is al-Qa'ida's high level of operational security. All terrorist groups need to keep their operations covert. Without secrecy they would not survive.[24] They need to ensure that police and intelligence services do not place a spy in their midst. They must be wary of having their phones tapped. Terrorism scholar David Rapoport notes that approximately 90 percent of all terrorist groups collapse within a year, and only half of the hardy remainder make it through another decade.[25] Al-Qa'ida has avoided this fate by focusing intensely on operational security. All operatives are ordered to blend in with local populations. Members are told to be wary of intelligence and police services, to speak only in code, and to avoid mentioning specifics unless absolutely necessary. For example, one member of the cell in Kenya that carried out the bombing of the U.S. embassy in Nairobi in 1998 noted, "We, the East Africa cell members, do not want to know about the operations plan since we are just implementers."[26] Similarly, bin Ladin has said that the September 11 hijackers did not know the details of their mission until "just before they boarded the planes."[27]

Yet another of Al-Qa'ida's strengths is its skill in adapting to changing circumstances. It has shown an ability to revise its methods and structure in response to setbacks or failures. As it plotted global operations, al-Qa'ida often drew on several regional hubs and allowed local groups to carry the banner in its name. But it proved willing to shift these hubs, moving responsibilities from one country to another according to the changing security environment. One of its manuals, *Declaration of Jihad against the Country's Tyrants*, calls for evaluating operations after they are carried out in order to learn from them. This willingness to confront mistakes gives the organization the ability to recuperate quickly from an operation gone awry or from successful government counterterrorist measures. Al-Qa'ida leaders do not rely only on faith to move their agenda forward. Terrorism analyst Rohan Gunaratna recalls hearing from one jihadist that "Bin Laden trusted in God but tied the camel tight."[28]

Al-Qa'ida seems to have an endless chain of leaders. Like a salamander regrowing its lost limb, the organization quickly finds a replacement for those fallen on the battlefront. Al-Qa'ida's number three leader, Mohammad Atef, was killed in Afghanistan, and the next three replacements—Abu Zubaydah, Khalid Shaykh Moham- mad, and Abu Farraj al-Libbi—were captured in Pakistan after intensive searches. Yet the organization continues to thrive even after these major losses.

In contrast to the eagerness of most terrorists, al-Qa'ida's lead- ers are unusually patient. Al-Qa'ida is willing to promote operations that take years to bear fruit, such as the September 11 attacks and the 1998 embassy bombings. To bolster their long-term position, the organization painstakingly penetrates local military and intelligence services, where they often receive advance information about pending arrests from sympathetic police members.[29]

For an organization that inflicts violence to enforce its goals, al- Qa'ida is remarkably tolerant. It is an odd characteristic for a terrorist group. Many extremist organizations—some of which are now affil- iated with al-Qa'ida—view competing radical organizations as more dangerous than the regimes they oppose. The Egyptian Islamic Jihad and the Gamaat Islamiyya, both of which advocated Islamic rule in Egypt and the violent overthrow of the Mubarak government, reserved much of their invective to fighting each other.[30] Many religious groups that are derived from one ethnic group regard others with suspicion.[31] Al-Qa'ida draws from a larger and diverse base and forges ties to revolutionaries whether they share all or only part of its goals. In a movement prone to divisions, al-Qa'ida is a unifier. Even if this bridging effort fails, cooperation continues. Al- Qa'ida is reported to have worked tactically with the Lebanese Hizballah, despite other salafi groups that regard Shi'a Hizballah members as apostates. As long as the group targets apostate Muslim regimes rather than the United States, al-Qa'ida feels free to work with them.

Al-Qa'ida's use of terror is different from that of other jihadist organizations. Their leaders view it strategically, as a means to an end rather than as an end in itself. Bin Ladin sees the Muslim world as artificially weak, bogged down by the United States and its puppet regimes. Al-Qa'ida attempts to provoke the United States into retaliating against the group and, in so doing, reveal America's true colors as an oppressor of Muslims. At the same time, al-Qa'ida works with local groups to pressure and topple the regimes they regard as corrupt. Bin Ladin sought to instigate a heavy U.S. military retaliation against Afghanistan in response to the September 11 attacks, believing, thus far incorrectly, that this would precipitate a broader clash between the West and the Islamic world that the United States would lose.[32] By hitting America hard and then trapping it in a quagmire, the United States would therefore be forced to withdraw from the Muslim world. On the other hand, the U.S. entry into Iraq appears to reinforce bin Ladin's master plan.

Al-Qa'ida believes it is winning.

Saif al-Adel, a senior al-Qa'ida leader, articulated a multiphase strategy that would culminate in victory in about 2020. Al-Adel contends that when al-Qa'ida or like-minded groups control a government, they can use this power as a stepping-stone to establish the global caliphate. Once the Muslim world is stronger and more united, the West can be attacked in a more conventional matter. Afghanistan was to be the first foot in the door, but after 9/11 and the U.S. occupation of Iraq, the stepping-stone became Iraq.

Al-Qa'ida Is Dead, Long Live al-Qa'ida

Despite its many strengths, the al-Qa'ida core was hit hard after 9/11. Most obviously, the United States and its Afghan allies ended al-Qa'ida's sanctuary in Afghanistan. Bin Ladin attempted to draw the United States into a debilitating and bloody conflict in Afghanistan. With only a few losses, the United States and its Afghan allies quickly routed the Taliban and killed or dispersed much of al-Qa'ida's cadre.

The loss of the Afghan haven was devastating. Afghanistan had been a hub for recruitment as well as planning. Al-Qa'ida and its supporters sent thousands of radicals to Afghanistan, allowing the group to choose the most skilled and dedicated to conduct operations. A sanctuary in Afghanistan made it far more difficult for counterterrorism officials to operate. Before their base was destroyed, a senior al-Qa'ida planner could quickly flee to Afghanistan whenever the heat grew unbearable. The congressional September 11 inquiry quoted one counterterrorism official as stating that al-Qa'ida's haven in Afghanistan gave the group a head start. It prevented the U.S. intelligence community from doing more than reacting to its constant plots. In the official's eyes, the world was "trying to chop down a tree by picking the fruit." Now al-Qa'ida members must often be on the run, unable to relax or to vet new recruits with the same thoroughness.

The immunity from attack in Afghanistan also gave the terrorists an important psychological advantage. In Afghanistan, a terrorist could make phone calls to his mother, relax with comrades after a day of training, and stay close to his wife and children. In the camp he could find family, sex with a spouse, companionship, and other human needs. Without a haven, all these normal human activities are lost, and a solitary life is difficult to endure.

A second, less noticeable advance is the worldwide police and intelligence campaign against al-Qa'ida. Before the attacks, counterterrorism was low on the list of world priorities. Even when senior U.S. officials did raise the issue of counterterrorism, foreign governments did not appreciate the degree of danger. Al-Qa'ida reaped the rewards of this shortsighted vision. Many governments around the world allowed al-Qa'ida a permissive environment in which to operate. Then deputy secretary of defense Paul Wolfowitz testified in 2002 that "even worse than the training camps [in Afghanistan] was the training that took place here in the United States and the planning that took place in Germany." Although these governments in no way supported Islamic radicalism, their own indifference and legal restrictions allowed al-Qa'ida operatives to recruit, train, and plan with impunity.

No more. Allied governments have made al-Qa'ida a priority. Though intelligence services possess different degrees of skill and government officials face varying degrees of political pressures, all are intent on preventing al-Qa'ida from obtaining a foothold in their country. In Europe and in Asia, security services are now far more willing to monitor and act against suspected radicals. Several countries have scrutinized their legal codes to ensure that terrorists do not exploit various loopholes. Then director of Central Intelligence

George Tenet testified on February 11, 2003, that more than a hundred countries have been involved in the capture and arrest of al-Qa'ida members. Proof of the effectiveness of this approach can be found in the statements of al-Qa'ida leaders. An al-Qa'ida "political bureau" statement declared that "The entire world became a CIA office, following America around everywhere on earth."[33]

The United States has either killed or arrested several thousand members of al-Qa'ida. These advances often receive little notice, and when they do appear in newspapers or on television, they are described as yet another unknown person sent to an undisclosed facility where it is unclear what would be revealed.[34] But these measures are the building blocks of counterterrorism success. Each individual arrested brings with him the potential to disclose information regarding the broader terrorist network, helping U.S. and allied intelligence to prevent the next attack.

Even when they are not killed or arrested, constant global pressure makes it far more difficult for terrorists to operate. Al-Qa'ida leaders must spend much of their time hiding. Communicating, recruiting, and fundraising, which are necessary to conduct operations, are far more difficult when the world's intelligence agencies are constantly on the alert.

Not surprisingly, the group's finances have fallen with these reverses. The 9/11 Commission staff found that al-Qa'ida's budget may be down to a few million dollars a year, in contrast to approximately $30 million per year before 9/11.[35]

A major shift in the terrorists' means of operation is their growing dependence on local groups. It is harder now for al-Qa'ida to conduct sophisticated attacks that involve global preparation—attacks such as 9/11 and the 1998 embassy bombings. Al-Qa'ida has downsized its targets. Local attacks with local perpetrators—scaled-down versions of 9/11—are more likely. Attacks are directed toward symbols of U.S.-Zionist hegemony, but they are more likely to be synagogues and Kentucky Fried Chicken outlets instead of warships or embassies. Many of the post-9/11 attacks were conducted by individuals with few contacts to bin Ladin himself. This shift is small comfort, but it suggests that bin Ladin finds it difficult to control the movement. For example, al-Qa'ida announced a "truce" with Spain

after a new government won elections there and promised to withdraw troops from Iraq. But local jihadists still tried to conduct
an attack there.[36] Given these problems, it is no surprise that the
number and scale of attacks directly linked to al-Qa'ida also have
fallen. Unlike the bloody pre-9/11 attacks, several of the most violent
attacks since 9/11—Bali, Madrid, and Beslan—were not planned
and orchestrated by the al-Qa'ida core.

So is al-Qa'ida dead? John Negroponte, the director of National
Intelligence, testified in February 2006 that while the al-Qa'ida
leadership is diminished, it still plots and prepares attacks, often
operating from ungoverned areas along the Pakistani-Afghan border.[37] This alone is of concern, but its current capacity for attack
is only one issue. More important, bin Ladin and his organization
retain their prestige, their Rolodex and a steady stream of willing
recruits. Many jihadists admire al-Qa'ida and would join the organization more formally if they could figure out how to approach the
leadership. Unless sustained and unrelenting pressure is placed on
its leaders, they will again be able to recruit and plan more attacks.

Even though the al-Qa'ida core has become weaker since 9/11,
bin Ladin's stature has increased. Bin Ladin himself is a giant today.
Few question his personal piety and courage. In Saudi Arabia,
younger Saudis lionize him. They view him as a giant compared with
the "pygmies" of the al-Saud.[38] Even if bin Ladin dies, al-Qa'ida,
and its brand of jihadist Islam, would live on. Al-Qa'ida has many
talented lieutenants who would step up to fill bin Ladin's role as
leader. Bin Ladin himself has prepared for his own demise, stating
that "my martyrdom would lead to the birth of thousands of
Osamas."[39] And in this he appears correct. Bin Ladin's image is
far more powerful than the man himself.

Even more chilling is the impact of bin Ladin's worldview. His
belief that the United States is the root of the Muslim world's problems has gained remarkable currency, just as his use of violence
against regional governments has helped many Muslims legitimize
terrorism.

Finally, the weaker core remains active and could easily regenerate should pressure lift. Since 9/11, al-Qa'ida conducted attacks in
Pakistan and plotted several operations in Europe (and, as noted

above, may have links to the July 2005 bombings in London). In addition, al-Qa'ida has been devoted to helping anti-U.S. forces in Iraq, Pakistan, and Afghanistan—major undertakings that have seriously set back U.S. interests in these countries and in the region.

Perhaps most ominously, the core seems to be reconstituting itself in tribal areas along the Afghan-Pakistani border. For five years after 9/11, the government of Pakistan made several serious efforts to gain control of this area and reduce al-Qa'ida activity. These efforts failed. Moreover, they were bloody, with Pakistan's military and police taking hundreds of casualties. In late 2006, fearing more losses and worried that continued pressure was angering anti-U.S. factions within the rest of the country, the Musharraf government agreed to curtail its attacks. Al-Qa'ida may now have a new haven. From this new haven, bin Ladin is planning spectaculars and working to knit together the various strands of jihad that have emerged in recent years. The plot revealed in August 2006 to bomb ten airplanes over the Atlantic Ocean as they flew from the United Kingdom to the United States looked professional and carefully planned. Particularly worrisome was the planned use of sophisticated liquid explosives. Several of the plotters, including Rashid Rauf, the alleged leader, had links to Pakistan-backed Kashmiri terrorist groups. A former Egyptian paramilitary commander turned jihadist reportedly orchestrated the attacks for al-Qa'ida from Pakistan.[40]

The Second Circle: The al-Qa'ida Periphery

Ammari Saifi was a rebel out of legend, as daring and charismatic as he was brutal. He was a leader of the Salafist Group for Preaching and Combat (in French, Groupe Salafiste pour la Prédication et le Combat, or GSPC), a salafi jihadist group that shares many of al-Qa'ida's goals and in January 2007 changed its name to al-Qa'ida of the Islamic Maghreb. GSPC is best known outside Algeria for having taken thirty-two European "adventure travelers" hostage for almost half a year. Surrounded by poor and strife-torn lands, Saifi's refuge was the Sahara, one of the most desolate regions on Earth. For several years he played hide-and-seek with U.S. and African troops, leading them on wild chases throughout the Sahara. He slipped from Algeria to Mali to Niger just ahead of the local forces. In 2004, Chadian rebels finally captured him, leading, eventually, to his imprisonment in Algeria in 2005.

Saifi did not begin as an international terrorist. For most of his career he focused on local issues, like other Algerian jihadists. He was born in Algeria in the late 1960s. His mother was French and his father Algerian. He joined the Algerian military and became a para-trooper, giving him his future nickname "al Para." Saifi joined the ranks of the Islamists when they went underground following the military seizure of power in 1991.

By any standard, the civil war that followed this seizure was horrific. Roughly 150,000 Algerians died, many in gruesome ways. The Armed Islamic Group (in French, the Groupe Islamique Armée, or GIA), the leading Algerian resistance group for several years in the mid-1990s, was extreme even by jihadist standards. GIA leaders included many Algerians who had fought in Afghanistan against the Soviets. They embraced violence in 1992, castigating not only the Algerian military for its coup but also Islamists who supported electoral politics. They argued that the Islamists were naive and that democracy itself was anti-Islamic. As the years wore on, the GIA became more radical. In the areas it controlled in Algeria, it imposed a brutal form of Islamic law. The group attacked not only soldiers but also foreigners, teachers, artists, and govern-ment employees. In 1994 and 1995 the GIA was implicated in a series of terrorist attacks in France, including the hijacking of Air France flight 8969 and bombings in the Paris Métro. Over time, its rejection of democracy became a bloody passion. The GIA's slogan for those who voted was "one vote, one bullet."

By 1996 the GIA had declared total war on all Algerians who did not support it, and it slaughtered Muslims who refused to join the group. Within the group, it purged more moderate members and even murdered their families. The GIA declared Algerian society to be *kuffar*—apostates, who had turned away from the word of God—and, as such, legitimate targets to be killed. The GIA wiped out whole villages. To terrify all of Algeria, the GIA made a point of killing people in appalling ways (disemboweling pregnant women, among many other horrors). For many among the GIA, imposing a salafist credo on areas it controlled was more important than fighting the government.

It took a lot to legitimate the corrupt, brutal, and despotic junta that overturned the 1991 elections. But the extent of the GIA's brutality alienated most Algerians. They did not want to see their country turned into a charnel house. The violence appalled not only the Algerians but also the international community, which shunned antigovernment fighters. Despite the international community's condemnation of the junta's military coup and repression, over time they supported the Algerian regime as the lesser of two evils. The GIA's violence backfired even within the Islamist community. Donations to the popular Algerian cause dried up as the once-heroic rebels were revealed as brutal thugs.

Torn by factionalism, the GIA began to spiral down. Personal rivalries, differences over obscure points of doctrine, and deliberate government efforts to encourage infighting led to internal purges and the creation of breakaway factions. Appalled by the GIA's ferocity and brutality, dissident Islamists led by Hassan Hattab, a former GIA regional commander, formed the GSPC in the late 1990s, a move that bin Ladin himself supported. Even bin Ladin, no stranger to horrific violence, turned away from the GIA's extreme brutality. Al-Qa'ida did not share the GIA's vision that all of society was apostate. With support crumbling and its members defecting, the GIA fell apart.

The GSPC then became the dominant group, and like the GIA, the GSPC went through several commanders. But the damage had been done. The GSPC steadily lost ground in its battle with Algerian forces. With its local hopes dashed, group leaders moved away from Algeria toward bin Ladin's more global agenda. One commander, Nabil Sahraoui, who was later killed, announced in 2003 that the group leaders "strongly and fully support Osama bin Ladin's jihad against the heretic America."[41] Several senior GSPC leaders also worked closely with al-Qa'ida, and other reports indicate that the GSPC has ties to networks linked to Iraqi jihadists. In January 2007, GSPC embraced al-Qa'ida formally with a name change, becoming al-Qa'ida of the Islamic Maghreb. As the new name suggests, the group's agenda includes radical change in Morocco and Tunisia as well as Algeria.

As various leaders died or defected, Saifi became more and more important to the GSPC. He was the group's chief commander for northeastern Algeria. The Algerian government, however, steadily gained the upper hand against the militants, and Saifi was forced to flee.

As his efforts to overthrow the Algerian government faltered, Saifi embraced banditry and international terrorism. His capture of thirty-two European tourists who were traveling through the Sahara in Algeria brought him worldwide attention. Journalist Raffi Khatchadourian speculates that Saifi may have had two reasons for taking the tourists hostage: one reason was to dramatically demonstrate that the GSPC was still strong; a second reason was to follow the al-Qa'ida leadership's 2002 call to strike at "the enemy's tourist industry." Eventually the German government ransomed the tourists for 5 million Euros, a staggering sum in a region that includes several of the poorest countries in the world. Saifi used the money to buy weapons and vehicles and soon had a small militia that was a match for local military forces.

Because of Saifi's brutality and anti-Western agenda, the American military joined local governments in pursuing him. That proved his undoing. With nowhere to hide, Saifi was captured by Chadian rebels, who passed him to the Algerian government.

Saifi's odyssey illustrates two sides of local groups—their parochial goals as well as their global aspirations. Saifi had loose connections to al-Qa'ida, but his men were locals.[42] Al-Qa'ida has long devoted much of its energies to supporting local jihadists fighting what they see as oppressive regimes. An obvious front was Algeria, where an avowedly secular military government was crushing rebels acting in the name of Islam. To this day, GSPC terrorists conduct attacks in Algeria. In exchange, many of the Algerian operatives entered al-Qa'ida's network, particularly in Europe. Sometimes the Algerians acted as minor functionaries, helping al-Qa'ida with acquiring documents, hiding operatives, or otherwise preparing for attacks. But they have also been connected to major terrorist acts. Ahmed Ressam, the so-called Millennium Bomber, who planned to bomb Los Angeles International Airport on New Year's Eve 1999, was one Algerian who gravitated to al-Qa'ida. Fighters from Algeria have been linked to numerous plots in Europe, including the March 11, 2004, commuter train bombings in Madrid, and to plots against the United States.

Peter Bergen compares al-Qa'ida to a holding company that exercises varying degrees of control over other groups.[43] When these groups are factored in, al-Qa'ida's manpower increases dramatically. Thus we are required to dramatically expand our estimate of the size and appeal of the adversary. These large numbers, however, are not necessarily indicative of al-Qa'ida's strength. Even when the leaders of these groups profess loyalty to bin Ladin, their agendas may be local or regional. Particular ideological visions may differ from those of bin Ladin. Some are not focused on the United States; others vary in their interpretations of jihad. These distinctions have implications for the struggle against terrorism. If these disparate groups join the al-Qa'ida core or embrace its agenda, bin Ladin's legions will have multiplied and his reach will have expanded greatly. On the other hand, if they focus entirely on local concerns, or if their actions discredit the jihadist cause in general, then the fight against al-Qa'ida becomes largely a manhunt for the relatively small number of members in the al-Qa'ida core.

The mountains of the Caucasus and the desert of Africa are geographical extremes, but affiliates of al-Qa'ida are found in both. In the cold reaches of Chechnya, far from the desert heat of Algeria, Vladimir Khodov fought the Russians. He, too, made headlines in the West, even though he never went after Americans or Europeans. On September 1, 2004, the first day of school, Vladimir Khodov and thirty-one other terrorists stormed Middle School 1 in Beslan, a town in the North Ossetia region of Russia. The attackers were a mix of individuals drawn from different parts of the Caucasus, particularly from Chechnya and Ingushetia, though ethnic Russians and others, including one or two Arabs, also took part.[44] The terrorists' demands were extensive. They called for Russia to immediately end its war in Chechnya and withdraw its troops from the province. They also insisted that Soviet president Vladimir Putin resign.

Even by the standards of a region accustomed to remarkable brutality, the Beslan attack was horrific. The gunmen took 1,200 hostages, most of whom were children. When Russian security forces stormed the building, at least 331 hostages died, including 186 children. Only one terrorist survived.[45]

Survivors of the Beslan attack say Khodov was "one of the most ruthless of the gang." He died, either at the siege itself, or a day later, in police custody—an uncertainty that is typical of the Beslan incident, which is clouded by propaganda on all sides.[46] But before his death he succeeded in sending a chill down the spine of parents around the world.

Vladimir Khodov called himself Abdullah. His embrace of jihad is more reminiscent of the Columbine school shootings in Colorado in 1999 than the daring deeds of Saifi. Khodov's father was a Soviet Army officer from Elkhodovo, a village near Beslan. As a boy, Khodov was a poor and sickly student who was regularly beaten by other boys. When his brother Boris went to jail for murder, he converted to Islam. Vladimir followed suit. Later he went to Dagestan, a neighboring province that has suffered violence linked to Chechnya, and became involved in violence there.

Khodov's transformation from ninety-eight-pound weakling to international terrorist occurred against the backdrop of a war that rivaled the Algerian conflict in its horror. The Chechen rebellion against Russia mixes a dash of al-Qa'ida-style religious fanaticism with old-fashioned nationalism and tribalism. The roots of the conflict date back decades if not centuries. It is tied to Russia's brutal subjugation of the Chechens. Russia first took over Chechnya in the late eighteenth century, and it fought resistance there for decades. When the Chechens rose up against the Soviets in the 1940s, Stalin deported the entire Chechen population to Siberia, where a quarter of their number died. The Chechens were only allowed to return after 1956.

After the collapse of the Soviet Union, Chechens hoped to gain independence, following the example of other ethnic groups long dominated by Russia. In 1991, when the Russians refused to grant them independence, the Chechens rebelled and declared themselves independent, free from the shackles of the Russian oppressors.

Russia "invaded" its erstwhile province in 1994 but withdrew in 1996. For reasons that remain murky, the Chechens subsequently led an incursion into neighboring Dagestan and conducted additional violence in Russia. Russia invaded Chechnya again in 1999. The violence inflicted on both sides was horrendous. Chechens claim that more than 200,000 people died—that out of a total population only slightly higher than 1 million—and more than 20,000 Soviet troops were killed. Hundreds of thousands of refugees fled because of the conflict. Meanwhile, the violence spread to nearby regions such as Dagestan, Ingushetia, and North Ossetia.

On the surface, this struggle would seem to have little to do with al-Qa'ida. The Chechen revolt has more in common with rebellions against colonial rule after World War II than terrorism in the twenty-first century. There are differences. Unlike al-Qa'ida, there is a strong criminal element in the Chechen insurgency that takes advantage of indigenous violence to run drugs and kidnap wealthy locals. Local Chechen leaders constantly joust for power. In the environment of Russian brutality, these differences, combined with strong popular opposition to Russian dominance, would be enough to foment rebellion regardless of what the jihadists do.

And yet al-Qa'ida has inserted itself. Most Chechens are Sunni Muslims. Thus many Islamists saw the Russian-Chechen conflict as yet another attempt of the Christian world to conquer Islamic lands. For the Islamists, Chechnya was a logical next step after liberating Afghanistan from Soviet rule. Starting in the mid-1990s, Chechnya became a cause célèbre among jihadists. Some commanders, such as Khattab, had close personal ties to the al-Qa'ida leadership and began to draw upon them for funding. Responding to the call to liberate oppressed Muslims, jihadists flocked to Chechnya from Central Asia, the Arab world, and even Europe. Al-Qa'ida quickly saw the struggle in Chechnya as part of its overall agenda.

Chechnya, in turn, proved a fertile recruiting ground for al-Qa'ida. Russian atrocities in Chechnya, both real and imagined, became the grist for al-Qa'ida's propaganda mill, and the conflict became one of the most prominent struggles in jihadists' eyes until the U.S. invasion of Iraq. Al-Qa'ida videos and propaganda endlessly highlighted the horrors Russia inflicted on the Chechens. According

to al-Qa'ida's leaders and the words repeated by Imams and propagandists throughout the Western and Muslim worlds, Russia
invaded Muslim lands, raped the women, and wantonly killed the
men. Sadly, many of the accusations of brutality are well founded. In
response to the call, the Chechen cause attracted volunteers and
foreign financial contributions. Al-Qa'ida facilitated this flow of
money and people. At times they diverted potential recruits and
money for their own purposes. The infamous 9/11 leader, Mohammad Atta, originally intended to go to Chechnya but was persuaded
by an al-Qa'ida facilitator to go to Afghanistan instead.

Al-Qa'ida neither controlled nor directed the Beslan attack
nor the kidnapping of Western hostages in the Sahara. Chechen
and Algerian commanders, even though openly sympathetic to
al-Qa'ida's global agenda, appear to have acted independently
of bin Ladin. It is likely that he didn't know about these outrages before they happened. Other affiliates are even further removed from al-Qa'ida's objectives and priorities. For example, the
Islamic Movement of Uzbekistan is focused largely on Uzbekistan,
and to a lesser degree Central Asia—not the struggle against
America.

Given al-Qa'ida's ties to a range of insurgencies and local groups,
a key challenge for counterterrorism operatives is determining
where the organization's influence stops. How many additional radical groups and ideologues share al-Qa'ida's objectives and worldview? And what impact has al-Qa'ida had on each local group's
ideology? Initially jihadist ideologies played little or no role in
the conflicts in Afghanistan, Bosnia, Kosovo, Chechnya, Iraq, and
Kashmir. With time and al-Qa'ida's encouragement, radical ideologies became a major component of these conflicts.

Al-Qa'ida successfully convinced many local insurgents the
world over that all Islamic insurgents are fighting individual battles
that are part of a larger worldwide war.

Today al-Qa'ida has wide appeal and influence throughout the
struggles it sponsors. This mutual cooperation benefits both sides.
Local groups have much to gain by association with al-Qa'ida.
Al-Qa'ida assists groups with logistics and skilled personnel to encourage cooperation and unity of purpose.[47] By organizing and

training jihadists, al-Qa'ida makes local conflicts more deadly. And as a result of their association with al-Qa'ida, the local groups become more prestigious.

Al-Qa'ida in turn benefits from additional venues for proselytizing. The local conflicts produce alumni who greatly expand the reach of the broader jihadist cause. Literally tens of thousands of Muslims have fought in conflicts on the antigovernment side in Algeria, Chechnya, Kashmir, Indonesia, and so on. Not all, or even most, of these local insurgents are al-Qa'ida. But al-Qa'ida can reach out to these people when it wants to conduct a local operation. A major strength of al-Qa'ida is its ability to link diverse jihadist elements into a broad network capable of working together for common goals, even though these groups are barely unified.

To understand al-Qa'ida, it is important not only to see it as a terrorist group such as the Weathermen or the Abu Nidal Organization but also as a "worldwide, religiously inspired, and professionally guided Islamist insurgency promoted by bin Ladin."[48] Although the spectacular terrorist attacks are what garner the most U.S. attention, these grinding low-intensity conflicts are what cause the most suffering and have the greatest potential for dramatic change. Because many of these conflicts are seen as legitimate liberation struggles, even by Muslims who reject terrorism, the jihadists' appeal is greatly expanded.

Unfortunately, the number of local groups embracing al-Qa'ida's global agenda may be increasing. Then director of National Intelligence John Negroponte testified in 2006 that several Sunni jihadist groups are expanding outside of their traditional area of operations. Indonesia's Jemaah Islamiah; the Islamic Jihad Union, which operates out of Central Asia; the Libyan Islamic Fighting Group; and various Pakistani groups all have used Iraq as a rallying point for fighting the United States. It appears that the call has been answered. Fighters from several such groups have shown up in Iraq as well, which suggests that even if al-Qa'ida itself is not growing, its appeal has widened.

The jihadist network may be bin Ladin's most enduring legacy. As former CIA official Paul Pillar argues, "This network is something like the Internet: it is a significant transnational phenomenon that has grown in recent years and that some determined people have used to their advantage, but nobody owns or controls it."[49] Bin Ladin's capture or death would not dismantle the thousands of personal relationships he helped forge in the past decade. The groups may be separate but the individuals are now connected.

The Third Circle: Unaffiliated Activists

Even more worrisome than the expanding web of bin Ladin's radicals is the explosive growth of unaffiliated activists. Throughout the world, increasing numbers of independent, insurgent, and terrorist groups are embracing al-Qa'ida's vision. The State Department's 2004 annual report on terrorism describes this trend:

> The global jihadist movement—including its most prominent component, al Qaeda—remains the preeminent terrorist threat to the United States, U.S. interests, and U.S. allies. While the core of al Qaeda has suffered damage to its leadership, organization, and capabilities, the group remains intent on striking U.S. interests in the homeland and overseas. . . . At the same time, however, al Qaeda has spread its anti-U.S., anti-Western ideology to other groups and geographical areas. It is therefore no longer only al Qaeda itself but increasingly groups affiliated with al Qaeda or independent ones adhering to al Qaeda's ideology, that present the greatest threat of terrorist attacks against U.S. and allied interests globally.[50]

These individuals would join al-Qa'ida formally if they could. But in much of the Western and Muslim world, the local affiliates of al-Qa'ida are weak: they receive limited support from local Muslim communities, or their governments have crushed them decisively. So these local individuals often act on their own.

The commuter training bombings on March 11, 2004, in Madrid—or "3/11"—is instructive. The attacks killed 191 people and wounded more than 2,000. As Daniel Benjamin and Steven Simon note, the attacks had "all the qualities of an al Qaeda operation": the perpetrators endorsed bin Ladin's ideas, the attacks were simultaneous (ten bombs were set off), and the goal was mass casualties.[51] Yet al-Qa'ida did not orchestrate the attack. Instead, Benjamin and Simon declare 3/11 to be a "homage" to bin Ladin. The attackers were a motley collection of petty criminals and jihadists of different persuasions. Only one member had any past jihadist experience to speak of.

Since 9/11, many of the attacks and plots in Western Europe and parts of the Middle East fall into this category of unaffiliated activists. At best, the insurgents maintain loose contact with the al-Qa'ida core. Terrorism expert Marc Sageman articulates this view when he notes, "The old Al Qaeda is hiding away in caves someplace."[52] Sageman's claim overstates al-Qa'ida's decline, but his basic point that the core is less capable is true. Nevertheless, the ranks of sympathizers swell even more.

Although al-Qa'ida's model is proliferating, these sympathizers are less skilled than the al-Qa'ida core. The Madrid cell had planned even more attacks after the subway bombings but was incapable of implementing them. Its members were quickly arrested or killed. The attackers in Morocco who killed thirty-three people in a series of attacks on Jewish, European, and Kuwaiti targets in 2003 fell far short of their goals: despite the carnage, they only managed to kill five Westerners and no Jews. Benjamin and Simon report that Europe has had fifteen major conspiracies for every successful attack, an impressive show of force by European security officials.[53] In other words, the intention is there but the capability is not.

This loose network of al-Qa'ida sympathizers presents a major problem for counterterrorism officials: there is no way to draw a profile of an archetypal terrorist. These members arrive on the scene from different countries, different economic and educational backgrounds, and with varying degrees of assimilation into their host country. The perpetrators of the July 7, 2005, attacks in London were primarily second-generation Pakistani immigrants, but those who attempted a follow-up attack two weeks later were first-generation immigrants from East Africa. The uncle of Abdelhalim Badjoudj, a French Muslim of North African extraction who blew himself up in Iraq, claimed that "If he had work, this wouldn't have happened."[54] But a British report on extremists in the United

Kingdom found that radicals came from both the deprived and the dispossessed and within universities. Among the individuals there is often no asocial behavior. Mohammad Sidique Khan, one of the July 7 London bombers, used to take time to help his neighbor's child with his homework.[55] Nor do the individuals necessarily display a high degree of religiosity before they turn to violence. Badjoudj, for example, drank beer and smoked hashish regularly. Despite their embrace of violence, they do not appear to be sociopaths.

In Europe, the emergence of unaffiliated jihadists is bolstered by their deep-seated belief that Muslims are not accepted as citizens in their new countries and that they are disenfranchised economically. A British Home Office report found that many European Muslim radicals were alienated because they were not participating in mainstream public and political life as well as "Islamophobia" in British society, among other issues.[56] Even those Muslims who abhor violence share the radicals' complaints. And there is truth to these feelings of unfairness. In most European countries, Muslim communities experience far higher levels of poverty and unemployment than do non-Muslims. Majorities of the public in Spain, Germany, and France believe that there is a conflict between being a devout Muslim and living in a modern society—a view that many Muslims living elsewhere in Europe also endorse. Spaniards, Germans, Russians, and Frenchmen often see Muslims as fanatical and violent.[57] The Home Office report found that Muslims experience three times as much unemployment as do non-Muslims in Britain.[58] European Muslims feel dislocated and uncomfortable in Europe as well as in their native country. Dominique Many, a French lawyer involved in the trials of several militants, noted, "In Tunisia they are considered foreigners. In France they are considered foreigners."[59] One study of British Muslims found that 80 percent see themselves as Muslims before they are British, and another found that 26 percent do not feel loyal to Britain.[60] In Spain and Britain, 16 and 14 percent, respectively, of Muslims polled have confidence in bin Ladin—a large number that is only slightly less than the 26 percent of Egyptians who do.[61]

Fanning the flames of fanaticism are the vitriolic sermons delivered in neighborhood mosques. Because of a shortage of religious leaders, European Muslim communities looked to the Middle East for their local religious leaders. Rather than sending imams who would calm the troubled waters, the native country often sent firebrands to European mosques. French intelligence estimates that 150 of the country's 6,000 mosques are under the control of extremists—a small overall percentage, but a tremendous number given the damage that only a few radicalized individuals can wreak. Similarly, the British government estimates that between 10,000 and 15,000 British Muslims support radical groups—a fraction of the overall Muslim community of almost 2 million, but a significant number nonetheless. Of these, the British security services believe that potentially hundreds might commit terrorist attacks.[62]

The Iraq debacle has encouraged these unaffiliated radicals on their path to violence. A British government analysis found that Iraq was the "recruiting sergeant" for extremist groups.[63] The war and subsequent occupation have "proven" that the United States and its allies seek to subjugate the Muslim world. Those who go to Iraq may find it to be as fertile an al-Qa'ida training ground as Afghanistan once was under the Taliban. Roland Jacquard, a French terrorism expert, declared, "Those who don't die and come back will be the future chiefs of Al Qaeda or Zarqawi [groups] in Europe."[64]

For now, European Muslims appear caught between the harsh Middle Eastern views of the West and more positive experiences that many Westerners assume come with living in a Western society. As a report by the Pew Global Attitudes Project notes, "While Europe's Muslim minorities are about as likely as Muslims elsewhere to see relations between Westerners and Muslims as generally bad, they more often associate positive attributes to Westerners— including tolerance, generosity, and respect for women."[65]

Criminal activity is another common characteristic among those active in jihadist violence in Europe. Before Richard Reid tried to set off a bomb in his shoe on a transatlantic flight in December 2001, he had been in jail for muggings and other petty crimes. It was there that he converted to Islam. Many radical groups have members who are common criminals like Reid and use their illegal activities to pay for violent acts. A group of French radicals linked to the financing of Iraqi insurgents conducted armed robberies and forged passports to finance its activities. Not surprisingly, the group also proselytized in prisons.[66]

A look at the major terrorist attacks since 9/11 suggests the complexity of discerning these three circles in practice. Some cases are clear: al-Qa'ida leaders appear to have directly organized the attack on a synagogue in Djerba, Tunisia, on April 12, 2002. But many of the most prominent attacks were done by locals who had cloudy links to al-Qa'ida. Other attacks, particularly those in the Middle East, often involved local affiliates of al-Qa'ida based in the country in question ("al-Qa'ida of the Arabian Peninsula" or "al-Qa'ida in the Land of the Two Rivers") rather than involving the sort of top-down planning that characterized 9/11 and several major plots before that, such as the attack on the USS *Cole* in 2000 and the 1998 bombings of U.S. embassies in Africa.

The Fourth Circle: Sympathizers around the World

Speaking to Congress and the nation in the immediate aftermath of the 9/11 attacks, President Bush declared: "The terrorists practice a fringe form of Islamic extremism that has been rejected by Muslim scholars and the vast majority of Muslim clerics—a fringe movement that perverts the peaceful teachings of Islam."[67] This view is reassuring but simplistic. If the views of al-Qa'ida and its fellow travelers exist only on the fringe, the organization's ability to sustain itself in the face of a worldwide manhunt would be greatly diminished.

Bin Ladin, unfortunately, is not a voice in the wilderness. That Muslim governments collaborating with the West are illegitimate, formerly a radical view, appears to be gaining ground, particularly as these governments rely on repression while failing to deliver economic progress.[68]

Many Muslims, particularly Arabs, share al-Qa'ida's resentment of the United States, especially its Middle East policies. They also disdain the tolerance of free artistic expression and homosexuality. Poll results released after the end of major combat operations in Iraq indicated that "people in most predominantly Muslim countries remain overwhelmingly opposed to the U.S., and in several cases these negative feelings have increased dramatically."[69] A 2006 Pew poll found that fewer than half of the citizens in Indonesia, Morocco, Jordan, Lebanon, Turkey, and Pakistan had a favorable view of the United States. Surprisingly, Jordan, a long-time U.S. ally, had the least favorable opinion, with only 21 percent viewing America positively.[70]

Al-Qa'ida's appeal goes beyond the Arab world. After 9/11, many new babies in Muslim parts of Nigeria are named Osama.[71] Jihadist appeal is very strong in Europe as well. Benjamin and Simon cite a *Times* of London poll that found that an astonishing 40 percent of British Muslims supported bin Ladin's attacks on the United States.[72]

Increasingly, this hatred is directed beyond current disputes. Sayyid Qutb, a leading Islamist thinker who inspired many al-Qa'ida officials, warns of the "Crusader spirit which runs in the blood of all westerners."[73] Radical Islamists combine this vision of eternal conflict with the West and virulent anti-Semitism (historically rare in the Muslim world). They view all current events through the lens of a broad conspiracy against Islam. Armed with these "facts," they conclude that the United States is truly evil rather than merely misguided.

The picture is ominous. It suggests that al-Qa'ida's ideology runs deep. Bin Ladin believes that by making America react forcibly to violence, America's true colors will be revealed. Then Muslims will take part in the cosmic battle between the East and the West, between Muslims and Christians, and between secularism and Shari'a. Unfortunately, bin Ladin's vision is gaining acceptance. As Scheuer notes, "with or without bin Laden, and whether or not the West accepts it, many Muslims appear to think a war against Islam is underway."[74]

Even nonjihadists believe that there will be an ultimate schism between East and West in which the Muslims will emerge as the victors. Gunaratna points out that mainstream Islamist groups did not condemn al-Qa'ida after September 11 because the attacks were wrong, but rather criticized the organization for attacking before the time was right and for risking American retaliation.[75] In particular, several Islamist leaders have argued that jihad will inevitably fail until the Muslim world is united. Such criticism of bin Ladin is small comfort to Westerners seeking amity.[76]

Divisions among the Ranks

Our enemy multiplies. To the few hundred members of al-Qa'ida's core we have added the tens of thousands of insurgent fighters who share jihadist goals. And to the mix are perhaps thousands more unaffiliated activists. Most menacing, the polling data of Muslims around the world suggest that millions more have sided against us.

Yet despite the growing number of jihadists, we must remember that as the number of the enemy grows larger, so does its potential for division. Though myriad groups—the Islamic Movement of Uzbekistan, for example—may sympathize with al-Qa'ida, they have different goals, motivations, skill levels, and degrees of dedication. Indeed, the jihadist community is rife with dissension. Many of these internal struggles have become violent. Beyond jihadist circles, among the Islamist community or Muslims in general, the differences far outweigh the similarities. Indeed, U.S. strategies for victory depend heavily on understanding and exploiting these divisions successfully.

One of the most basic divisions among the jihadists concerns the nature of the perceived enemy. Most jihadists would agree that the governments of the United States, Israel, Russia, the United Kingdom, Saudi Arabia, Egypt, and numerous other countries are immoral and hostile to Islam. But where to begin? What country deserves the groups' priority? Traditionally, most groups focused first on their home country. And despite bin Ladin's efforts to make the "far enemy," the United States, the priority over the "near enemy," Egypt and Saudi Arabia, most groups still see their local struggle as a top priority.[77] In Saudi Arabia militants split between those heeding al-Qa'ida's call to fight Americans in Iraq and those focusing first on overthrowing the al-Saud regime. In fact, al-Qa'ida has not yet resolved this basic question within its own ranks. Journalist Lawrence Wright reports that an al-Qa'ida training school in Afghanistan listed its heretical enemies: Mubarak and his ilk first;

followed by the Shi'a; then America; and finally Israel. Wright adds that the order would vary depending on who was teaching.[78]

The question of methods also divides potential sympathizers. Many Islamist political movements share their violent coreligionists' ultimate objective of establishing a government of God but disagree strongly on the means of achieving that goal.[79] Modern Islamists advocate three different approaches to advancing the faith: the political process, social change, and finally violence.

Those who view Islamists as a fringe group may be surprised to discover that the Islamists view politics as a promising path to power. In the Arab world, Islamist political parties have done quite well in elections. A common maxim for watchers of Arab politics is that the freer the election, the better the Islamists are likely to do. In Iraq, Lebanon, and the Palestinian territories, the dominant political victors turned out to be the Islamist parties, including two terrorist groups: Hizballah in Lebanon and Hamas in Palestine. In Saudi Arabia, Egypt, Kuwait, Yemen, and other countries there has been more limited political participation, but Islamists have done quite well, given the constraints and government vote manipulation they faced during campaigning. For these Islamist parties, the vote is the key to power and change. Millions of Muslims have endorsed this position simply by casting their ballot.

The jihadists, however, viscerally reject democracy. In their eyes, democracy places the law of man above the law of God. A legislature, for example, could legalize drinking. Or it could grant women the right to vote. Both measures would be anathema to jihadists. For the extremists, the Koran is the foundation of all law. Any other source of law is blasphemous. Yet democracy is exceptionally popular among Arab publics, perhaps because they understand firsthand the costs of tyranny. Thus the jihadists' position puts them at odds not only with the vast majority of people in the Muslim world, but also with the numerous Islamist parties and movements that stand to do quite well through the ballot box. Not surprisingly, when elections have happened, they have caused rifts in the movement.

Many *salafis* also are highly skeptical of political organization. Their dreams are personal and spiritual. To realize God's will, they must make themselves and their acquaintances better Muslims. Then society will improve, slowly and steadily. Their emphasis on religion places them at variance with groups or social movements that seek political change. They disapprove of prominent jihadist theologians such as Sayyid Qutb, who emphasizes political rather than religious advancement. The salafis' wariness of political organization places them at odds with mainstream political movements and terrorist groups. The salafis disdain the political savvy and tremendous organizational skills that are required to mobilize people and force governments to capitulate. Their dismissal of politics in turn drives a wedge between them and al-Qa'ida, which is intensely political.

Many salafis also define jihad as a struggle to strengthen one's own religious convictions rather than just violence. Salafis do accept that violent jihad is at times appropriate, but they are skeptical of how groups like al-Qa'ida use it. Jihad, in the eyes of most salafis, is appropriate only under rare circumstances and should not involve taking innocent blood. In the absence of a consensus regarding a commander of the faithful, they believe jihad should only be defensive. Iraq today is seen by many salafis as a legitimate place for jihad, but they would disagree with other calls to take jihad to fight for Muslims throughout the world. Salafis are not alone in criticizing the jihadists. Other Muslims see their violent coreligionists as unschooled and too political. In their eyes, social change and personal purification should be priorities.

The jihadist violence often backfires. After the bombings of hotels in Jordan in 2005, the Jordanian public's support for suicide attacks as a justifiable tactic plunged from 57 percent to 29 percent and public confidence in bin Ladin fell from 60 percent to 24 percent.[80]

Another key area of disagreement is the question of *takfir*, the act of declaring an individual (or government) to be an unbeliever, or *kafir* (plural, *kuffar*). The charge is serious and punishable by death. Sinful behavior such as murder or rape is not enough to make an individual a kafir. The individual charged must also make a deliberate decision to deny the faith, thus becoming an apostate. Because the charge is so serious, overwhelming evidence is required to prove that an individual is a kafir. That person is guilty only after this evidence is presented. Many Muslims refer to jihadists and their supporters as "takfiris" because they have the audacity to declare other Muslims to be apostates.

A number of jihadists have expanded the definition of takfir from individuals to governments throughout the Muslim world. As such, devout Muslims do not owe them loyalty, but in addition are obligated to rebel against them. In contrast, traditional Islamic teachings emphasize the value of a civil peace, even at the price of tyranny.[81] The International Crisis Group points out that salafis in general are highly skeptical of the legitimacy of rebellion against a Muslim government, even if it does not follow salafi teachings. "Most salafists, if forced to choose between the Saudi government and Osama bin Laden, would choose the former."[82] In Saudi Arabia, many salafis reject politics altogether; they may reject the Saudi state and its authority, but they also reject the rival claims of various religious organizations.[83]

Some groups have taken their view of takfir to such extremes that even jihadists find them intolerable. The GIA in Algeria, for example, declared all of society apostate: in short, those who were not jihadists were kuffar, and the group had the right—indeed, the obligation—to kill them.

Bin Ladin has fought against this narrow approach. In particular, he has tried to discourage attacks on other Muslims, whether they are Sufis, Shi'a, or other groups that many salafis view with suspicion. He has tried to unify different Sunni jihadist groups, urging them to go beyond their differences. Much of the global jihad, however, rejects this big-tent approach. Believing they have a duty to kill apostates, jihadists in Iraq regularly target the Shi'a.

As a result of these differences, many jihadists reject al-Qa'ida's call to focus on U.S. policy. Mohammad Bouyeri's 2004 attack on Dutch filmmaker Theo Van Gogh or the violent demonstrations over the cartoons ridiculing the prophet Mohammad in a Danish newspaper are, for many European Muslims, more salient issues than U.S. support for corrupt regimes in the Arab world. (The al-Qa'ida core is trying to reach out to these would-be affiliates. Although bin Ladin has historically focused on policy more than values, Ayman al-Zawahiri released a videotape in March 2006 that railed against Danish cartoons mocking the Prophet Mohammad.) The Taliban in Afghanistan and Jemaat Islamiyyah in Indonesia are concerned about the penetration of Western popular culture, as suggested by its attack on the Bali discotheque. Protests ensued immediately after *Playboy* went on sale, even though the Indonesia version lacked unclothed women (raising the unrelated question of why anyone would purchase the magazine). In Southeast Asia and Egypt, insurgents burn churches and attack Christian businesses. Sectarian issues often stir more passions than bin Ladin's global, U.S.-focused agenda.

Nationalism still divides many Islamist movements, with Hamas focused primarily on Palestine, the Islamic Group focused primarily on Egypt, and so on. Nationalism is an issue even within al-Qa'ida, where the prominence of Egyptians in its senior ranks has bred resentment. In London the presence of representatives from a wide range of Islamist groups has "led to a tempest of reciprocal excommunications and anathemas."[84] National sentiment is an exceptionally strong form of identity, and it has defeated international communism, Arab unity, Christendom, and other past pretenders to universalism.

Because ideology is so malleable, it is tempting to dismiss these differences as irrelevant to the world of terrorism operatives. That would be a mistake. Ideology helps the movement raise money and recruit members. Those who contribute or join usually do so because they genuinely believe in the cause. But the differences do not necessarily end once the recruits join the group. Assuming that most terrorists conclude that violence is justified, many will then disagree about the level of intensity. The al-Qa'ida–supported struggles in Algeria and the Caucasus involved levels of bloodshed that far exceeded anything al-Qa'ida itself has committed. The French scholar of Islam Gilles Kepel contends that the "savage violence" of terrorist organizations has worked against them. Rather than inspire other Muslims to take up arms against the West or apostate regimes, they have instead disgusted their coreligionists, leading them to reject extremism. The GIA justified the mass murders of Algerian villagers because they believed that the villagers were kuffar. Instead of helping the GIA's cause, the murders led to worldwide repugnance. Egyptian Islamic Jihad's bombing of the Egyptian embassy in Pakistan in 1995 led to considerable criticism among supporters, who claimed that the innocent died along with the guilty.[85]

While resentment and disdain toward the United States from the Muslim world have not declined in recent years, there are signs that support for bin Ladin and terrorism has fallen. A 2005 Pew opinion survey of the Muslim world found that in many countries support for terrorism and Osama bin Ladin was on the decline. Indonesia and Morocco exhibited the biggest change since 2003, with the percentage of respondents displaying "a lot" or "some" confidence in bin Ladin falling by almost half, from 58 percent and 49 percent to 35 percent and 26 percent, respectively.[86] Moreover, support for suicide bombs against civilian targets in Pakistan dropped from 41 percent in 2004 to 25 percent in 2005. In Indonesia, the figure fell from 27 percent to 15 percent.[87]

According to Middle East expert Augustus Richard Norton, these results are not surprising: "Muslims, like non-Muslims, are plugged into the world. . . . It is one thing to be caught up in the supposed glamour of attacking the superpower or global bully, but it is quite another to have to pay the consequences economically, politically, not to mention personally. This is what has happened in places like Indonesia, Morocco, Pakistan and Turkey, where many people now see extremist Islam as a threat to their lives, not a fantasy game of kick Uncle Sam."[88] While many Muslims in 2003 "saw a worldwide threat to Islam and [bin Ladin] represented opposition to the West and the United States" says Andrew Kohut, president of the Pew Research Council, "tempers have since cooled."[89]

Personal rivalries among leaders compound these differences. For many years Egyptian militants were divided into two camps: those who followed the blind sheikh Omar Adbel-Rahman, the man who inspired the 1993 World Trade Center attack, and those who rejected his leadership. This dispute between like-minded groups produced polemic after polemic. Some salafis in Indonesia have branded bin Ladin a *khawarij*, essentially labeling him a deviant who can be killed with impunity.[90]

Once a person leaves the salafi community and enters the broader world of political Islam, the differences loom even larger. The Islamist community shares the jihadist belief that Islam should play an important role in politics, but like any large religious community, they are divided on a wide variety of issues. Some leading Islamists seek harmony with the Shi'a and other sects. Others preach that only one school of thought is legitimate. Islamists disagree on the value of democracy, the role of women, the level of tolerance toward different sects within Islam, the proper role of government in the economy, and other core issues. The vast majority oppose violent rebellion against their own governments.

When the Islamists are successful in gaining power, their record so far has been unimpressive, which suggests that the model they champion may have inherent limits. Two self-declared "Islamic states"—Sudan and Afghanistan—have become remarkably less "Islamic" in recent years. In December 1999, Khartoum jailed the prominent Islamist Hassan al-Turabi, though they later released him. Two years later, the Taliban regime in Afghanistan fell to U.S.-backed forces. The much-feared "Talibanization" of Pakistan has been checked, though it remains disturbingly plausible. Attempts to overturn the government of Egypt, Algeria, and Saudi Arabia, among others, have failed. Iran's "government of God" is in crisis, with widespread disillusionment throughout Iranian society and much of the religious establishment.[91]

Implications for Counterterrorism

There is no single strategy that can successfully defeat the jihadists. All heads of the hydra of terrorism must be attacked. It is precisely the divisions among the groups that suggest the means in which the battle against terrorism can be successful. (Some of these points will be discussed later, but they are worth mentioning now.)

Al-Qa'ida's size, discipline, and skill make it a formidable intelligence challenge. Early terrorist groups such as Germany's Red Army Faction or November 17 in Greece were small and limited in scope. Unlike al-Qa'ida, they did not pose a global threat, nor were their techniques especially innovative. They lacked the ability to regroup when their leaders were killed or arrested. Even the activities of larger and more competent groups such as the Provisional Irish Republican Army and the Lebanese Hizballah are far smaller and more geographically focused than al-Qa'ida. The most important difference between these groups is that al-Qa'ida is willing to inflict mass casualties on U.S. soil. Few other organizations are willing to embark upon such a horrific quest.

So the first challenge to U.S. intelligence is collecting in-depth information about the areas in which al-Qa'ida and its affiliates function. But counterintelligence operatives cannot stop there. The United States must also be able to connect disparate pieces of information from a wide swath of countries across the world. Information from a cell in Algeria may be relevant to terrorists in Europe, who in turn may be in touch with radicals in Iraq. The United States must go beyond the al-Qa'ida core. In the countries they investigate, operatives must obtain knowledge about each local group and each relevant individual. Though many of the locals have done little to threaten the United States, they may possess a small nugget of information that can lead to the terrorist networks within their midst.

Militarily, the United States will have to ensure that there are no more Talibans: no regime should be allowed to support, or even knowingly tolerate, a jihadist presence. In addition, the military will be called on for narrower, nontraditional roles that differ from its traditional emphasis on conventional war. Conducting or assisting targeted killings may be one role. Given the importance of insurgent groups to the global jihad, the most important function of the military should be counterinsurgency.

Diplomatically, the United States must redouble efforts to gain strategic allies in the fight against terrorism. Allies in the Muslim world are of paramount importance. But so, too, are traditional allies. Europe was a staging ground for the September 11 attacks, and its large Arab and Muslim population represents a pool of potential recruits for al-Qa'ida. Similarly, allied police and intelligence services offer additional (and sometimes superior) intelligence to complement U.S. efforts.[92]

So far, al-Qa'ida is winning the battle of ideas: its concept of defensive jihad is gaining authority, as is its credo that the United

States is at the root of the Muslim world's problems. If we do nothing to counter al-Qa'ida's ideology, the movement will gain a steady stream of recruits. And terrorists will be able to find refuge among a sympathetic populace. Public diplomacy should try to provide a competing narrative, one that calls attention to the acceptable positions of U.S. foreign policy and, most importantly, delegitimizes the jihadists' activities.

The United States must use extreme caution when it attempts to foster political reform. The grievances jihadists harbor against their own countries are often justified, and promoting reform may be necessary. But reform can backfire. Change can dislocate established elites. Reforms can create instability, particularly in the short term. If the dislocations resulting from reform are not addressed, they offer further openings for jihadists to exploit.

One issue stands out above all else: Iraq. All else pales beside the overwhelming quandary that Iraq has created for the United States. Al-Qa'ida has sought to make Iraq a new Afghanistan, and it appears to be succeeding. Iraq has inflamed the passions of millions of Muslims, and at the same time it has become a base for jihadists operating in the region. The fate of Iraq will be instrumental in determining the future path of the jihadist movement.

If the United States treats all insurgents as one group, it runs the risk of fulfilling bin Ladin's desire to elicit a heavy-handed U.S. response to terrorism, which will then generate more sympathy and support for his cause. In particular, policy must seek to avoid turning groups with primarily local aspirations into groups that share al-Qa'ida's global agenda. Indeed, equating al-Qa'ida and terrorism, and making any organization with sympathy for al-Qa'ida part of a monolithic terrorist *internationale*, may become a self-fulfilling prophecy by forcing us to take the government's side in every internal dispute. In the end, such a policy will bolster al-Qa'ida in places where its current presence is limited—the Xinjiang region of China, for example.

Al-Qa'ida's penchant for infighting and its limited mass support are internal weaknesses that are ripe for U.S. influence. Islamists, salafis, and salafi jihadists are divided on issues that range from ideology to tactics. The United States can take advantage of these differences to reduce contacts among groups, even turning one against another.

When possible, U.S. policy should try to distinguish between those groups supporting violence against the United States and those that simply dislike or denounce America. Fortunately, only some of the radical groups around the world are focused on the United States—though the number is growing. Some local groups, such as Algeria's GSPC, Egypt's Islamic Jihad, and Indonesia's Jemaah Islamiyya, have joined al-Qa'ida or otherwise embraced its global agenda. So, too, have many local cells such as the Madrid bombers, many of which do not formally belong to any long-standing group but nevertheless pose a deadly threat. But other terrorist organizations should not be as high on the list. Chechen fighters, for example, often share a similar outlook with al-Qa'ida, but their goals are primarily local. Attention should be focused on the more urgent threat—those groups that intend to harm the United States through violence.

A final necessity is education of the U.S. public and improved homeland defense. Given al-Qa'ida's lethality and appeal, we must expect further attacks. The president and other senior leaders must try to minimize the popular fear and the economic and political damage resulting from even a limited attack. Also vital is ensuring the continued goodwill of the U.S. Muslim community. Violence is almost certain to continue for at least the coming decade. If Americans can remain steadfast, the government can better avoid mistakes and overreactions that play directly into al-Qa'ida's hands.

2

What Is Victory and How Do We Achieve It?

Fighting an amorphous foe that strikes intermittently means having difficulty knowing when you've won. Most definitions of victory are either so vague as to be meaningless or so grandiose as to be impractical. Politicians of both parties regularly talk about "eliminating" terrorism, failing to recognize that the tactic has been around for literally thousands of years and is almost impossible to eradicate. Expecting groups to abandon terrorism completely is unrealistic, as desperate individuals will always resort to desperate means. As the strategist Stephen Biddle points out, dramatically reducing levels of terror might require fundamental regime and social changes throughout the Muslim world.[1]

The goal should be to defeat the jihadist terrorists at an acceptable price. Much of the focus should be on short-term efforts to imprison, kill, and disrupt those who would kill us. At the same time, the United States and its allies should try to combat the terrorists' ideology and encourage reforms that lessen popular support for radical activities—but these long-term measures must be done carefully, and their success is likely to be limited and will take many years to bear fruit even if all goes well. Thus our goals must be realistic even as they are ambitious.

A more nuanced definition of victory should look at several overlapping measures: physical security, psychological reassurance, impact on other policy goals, and overall cost.

Physical security can be measured in lives and property. There is no "acceptable" level of death from terrorism, but it is important to distinguish levels that can truly reshape our daily lives and those that, while horrible, are objectively extremely low. Until 2001, terrorism was a concern for most Americans, but one that remained in the background. The deaths of seventeen Americans in the *Cole* attack in 2000, eighteen in the embassy attacks in 1998, nineteen in Khobar Towers in Saudi Arabia in 1996, and six in the 1993 World Trade Center attacks were not enough to provoke widespread concern (and some attacks, such as the *Cole* strike, were barely noticed). So past experience suggests that if the threat is limited to perhaps the deaths of fewer than twenty Americans a year from terrorism, terrorism should be a policy concern, but not the dominant one it has been since 9/11. Moreover, the pace of attacks was limited—it did not involve constant strikes, but rather intermittent ones. Similarly, all these attacks involved destruction of U.S. facilities, but the costs were easily manageable for the mammoth U.S. economy. So part of "success" is reducing the threat of terrorism back to this manageable level.

Yet, as political scientist John Mueller points out, even the deaths of three thousand Americans is "manageable" from an actuarial point of view: we have at times lost more people in traffic accidents in a month than we have in the history of international terrorism, including 9/11. Here the problem is also one of perceptions and reassurance: the terrorist attacks must not be perceived as causing a lethal threat to millions or of posing a danger to governance.

Governments recognize this logic. The 2003 U.S. *National Strategy for Combating Terrorism* declared, "Our goal will be reached when Americans and other civilized people around the world can lead their lives free from terrorist attacks." The British government's definition of success also followed this logic of perceptions: it sought *"to reduce the risk from international terrorism so that people can go about their business freely and with confidence."*[2] Then secretary of defense Donald Rumsfeld expressed this view more vividly after 9/11, noting that the United States will have won "when you and I and our children get up and walk out the door and don't worry that an airplane is going to come down and hit us, or a truck bomb is going to drive into a building, or the World Trade Center is going to fall down."[3]

Psychologically, it is important to recognize that the "success" of terrorism is often in our own hands. Secretary Rumsfeld has noted that terrorists can win only if "we lose our will and surrender the fight."[4] This approach suggests that simply by keeping a stiff upper lip we will not fail.

This raises the question of how much fear is acceptable. By some measures, we are already there: people fly in airplanes, invest in businesses, travel internationally, and otherwise live their lives even with the threat of terrorism. And as Mueller notes, real estate prices in New York and Washington have only risen since 9/11, suggesting that people are willing to put their money and their lives at stake as well. National polls, however, suggest that terrorism remains in the forefront of most Americans' concerns. Success thus would involve a matching of perceptions and reality: people would not only be less at risk from terrorism, but they would also cease to see it as a necessary driver of U.S. foreign policy.

Moreover, although an American who dies in Yemen is no less a loss than one who dies in Topeka, the psychological difference is considerable. Thus, the bar for acceptable deaths at home should be lower than that overseas because of its psychological impact. Attacks that kill hundreds in the United States are thus not acceptable and require significant policy changes. Moreover, the murder of high-level officials is also a sign of failure, as it suggests a problem for governance even though the U.S. system is able to replace them.

A third dimension of success is the impact on other policy goals. The United States has other policy objectives that are vital, ranging from the health of the international economic system to stopping nuclear proliferation to preserving peace among the world's leading powers. A U.S. policy that led to a substantial decrease of the flow of goods around the world in order to reduce the danger of terrorist arms smuggling would only be a success in the narrowest terms: the loss of tens of billions of dollars in trade and thousands of jobs would be far more important overall to the health and well-being of Americans and our political institutions.

A fourth, related dimension is the cost of success. Conceivably, the United States might be able to reduce terrorism by withdrawing its military forces from the Middle East. If this led to the invasion of Saudi Arabia or internal strife there—and thus caused the price of oil to go to $200 a barrel—the cost would be too high. Similarly, constant U.S. military campaigns that lead to the deaths of thousands of Americans is a high price to pay. Although it is easy to use ringing rhetoric of "spare no cost" when it comes to lives lost from terrorism, additional levels of security are often more than Americans want to, and should, pay.

Taken together, these criteria suggest several metrics for victory:

1. *low levels of death* from international terrorism, numbering less than a hundred each year;
2. *the level of fear is reduced* so that Americans go about their lives with little concern about terrorism—this requires not only a low number of deaths in absolute terms, but also a particularly low level of deaths on U.S. soil;
3. counterterrorism *done at an acceptable cost* in dollars, lives, and other policy priorities.

When counterterrorism is going well, other foreign policy issues will, and should, rise to the fore. If the realistic danger is that dozens of Americans might die, as opposed to hundreds or thousands, it is appropriate for the government to concentrate on a range of other policy concerns.

How Do We Achieve Victory?

In the years since September 11, the Bush administration has tried, often commendably, to fight terrorism with efforts ranging from an aggressive intelligence and military campaign to trying to win over the youth of the Arab world through radio and television broadcasts. The 2006 *National Strategy for Combating Terrorism* emphasized killing and arresting terrorists abroad, denying them the support of states, preventing them from gaining access to weapons of mass destruction, and spreading democracy.[5] These efforts, however, are not part of an overarching strategic framework that lays out a path to victory. As a result, these different approaches are at best not integrated and at worst are working against one another.

The Bush administration's shotgun approach to counterterrorism reflects a broader confusion on how we win the war on terrorism. As pundits and policymakers endlessly remark, this war will not end with a World War II–like surrender on the battleship *Missouri*. The enemy is too diffuse to simply attack and conquer. That insight is important, but it raises the broader question of how victory may be attained. For many observers, victory in the war on terrorism bears a striking resemblance to obscenity: you know it when you see it.

Such vagueness can be disastrous for something as serious as terrorism.

Most elements of a strategy can be thought of as addressing one of two different goals: disrupting the group itself as it tries to conduct operations, or changing the overall operating environment in a way that defuses the group's anger or makes it harder for it to raise money or attract recruits. Moreover, various strategies affect different parts of the problem in different ways. Some hurt the al-Qa'ida core, while others affect its affiliates and sympathizers.

For example, we could accomplish our short-term goals by backing our most aggressive and capable allies who are committed to stopping al-Qa'ida, providing them with financial support, intelligence assistance, and other aid. In the long term, we could decrease political alienation in the Muslim world by spreading good government, reducing the level of popular grievance on which terrorists feed. Both approaches are good in theory, and in fact were endorsed in the White House's 2006 national security strategy policy.

Yet a closer look suggests some inherent tensions between these two apparently straightforward approaches. Egypt, for example, is one of our closest allies in the war on terrorism and has aggressively gone after al-Qa'ida and its affiliates, both for its own sake and on our behalf. At the same time, Egyptian president Hosni Mubarak is a turgid dictator whose cronyism, corruption, stagnation, and repression understandably alienate and anger many Egyptians and lead some to violence. Should we weaken this despotism to increase the chances of good government, or should we back it to crush al-Qa'ida cells by any means necessary?

Picking the right strategy is the difference between winning the war and losing it, and the answer is by no means obvious. Before we decide on how best to approach the problem of terrorism, let's consider the strategy alternatives.

Strategy One: Crush al-Qa'ida Ourselves

The most obvious way to defeat al-Qa'ida, and the one with tremendous emotional appeal, is to directly target al-Qa'ida and its supporters. The goal is to kill (or at times arrest) those who mean to do us harm. As Avi Dichter, the former head of Shin Bet and one of the architects of Israel's counterterrorism campaign, told me: "You try to find people who want to have you for dinner and you have them for lunch." For many Americans, such an approach means going well beyond current counterterrorism policies and using U.S. military forces to kill al-Qa'ida and large numbers of its supporters wherever they can be found. In his book *Imperial Hubris,* Michael Scheuer, who led the hunt for bin Ladin at the CIA for several years in the 1990s, notes that "unchanged U.S. policies toward the Muslim world leave America only a military option for defending itself" and that military force cannot be applied "daintily." Scheuer calls for the United States to return to a World War II–style use of force, with fast-paced killing and "extremely large" body counts.[6] Our allies, Scheuer contends, will not do this dirty work for us.

Though rare, there are some examples of instances where strong government campaigns have crushed terrorist groups. Turkey's campaign against the once-daunting Kurdish Workers Party (PKK) is instructive. For decades after the founding of the modern Turkish state in 1923, Turkey's Kurds had repeatedly chafed at the Turkish government's efforts to assimilate them. In 1984 the PKK launched a terrorism campaign and formed a large guerrilla army. Fighting in the name of Kurdish self-determination, the PKK sparked a mini–civil war, which by the time it diminished in 2000 had killed more than thirty thousand people. The Turkish government's response was a tough counterinsurgency campaign involving much of the Turkish army and intelligence service.

Concurrently, Turkey also pressed the PKK's two main sponsors, Iraq and Syria, to cease providing safe haven and to surrender the PKK leaders hiding in their countries, particularly the PKK's leader, Abdullah Ocalan, who for years benefited from Damascus's hostility toward Turkey. Turkey engaged in a massive war against PKK cadres, repeatedly crossing the border into Iraq to target PKK bases in the Kurdish areas there. In 1998 Turkey threatened Syria with military action (a position that the United States backed), and the regime sent Ocalan packing. He fled, going from Syria to Russia, Greece, and Italy, eventually ending up in 1999 in Kenya, where he was arrested and brought back to Turkey. This coincided with a period where the Turkish government became less repressive of Kurdish rights, allowing the use of the Kurdish language and otherwise lessening assimilationist pressure.

The Turkish government's strategy illustrates how a group can be crushed by force. After large numbers of cadre are killed or arrested, the organization is simply less able to function. Over time, would-be members are dissuaded from joining the group out of fear that they, too, will be killed, arrested, or otherwise punished. Particularly important was getting the PKK's leadership: as long as they were able to recruit, fund-raise, and train new cadre in havens outside Turkey, the group was able to survive despite the government's fierce counterterrorism measures.

A closer look, however, reveals that such a direct approach is a strategy founded on illusions when it is applied to al-Qa'ida. If the United States seeks to crush al-Qa'ida largely by itself, this has truly massive requirements. First and foremost, the intelligence capabilities needed are daunting. Because of al-Qa'ida's global presence (to say nothing of that of its sympathizers), the United States needs a massive intelligence presence in every country with a significant jihadist presence, including Pakistan, Afghanistan, Saudi Arabia, Yemen, and Indonesia. In all these countries, U.S. operatives would be spying on local mosques, tapping phone lines, trailing suspects, and otherwise doing the day-to-day work of counterterrorism. U.S.

operatives would be breaking local laws and thus having to hide their activities from the police and intelligence services—many of whom might be trailing the same suspects!

Although the United States can improve its capacity in various countries, it cannot summon the necessary manpower to do everything everywhere. To monitor subversive and criminal activity in the United States, the FBI in 2005 had just under thirty thousand total employees.[7] Many more are needed to gather intelligence in remote areas around the world where the police and people are not cooperative. But where would all those talented employees come from?

In 2001, fewer than a third of the CIA's new case officers had any foreign-language expertise.[8] Efforts to remedy the shortfall in the intelligence community have not met with much success. Finding Americans with the necessary foreign-language skills can be difficult. According to census data, only 1.6 percent of Americans speak critical foreign languages. And the number of those who have academic degrees concentrating in such languages, as Betsy Davis, the CIA's number two recruiting officer, recently noted, is "frighteningly small."[9]

To fight affiliates linked to al-Qa'ida, the United States would be engaged in several Iraq-like operations and many smaller ones as well. Kashmir, Afghanistan, Chechnya, and Algeria would all be theaters of action, as would Indonesia, Yemen, Nigeria, and other places. Maintaining more than a hundred thousand troops in Iraq has proven daunting for the U.S. military, which has found it hard to maintain readiness for other missions and to attract qualified recruits. Doing multiple Iraq-type operations would be overwhelming.

Strategy Two: Strengthen Allies and Crush al-Qa'ida Indirectly

Working with others would solve some of these problems. Rather than monitor mosques in Yemen with our agents or kill Algerian insurgents with our troops, we would rely on the forces of allies to act in our stead. The destruction of the Egyptian Islamic Jihad (EIJ) network in Europe and Egypt is one model that demonstrates the power of this approach. Like many Egyptian militant groups, EIJ grew out of Egypt's Muslim Brotherhood—a political organization that has flirted with violence repeatedly and has suffered from repression again and again since its founding in 1928. Along with the like-minded (but at times bitter rival) Islamic Group, EIJ led an uprising in the early 1990s that led to more than a thousand deaths. The militants attacked not only regime security forces but also writers, secular judges, Copts, and foreign tourists.

The Egyptian government steadily gained the upper hand over the militants. Through massive detentions and brutal interrogation, the regime rounded up most of the suspects—as well as thousands of other Egyptians. To take the wind out of the militants' sails, the regime also made numerous concessions to individuals affiliated with the more moderate Muslim Brotherhood (and often antijihadist) and to the religious establishment. The result was a more Islamicized Egypt, but a more peaceful one.

By 1996, the groups no longer posed a threat to the Mubarak regime's survival—but they remained lethal. The Islamic Group continued to attack Western tourists, most notoriously killing fifty-eight (along with four Egyptians) in an attack on the Hatshepsut Temple in Luxor in 1997.

But as EIJ wound down in Egypt, its international role expanded. One strand of the EIJ led by Ayman al-Zawahiri effectively merged with al-Qa'ida. This strand embraced al-Qa'ida's global agenda and came to see the United States, not the Egyptian government, as the primary enemy. (Others within the battered movement continued the struggle in Egypt, while still others called for a cease-fire.)

The United States worked closely with the Egyptian government and other allies to contain this international movement. For example, the *Wall Street Journal* reports that in July 1998 the CIA worked with the government of Albania to deport several members of an EIJ cell from the Balkans to Egypt. The CIA helped Albania's intelligence service with equipment to tap phones and trained them on surveillance. Their interrogation in Egypt, much of which was brutal, led to mass trials of alleged terrorists there.[10]

As the EIJ experience demonstrates, the United States can play multiple roles. With Egypt, the United States is a recipient of intelligence: information from interrogations goes to U.S. intelligence officials, who in turn use it in their efforts in other countries or to prevent terrorists from infiltrating the United States. At times the United States uses the intelligence it collects to direct allies like the Albanians to crack down on terrorist cells in their countries. As a result of this cooperation, more EIJ members are off the streets. They no longer pose a threat to the United States or its citizens.

Allied police, soldiers, and security services act in the stead of American agents to shut down fund-raising, proselytizing, and Web sites. The military equivalent of the CIA's Albania operation is working with local military forces against al-Qa'ida–linked insurgents. Instead of American special operations forces closing in on the al-Qa'ida camp in the North West Frontier Province, the uniforms would be those of the Pakistani military.

Because much of the heavy lifting is done by allies, the cost of this option is far less than crushing al-Qa'ida directly. The United States may pay to augment local capabilities, but this is a fraction of the cost of doing the work ourselves. Also, these allies are likely to be better in many respects than their U.S. counterparts at certain functions, particularly when it comes to gathering intelligence (i.e., they have the home field advantage). Allies can use their own laws to legally and easily acquire information, drawing on cooperation from local businesses and citizens. Their police know the communities well, and they have a massive presence simply to keep order (and, in many cases, to protect the regime from unrest).

One of the biggest problems of this reliance is competence. In some respects, allies are as good as Americans and, in several important ways, better. But in many instances they suffer in comparison. Militarily, few allies hold a candle to American forces, particularly elite special operations force units such as the U.S. Navy's SEALS or the U.S. Army's Delta Force. Most allies, particularly in the developing world where al-Qa'ida camps are most likely to be found, lack sophisticated technologies such as the Predator Unmanned Aerial Vehicle and often are not able to coordinate their forces well. Some members of allied security services may even be sympathetic to the jihadists, providing them with advance warning or otherwise assisting their efforts to escape.

Some allies might also hesitate to work with the United States. Open cooperation may draw the jihadists' wrath, turning allies from bystanders to targets. The good news is that most allies share our views on al-Qa'ida. For alliance purposes, bin Ladin's organization is in many ways an ideal ally: it hates everyone. Muslim regimes are corrupt and impious, Western states support a variety of decadent leaders and are oppressing the Muslim world, and so on. Al-Qa'ida's policy of supporting insurgencies means that many traditional non-Western major powers such as Russia, China, Indonesia, Nigeria, and India all have a strong interest in seeing the jihadists destroyed.

Another problem is that anarchy reigns in parts of the world, making reliance on allies at best a limited policy. Afghanistan, Mauritania, Somalia, Tajikistan, and Yemen are only a few of the countries around the world where the government's writ is limited to the capital and other major cities. In these areas, allies can (or will) do only so much. Thus, working through allies solves part of the problem, but huge gaps remain.

As with crushing al-Qa'ida directly, working through allies requires making counterterrorism a priority, albeit in a different manner. The challenge here is not dealing with the fallout of offending allies, but rather paying the price of their cooperation. If we rely on allies to cooperate because it is the right thing to do, we will be sorely disappointed. Some will do it fitfully, others on their own schedule, and still others not at all. To gain this support, the United States will often need to make concessions to allies. Pakistan may provide additional cooperation against various jihadist movements—but not if the United States is simultaneously punishing Islamabad for its nuclear program.

Strategy Three: Contain al-Qa'ida
An alternative to crushing al-Qa'ida completely is to try to contain it, transforming it from a grave strategic threat to a dangerous nuisance, comparable to the dozens of other terrorist groups around the world. Many of the particulars would be similar to other strategy options; the main difference would be in priorities. The struggle against the jihadists would join the host of other U.S. foreign policy concerns, at times taking precedence but often being secondary. With Pakistan, for example, the United States would prioritize its nuclear program; with Saudi Arabia, oil price stability.

Containment recognizes the difficulty in finding every terrorist or even of reducing group capabilities so that relatively low-tech attacks like the Madrid and London bombings are impossible. A containment strategy assumes the threat is manageable. As Philip Heymann, a former deputy attorney general of the United States, argues, "There will be terrorism. We can deal with it; we can discourage it; but we cannot end it completely."[11] Indeed, by some measures, the threat is more than manageable—it is negligible. John Mueller acidly notes that before 9/11, the number of Americans who died from international terrorism was less than those killed by lightning strikes or, less dramatically, drowning in toilets.[12] Excluding Iraq and Afghanistan, the number of Americans killed by al-Qa'ida-linked terrorism since September 11 is in the dozens (much depends on which groups are counted as al-Qa'ida). While tragic, losing relatively few people from terrorism in the five years since 9/11 suggests that from an actuarial point of view, more U.S. lives could be saved by putting resources elsewhere. Even in the month of September 2001 itself, more Americans died on the road or from cancer than died from terrorism.[13]

Containment does not mean ignoring terrorists, but rather not putting terrorism front and center in U.S. foreign policy. Containment, in essence, was the U.S. counterterrorism strategy for decades. The United States went after individual terrorists, be they members of the Abu Nidal Organization, the Lebanese Hizballah, Greece's Organization 17 November, or other groups whose members had killed Americans. In all these cases the United States tried to arrest particular individuals (or have its allies do so), but there was no pretense of going after the group as a whole. The Lebanese Hizballah, for example, has been nestled comfortably in Lebanon since its founding in the early 1980s. It killed Americans and took Western hostages in the 1980s, and since then continued to war constantly with Israel, but U.S. efforts were confined to pressing the group's state sponsors, Iran and Syria, and trying to disrupt and arrest individual members when they left the Lebanese sanctuary.

The exception to this limited focus was domestic terrorism. The FBI relentlessly tracked leftist groups such as the Weathermen or the Symbionese Liberation Army, driving them deep underground and eventually rounding up all their important members. When the threat from right-wing militia movements became clear after the April 19, 1995, bombing of the Alfred P. Murrah Federal Building in Oklahoma City—at the time the most devastating domestic terrorist attack in U.S. history, killing 167 people, including 19 children—the FBI moved quickly to penetrate, and then disrupt and arrest, various right-wing movements throughout the country.

In addition to seeing the risk itself as minor, containment has a strategy for victory: that the adversary has internal contradictions that, given time, will discredit and divide it. The adversary is divided on what target should receive priority, who is kuffar, whether it is against Western values or just U.S. policies, and other core issues. In addition, there are numerous leaders who will rise to the fore if bin Ladin cannot control the organization—and these leaders are bound to fight one another as they compete for power and prestige. All of these differences have the potential to divide the movement. A generation from now, these contradictions will not have destroyed the jihadist cause, but they may have weakened it dramatically. The jihadist movement will cooperate less internally. Moreover, parts of the movement may literally war on other parts, and some elements may work with foreign intelligence agencies against their rivals.

Equally important, containment recognizes the limits of many alternatives and that some of them may even backfire. Most of the ideas and policies outlined in this book are at best challenging and costly; at worse, they may fail or even backfire. One of containment's greatest strengths is that it avoids some of the risks from other policy alternatives. Containment is thus a relatively low-cost alternative: it demands less in the way of troops and intelligence. At home, less needs to be spent on costly homeland defense measures. Even more important, it requires few policy sacrifices. If Pakistan threatens to reduce its aid to the United States on terrorism because of U.S. pressure on its nuclear program, the United States can take that risk because counterterrorism is not the dominant policy.

Containment, however, is far from perfect. In the past, containment worked—but the reasons for this success should give us little comfort today. The primary target of most terrorist groups in the world is not the United States, but rather their local government or, in many cases, Israel. Thus while the Lebanese Hizballah has not been linked to anti-U.S. attacks for more than a decade (and its role in the 1996 attack on Khobar Towers where a member was implicated seems secondary), this is in large part because the organization prefers to go after other targets first, particularly Israel. Other groups, such as 17 November, are small and are only capable of mounting a few attacks.

Al-Qa'ida, however, both seeks to kill Americans itself and, equally important, turn more local groups against the United States. While it also has other priorities, it can and will kill large numbers of Americans if not confronted or disabled. This problem is particularly acute today. Containment's vision is a long-term one and, over time, the movement may focus elsewhere or collapse under the weight of its own divisions. In the short term, however—and the short term may last a decade or more—the jihadist cause is alive and well, and more attacks are likely to continue.

Containment's more realistic defenders would argue, correctly, that containment is not passivity. The United States would still work with allies (and indeed containment is a natural partner to an ally-based strategy), police its borders, and otherwise try to keep the jihadists off balance and weak. Moreover, the United States should focus particular attention on high-lethality attacks (or ones that would be psychologically devastating and cause panic), such as those involving chemical, biological, radiological, or nuclear weapons.

Getting some allies to cooperate with a containment policy would be difficult. Other states will naturally have their own security interests at heart and probably would resent our efforts, which are focused on protecting our citizens' lives, not theirs. Part of containment is simply keeping the lid on the pressure pot—preventing local insurgents from going global and attacking Americans. Such a policy will obviously not be viewed favorably by these countries' governments, which are looking for help in destroying the threat, not in just keeping it local.

One of the biggest problems with containment is the home front. Containment is the antithesis of a "crush" strategy and thus appears like weakness to audiences at home who are scared, angry, and hungry for vengeance after a terrorist attack. This public response is not based on a calculation of the risk of death. Yet terrorism scares people. Thus even a limited number of deaths, particularly if they occur on U.S. soil, has a disproportionate psychological effect. Work stops, and people refuse to travel. Public confidence in government plunges. All this may be irrational to statisticians, but policymakers must adjust policy to cope with the actual behavior of citizens. Moreover, every government must ensure the security of its citizens to be credible, and the deliberate murder of civilians is a direct challenge to a government's credibility and legitimacy.

It will be impossible for politicians not to respond to such provocations. The Bush administration has spent the years since 9/11 telling the American people how dangerous the threat is, and most Democratic politicians have joined in the chorus. When politicians have tried to soften their rhetoric on terrorism, they faced tremendous criticism. During the waning days of the 2004 elections, Democratic presidential candidate John Kerry told the *New York Times* that he wanted to turn terrorism into a "nuisance" like crime is; President Bush told reporters that the United States would never achieve a clear victory in the war. The public outcry forced both to "clarify" (i.e., disown) their statements.

You cannot take the politics out of counterterrorism. The painful answer might be that "doing something" (whether it is spending money on homeland security or acting aggressively abroad) is needed to reassure people after a massive attack on the U.S. homeland, since a perception that the government was passive could contribute to a massive overreaction. Reacting may be necessary to prevent overreacting.

In addition to preventing peace, terrorism also can spark a far more massive conflict. Indeed, terrorist groups often hope to provoke a larger popular struggle, seeing themselves as the vanguard of a broader movement that they can create through violence. Through the murder and intimidation of civilians—and by provoking a harsh state response—they force people to choose sides, shattering what was a peaceful accommodation. There may be few fatalities from such terrorism, but the strategic consequences are massive. Two of the world's most deadliest insurgencies in Kashmir and Chechnya began with limited terrorism and quickly escalated to conflicts that claimed hundreds of thousands of victims. Israel, Colombia, and other parts of the world have seen terrorists derail peace talks.

Indeed, small but violent groups can have an influence disproportionate to their size. In "The Banality of 'Ethnic War,'" John Mueller points out that demagogic politicians can use very small bands of thugs to spawn refugee flights, which in turn lead to a cycle of revenge. During the wars in the former Yugoslavia, in some towns in the Balkans little more than a dozen thugs forced thousands to flee.[14] In Iraq, limited violence in the summer of 2003 escalated just as the terrorists (now the insurgents) sought.

The lack of a response to terrorism can fuel this. Successful terrorism spawns imitation. (In contrast, devastating hurricanes don't tell their hurricane buddies that the U.S. coastline is wide open.) An ineffectual response can thus spawn more of the problem. In addition, no response can undermine the credibility of a government, beginning a cycle that terrorists exploit to build their organization and become a full-fledged insurgent movement.

Al-Qa'ida, of course, is well aware of ill-gotten rewards of terrorism and seeks to exploit them. The bulk of al-Qa'ida's activities are not related to anti-U.S. or even international terrorism. Rather, the organization proselytizes and fosters insurgencies around the globe. Chechnya, Algeria, Kashmir, Bosnia, the Philippines, Indonesia, and now Iraq are only some of the countries where the organization has focused. These insurgencies, of course, kill tens or hundreds of thousands—and terrorism is how several of them began.[15]

Here is where containment advocates overstate how well things are going today. Attacks on the U.S. homeland have not occurred, in part due to the changes the United States has forced on al-Qa'ida as well as due to increased vigilance. However, al-Qa'ida and affiliated groups have if anything become *more* active overseas in their pace of attacks since September 11. Algeria, Indonesia, Spain, Morocco, Saudi Arabia, Jordan, Yemen, Russia, Pakistan, Egypt, and the United Kingdom are only a few countries that have suffered terrorism. More important in many ways are the ongoing insurgencies in Iraq, Afghanistan, Chechnya, and Kashmir and the strife in Pakistan and Nigeria. In these countries, violence is constant and exceptionally costly.

Last, containment requires restraint—something difficult for politicians of all parties.

Strategy Four: Defenses

A good defense is the flip side of various offensive strategies and containment. Until jihadism collapses under the weight of its own failings or is decimated by killings and arrests, we still need to protect ourselves.

If terrorists could easily enter the country and operate here with impunity, the number of attacks would almost certainly increase. "Defenses" is a broad term, however. It can include emergency preparedness, domestic intelligence, better border control, port security initiatives, and other measures designed to make it harder for the terrorists to successfully attack.

Some of what is now "al-Qa'ida" is really an unaffiliated group of wannabes, inspired by bin Ladin's dream but not in touch with the broader organization. They might be able to scrounge together the money to fly to the United States for an attack (or, more realistically, seek to strike a U.S. target in their home country). While in the United States, they could probably acquire a weapon or materials for a bomb.

With better defenses, however, the chance of finding these amateurs is higher. Their shoddy passports will be inspected more carefully. Weapons dealers will be more vigilant with regard to individuals who might be terrorists, and illegal arms merchants will be under closer scrutiny. If the terrorists seek help from individuals in the United States who might assist them (providing them with a room to sleep in or helping them survey various targets), they are more likely to be caught, as these individuals are under surveillance from the government.

Effective offense cannot catch all these individuals. Many of them do not appear on the radar screen of intelligence agencies until after they commit attacks. However, it can help ensure that they are not linked to a broader operational (as opposed to ideological) network. In the absence of a local support infrastructure, terrorists must do everything on their own: acquire documents, raise money, find fellow travelers to help them live from day to day, and so on. Even more important, they are less likely to be trained and thus are more likely to make mistakes.

Perhaps the best example of how defense can work in a tactical sense is Israel's security barrier, which separates much of the West Bank and Gaza Strip from major Israeli population centers. The fence stopped many would-be attackers from penetrating Israel proper, forcing many to abandon their efforts or to go through checkpoints, where they were often detected. Others tried to circumvent the fence by traveling through areas where it was still incomplete. These detours added many miles and hours to their trips, however, and forced them to work with and inform more people about their activities—delays and opportunities that Israeli counterterrorism forces were able to seize on in disrupting attacks.

Defenses are necessary because intelligence, even if superb, is always incomplete. Investigations of attacks before September 11 emphasized that warning of a particular attack may be lacking even though there is broad recognition that an attack may occur. Even today, U.S. government officials regularly warn that terrorists could strike tomorrow with no warning.

One advantage of defenses over other strategies is they do not rely on as much cooperation with more distant allies as on those that border the United States. Regardless of the good opinion of Germany or the level of cooperation from Pakistan, the United States can still make itself safer by making its borders more secure. Canada and Mexico, however, must cooperate wholeheartedly for defenses to function to their full extent.

Yet a strategy of defense begs some rather obvious questions. First, what is to be defended? Some sites seem obvious. The White House and Congress, of course, should be well defended. So, too, should nuclear power plants and chemical manufacturing sites. But now it gets harder. Should state capitols be defended, or lesser federal government buildings (say, the U.S. Department of Transportation)? What about public transportation, which has long been a favorite target of terrorists around the world? Although difficult, choices must be made. For example, the cost of purchasing and installing explosives detection systems for Boston's Logan International Airport is estimated to be $146 million, while the cost for Dallas/Fort Worth International Airport will be more than $193 million, and the nationwide price tag is $3 billion. Is this the best use of tax dollars, or is it better spent on more border guards or on social welfare programs that decrease immigrants' alienation and thus make them less prone to terrorism?[16]

The more comprehensive the list, the more costly the defenses become. Increasing airline screening since 9/11 has cost more than $10 billion so far, and the Transportation Security Agency (TSA) expects to spend billions more in the coming years.[17] At the Rochester, New York, airport the cost of security screening in 2003 exceeded the cost of running the rest of the entire airport![18] Even after spending billions of dollars, however, airport security has not improved dramatically. A 2004 confidential report prepared for the House Homeland Security Committee found that screeners are failing to detect weapons at roughly the same rate as shortly after the 2001 attacks.[19] The TSA bought 1,344 high-tech baggage screening machines costing more than $1 million each but experienced false alarms in 15 to 30 percent of all luggage. The culprit? Yorkshire pudding and shampoo bottles, which happen to have similar densities to certain explosives.[20] The primary cost is not wasted dollars but lost time. Metal detectors for a subway, for example, would lead to massive delays and make what is supposed to be convenient transportation quite inconvenient. These delays, in turn, would create perverse effects that would almost certainly lead to more deaths. Less convenient subways would make more people drive, and driving is far more dangerous statistically than taking the subway.

As the billions mount, the figures that can be spent on defenses eventually become so large that they boggle the imagination. It is useful to think in terms of trade-offs. To cover the medically uninsured would require only $34 billion.[21] Tax cuts of hundreds or thousands of dollars could be given to all middle-class families.

Innovation is also a challenge. Israel has found that the security barrier has led Palestinian groups to shift their tactics. The barrier has contributed to a dramatic plunge in the number of Israeli deaths from Palestinian suicide attackers. But some attackers still get through. Moreover, Palestinian groups have increased their use of mortars, firing over the barrier to strike into Israel. To be clear, the mortar attacks are less successful than the suicide bombings, but it does demonstrate how terrorists will continue to innovate in response to defenses.

Similar, but more successful, terrorist innovation led to the failure of U.S. defenses on 9/11. With metal detectors and improved security, the United States and other countries greatly reduced the number of hijackings from the 1970s. Indeed, part of the reason for the success of the 9/11 plot was that the hijackers figured out a way to take over an airplane without guns—an innovation that would work only if they then crashed the airplane. (If they had landed the plane and negotiated, as past hijackers had done, rescue teams could have easily stormed the plane without fear of the hostages being shot.) U.S. airline defenses worked as planned, as no one smuggled a gun or explosive material onto an airplane, but the plan itself did not encompass the full range of possibilities.

The United States faces particular problems because, unlike Israel, its citizens and interests are global. Defenses, of course, do little to help critical allies in fighting terrorism. And while the United States defends its embassies and military bases around the world (and as a result many U.S. embassies resemble fortresses rather than outposts of civility), terrorists still can go after less prestigious targets. Rather than attack a military base, they can attack individual soldiers at a bar, as Libyans did in 1986 when they killed two soldiers and a Turkish woman at the La Belle discotheque in Germany; rather than blow up embassies, terrorists can kill individual diplomats in their homes, as they did to Lawrence Foley, a U.S. AID official in Jordan, in 2002.

Bureaucratically, improving defenses can be costly. The Department of Homeland Security (DHS) was created to better coordinate the myriad agencies that have a piece of the homeland defense puzzle, but it has suffered from poor morale and from confusion as to its mission. Moreover, the emphasis on terrorism has had dramatic costs. The Federal Emergency Management Agency (FEMA) was placed under DHS because a terrorist strike could involve catastrophic damage that requires a sustained effort to care for victims and restore services. Under DHS, however, FEMA lost personnel and budgets for its traditional role of responding to natural disasters, a problem that became painfully clear after its disastrous performance following Hurricane Katrina.[22]

One of the most effective forms of defense is domestic intelligence: identifying suspicious individuals and carefully monitoring their activities. The FBI currently is the leading domestic intelligence agency, along with serving as the leading criminal investigative agency. Improving domestic intelligence involves a raft of changes, some of which involve diverting the FBI from other priorities (such as white-collar crime).

But many of the biggest changes for domestic intelligence have costs in civil liberties and in the openness of our society. In December 2005, *New York Times* reporter James Risen published a stunning article disclosing that the Bush administration had used the National Security Agency to spy on suspected terrorists on U.S. soil without going through the congressionally mandated process that involved the Foreign Intelligence and Surveillance Act (FISA) Court. These revelations, and the lesser flap over the USA PATRIOT Act, highlighted a fundamental tension: gaining better information on suspected terrorists necessitates collecting more information in general, including on individuals who, in the end, may not be involved in terrorism.

Domestic surveillance of U.S. Muslim and Arab communities, which would be the communities from which al-Qa'ida would recruit and its sympathizers would emerge, may backfire in the end. Surveillance and official hostility may lead these communities, which for now are well integrated into U.S. society, to see a gap between being a Muslim and being an American.

Most proposed defensive measures come down particularly hard on immigrants and visitors. Reducing the number of visas to visitors from Pakistan, Saudi Arabia, Indonesia, Egypt, or other countries with al-Qa'ida–linked groups does reduce opportunities for radicals to slip in, but it also reduces opportunities for individuals who might be sympathetic to the United States to travel here. Students from the Middle East, for example, have increasingly chosen to study in Europe, Canada, and Australia rather than in the United States since 9/11. The number of students from the Middle East studying in the United States in the 2002–2003 academic year fell by 10 percent from the previous year. Saudi Arabia and Kuwait saw a decrease of 25 percent, while the number of students from the United Arab Emirates dropped by 15 percent. Other Muslim countries also were affected.[23]

In the long term this could increase hostility toward the United States, as many students to the United States are current or future elites back home—they typically have more money, are better educated, and are otherwise able to shape opinion. Turning them away or treating them poorly while they are here confirms their suspicions that the United States is hostile to Muslims. This can harm other policy goals as well, as these same elites might later help on trade, oil pricing, or other important U.S. interests.

If part of our plan is to sell our values and explain the U.S. system by exposing foreigners to Americans and the U.S. political system, closing off the United States is a problem. Indeed, this is a particular concern, as those we seek most to influence—Islamists of various stripes who are often highly critical of al-Qa'ida but also critical of the United States—face difficulty traveling here because of their views and thus are more likely to sympathize with al-Qa'ida.

Most important to remember, offense and defense work in tandem. If defenses make it harder for terrorists to enter the United States—and successful U.S. and allied strikes reduce the number of skilled terrorists—then the remaining amateurs are far more likely to fail. However, give terrorists enough time and freedom, and they are far more able to overcome even sophisticated defenses.

Strategy Five: Divert al-Qa'ida

A fifth, and much nastier, approach to counterterrorism is to sic the jihadist dog on someone else—the "campfire strategy." (When a bear attacks you and your friends when you are sitting around a campfire in the woods, you don't need to run faster than the bear, just faster than your friends.) This is a strategy of diversion. Though the jihadists may loathe you, they will not target you because they have other priorities.

Diversion would involve playing up other conflicts that inflame the enemy. The United States would criticize Russia openly and frequently in Chechnya, play up the problems Muslims face in Europe, cluck sadly over India's abuses in Kashmir, and otherwise portray itself as sympathetic to the Muslim world, highlighting those causes on which jihadists focus. At the same time, the United States would back away from policies (support for Israel, presence in Iraq, backing authoritarian Muslim regimes, etc.) that most anger the jihadists. Over time, other countries would enter the jihadists' crosshairs.

Diversion is an exceptionally common strategy, but one that few leaders articulate because its goal is to cause problems for others rather than for one's own country. France in the 1970s and much of the 1980s deliberately allowed terrorists a sanctuary on its soil, believing (at times correctly) that as a reward for its cooperation, terrorist groups would not attack French citizens or interests.[24] Arab governments in the 1980s tried to send potential young troublemakers to Afghanistan, lauding them as heroes for their efforts against the Soviets but all the while hoping that the youngsters would achieve their goal of martyrdom in the struggle. Inadvertently, the United States follows this logic with many terrorist groups around the world. The Liberation Tigers of Tamil Eelam in Sri Lanka (arguably the most capable group in the world) or Chile's Manuel Rodriguez Patriotic Front-Dissidents (FPMR-D) both are hostile to U.S. influence and U.S. policies, but they focus first and foremost on their home countries. Even an explicitly anti-U.S. (and quite dangerous) group such as the Marxist group Devrimci Halk Kurtulus Partisi-Cephesi (DHKP-C) in Turkey is of only limited concern because it is focused primarily on the Turkish government. Such groups have other fish to fry, and the United States is quite content to let them do so.

Even in Iraq, some commentators argue that it is possible for terrorists to become engaged in a civil war there rather than going after the United States as international terrorists.[25] If the United States left Iraq, or perhaps if it lowered its profile there considerably, Sunni jihadists might focus even more on killing Shi'a, whom they see as apostates. In Iraq, the terrorists' propensity for internecine warfare may lead them away from U.S. targets.

Iraq also has been justified as a way of diverting terrorists from attacking the U.S. homeland. As President Bush argued in a 2005 speech about Iraq, "There is only one course of action against them [the terrorists]: to defeat them abroad before they attack us at home."[26] By this logic, jihadists from around the world who would otherwise plot attacks against New York, Washington, or other cities are instead sending their best people and devoting their time to defeating the U.S. military in Iraq. No one wants to make U.S. soldiers targets, but even (or, in my experience, especially) most soldiers would prefer that the military be attacked than civilians.

Arab governments in particular are ripe for diversion. Many are already engaged in harsh repression against jihadist movements in their countries: Jordan, Morocco, Syria, Egypt, Tunisia, and Libya are all good examples. In countries such as Algeria, Iraq, and to a lesser degree Yemen and Saudi Arabia, the governments are fighting full-blown or protoinsurgencies. These conflicts have led to thousands of deaths and imprisonments, as well as full-scale suspensions of human rights. Not surprisingly, many Arabs are bitter at their governments and thus vulnerable to having jihadist movements focus more on them than on the United States.

Nor are non-Arab Muslim countries off the hook. Indonesia, Pakistan, and Bangladesh, the largest Muslim countries in the world, all face local terrorist groups linked to al-Qa'ida, and Afghanistan faces the remnants of the Taliban. Pakistan, of course, is home to myriad jihadist groups. None of these governments is accepted as legitimate by the jihadist community: some are too democratic, some are too close to the West, and none is sufficiently Islamic.

Even countries on the periphery of the Muslim world are ripe for diversion. India in Kashmir, Russia in Chechnya (and in other parts of the Caucasus), China in Xinjiang Province, the Philippines, Thailand, Nigeria, and of course Israel are all countries where the non-Muslim government (secular, Hindu, Christian, or Jewish) is facing internal dissent from a Muslim community, often assisted by people on the borders. These are logical places for the next jihad if the goal is removing foreigners from the lands of Islam, or Muslims from the dominance of other religious communities.

The above sources of diversion are political, but even if the issue is values rather than policies, the United States has some advantages. Admittedly, Hollywood, American television, and American music send to the world such blasphemous ideas as free speech, women's equality, and the rights of homosexuals as well as a steady diet of teen sexuality and the subversion of the traditional family hierarchy. However, many of the issues that have caught Muslim extremists' ire in recent years have been in Europe. Dutch filmmaker Theo Van Gogh's graphic film criticizing the treatment of women under Islam, France's ban of head scarves for Muslim girls in school, or the publication of cartoons mocking the Prophet Mohammad in Denmark are a few of the most explosive issues in recent years. Because, unlike Europe, the United States does not face significant tension from a large Muslim population, such events are less likely (though still not impossible) in the years to come.

Diversion is likely to work particularly well against potential al-Qa'ida affiliates and the loose network of bin Ladin admirers. The affiliates are usually engaged in bitter wars against local regimes, and this already takes most of their attention. These individuals are not yet fully committed to attacking the United States. Diversion would make the United States even less attractive as a target. Similarly, the imaginations of individual jihadists in Europe or in the Muslim world would be seized by the supposed outrages of other countries, not America.

The advantages of diversion can be measured in saved American lives and dollars. To be blunt, others will die so Americans will live. Al-Qa'ida and local movements will attack in Britain, Russia, Indonesia, Egypt, Saudi Arabia, and so on—but not in the United States (or, more realistically, will do so less frequently). Nor will the United States have to undertake as many costly defensive measures. In addition, other policy concerns, such as trade and nuclear proliferation, can receive the attention they deserve.

Over time, diversion might exacerbate fault lines within the jihadist movement. Without a single enemy on which to focus their anger, jihadists might start to fight one another over priorities and resources.

Needless to say, a diversion strategy has several severe problems. Diversion, of course, requires policy changes—in short, concessions—to be meaningful. Parts of the jihadist movement may decide that the United States is no longer public enemy number one, but only if U.S. policies and values give less offense or another state commits a grievance that rises to the level of perceived U.S. crimes. Most important today, the United States would have to withdraw from Iraq (ideally, from the jihadists' point of view, with its tail between its legs). The United States would also have to cut off Israel. Being more sympathetic to the Palestinians and pushing hard for a two-state solution is not enough; the United States must be seen as a foe of Israel, not a friend. Washington must also be more like Japan in its foreign policy toward the Muslim world: trade is okay, but political and military influence is not.

Even if these policy transformations occurred, parts of the jihad would resist being diverted. It would take many years to convince skeptical and conspiratorial jihadists that the United States was showing new colors. Moreover, the list of grievances against the United States is exceptionally long. Even some who would be diverted might be distracted only temporarily. The Arab regimes' efforts to divert their homegrown jihadists to Afghanistan to fight and die in the struggle against the Soviets worked in the short term. But when that struggle ended, they found themselves confronting a far more dangerous foe. As former CIA officer Milton Beardon noted about these fighters, "they didn't die in great numbers. They died in tiny numbers, and they did come back."[27]

Diversion also would relieve pressure on the al-Qa'ida core, perhaps enabling it to reconstitute itself. Because the jihad is global, keeping it down requires a global response—something the United States now orchestrates. Equally important, U.S. pressure greatly reduces other countries' incentives to look the other way at jihadists on their territory. Although the jihadists may intend no harm to their host, many states avoid tolerating them for fear of infuriating the United States—a risky move for any state.

Conversely, if the United States tried to divert the jihadists, it would infuriate U.S. allies and other countries. In essence, the United States would be inviting terrorists to focus on killing other people, just not Americans. Even if this were not a declared U.S. policy, its contours would become known to a degree, and gaining diplomatic support from the affected countries would be far more difficult.

Even more important, while diversion reduces the threat to U.S. citizens, it does not diminish (and is in fact intended to increase) the threat to other countries, thus implicating many U.S. interests around the globe. The stability of Iraq and the security of Israel are both U.S. interests. Even outside these issues, a greater al-Qa'ida threat to Saudi Arabia risks instability in the world's largest oil producer. If the already strong Pakistani jihadist movement grew, it would further threaten stability in an already tottering state suffering from rampant corruption, severe economic problems, ethnic strife, and a border war with India. Add to this lethal mix Pakistan's nuclear program and you have the stuff of nightmares.

Diversion is in essence a neoisolationist approach to the problem of terrorism. The track record of neoisolation, however, is poor. Historically, U.S. attempts to avoid the burdens of being a great power usually failed. Too often the United States is forced to pay attention to the problem it is dodging but has had to do so years later, when it is even harder to stop. As the world's only superpower, such shirking is even more difficult today.

It would be disastrous should the jihadists ever capture a state, or even gain significant influence over one, as they did in Afghanistan under the Taliban or before that in the Sudan. Al-Qa'ida was able to use a base in these countries, remote and poor as they were, to construct a global army. The organization was able to make its network far stronger and to bolster like-minded groups around the world. Recruitment, training, propaganda, indoctrination, and other vital organizational efforts became far more effective when the groups had the security of a state to exploit. Within these countries, the humanitarian costs were high. Afghanistan continued to be racked by civil war, and the Taliban turned away international aid organizations trying to help its desperate citizens. Citizens who did not share the Taliban's extreme credo suffered brutal repression.

These problems would grow exponentially should jihadists come to power in a rich state such as Saudi Arabia or a powerful one such as Pakistan. Al-Qa'ida's yearly budget at its peak was about $30 million; the Saudi state in contrast, took in revenues of almost $150 *billion* in 2005. Spending a fraction of that money on advancing the jihadist cause would transform the movement's capabilities and size. Pakistan's situation is even more troubling. Pakistan's government budget is "only" about $15 billion (fifty times al-Qa'ida's peak). However, Islamabad controls a large army and several nuclear weapons. A nuclear exchange with India that would kill tens of millions is one possibility, as is a launch against Israel or a Pakistan-backed terrorist strike on the United States.

Diverting jihadists away from the U.S. homeland to Iraq is particularly dangerous. This strategy assumes a finite number of jihadists who, logically, can be in only one place at a time. However, the Iraq war has proven to be a generator of terrorism, inspiring thousands of young Muslims against the United States. Thus there are more than enough jihadists to go around. Moreover, in Iraq the jihadists are picking up new skills and joining a dangerous network that makes them exponentially more dangerous. And they will use these skills as they take jihad to Saudi Arabia, Kuwait, and other key U.S. allies.

It is difficult to pursue diversion and not run these risks. U.S. efforts to weaken the jihadists, even if done surreptitiously, will still surface through leaks at home and the occasional statements of allies. Over time, it would be impossible to carry out this policy covertly. In addition, the United States can't simply pick and choose and hope to appease the jihadists. Though leaving Iraq would address one grievance, the al-Qa'ida list was drawn well before the U.S. invasion and would remain after the last U.S. soldier leaves Iraq.

However, one aspect of diversion should be kept in mind even as the strategy as a whole is rejected: the United States need not fight every battle. Many local groups are for now focused on local governments. Unless there is good reason to think these groups will soon join al-Qa'ida, the United States should be leery of confronting them directly or otherwise making new enemies.

Strategy Six: Delegitimize

A sixth approach takes a quite different tack from the more immediate courses of action presented so far: trying to undermine support for the terrorists by delegitimizing their tactics and ideas. Simple antiterrorist propaganda can often be quite effective (while pro-American propaganda is not). Explaining government positions, highlighting the extreme views and brutality of the terrorist group, and otherwise employing standard political campaign tactics of making yourself look good and your opponent bad are invaluable. Governments may also use moderate and respected voices in the relevant community (Muslim preachers for the jihadists, labor unions for leftists, cultural heroes for ethno-nationalist groups, and so on) to condemn the terrorists. Governments also have shined a spotlight on defectors from the group.

Saudi Arabia has pursued this strategy successfully in its antiterrorism campaign that began in earnest after the May 2003 attacks in the kingdom. At the behest of the regime, Saudi Arabia's usually bland media explicitly portrayed the gruesome impact of attacks by al-Qa'ida of the Arabian Peninsula on Muslim civilians. The result was a wave of popular revulsion against the jihadists. This forced them to shift attacks away from Muslim civilians, a shift that made operations much harder and demonstrates that damage has been done to their credibility. Saudi Arabia also was able to convert several prominent clerics from adversaries and critics into regime supporters. This campaign helped convince many Saudis to reject the radicals, hurting their efforts to recruit and fund-raise and giving the Saudi regime the ability to better solicit information from the populace.

Terrorism requires the deliberate killing of noncombatants. This is rarely popular. Few publics, no matter how bloodthirsty, want women and children to die. (An exception may be attitudes in the Arab world toward attacks in Israel, where terrorists' killing of women and children is widely seen as legitimate, or at least forgivable.) Thus terrorists start out at a disadvantage in convincing the public to see them as just.

Even the terrorists' ideas, while less controversial than their use of violence, can be attacked with relative ease. Some terrorists consider the vast majority of Muslims to be apostates, hardly a viewpoint that will make them popular. Most jihadists roundly condemn the concept of democracy, even though it is supported widely in the Arab world. In addition, jihadists have declared many popular activities such as sports and music to be deviations from true Islam. Such positions greatly affect the level of public support the jihadists receive.

Theologically, the terrorists are on thin ice. The vast majority of Muslim scholars have different interpretations concerning the declaration of jihad, the role of popular input into decision-making, the legitimacy of various regimes in the Muslim world, and the permissibility of deviancy from the strict codes the terrorists proclaim. Many of these clerics have views on these issues that would not comfort Western audiences, but they are far removed from those of the terrorists.

One common criticism of efforts to delegitimize terrorists is that no amount of propaganda would convince someone like Osama bin Ladin and his diehard followers to lay down their arms. This criticism is true, but it misses the point. Delegitimizing terrorists has little impact on those already in the organization. They have already drunk the Kool-Aid. Rather, efforts to delegitimize terrorists affect both would-be recruits and potential financiers. In addition to shaping the attitudes of these more active parts of the jihadist movement, delegitimizing the terrorists also shapes the public mood, which has profound effects on the ability to gather intelligence and on the long-term desirability of reform.

One of the biggest advantages of delegitimation is that it has relatively few costs. The investments are in people and changing tactics. The United States does not have to deploy troops, change its alliance structure, or otherwise shake up its security to engage in delegitimation.

Delegitimation, however, will be less effective if it is not tied to policy changes. Perceived U.S. atrocities in Iraq or more images like those from Abu Ghraib will drown out outrage over a terrorist atrocity like Beslan or disagreement with the jihadists' condemnation of democracy. Even if other governments are the messengers, the anger U.S. policies generate will make it difficult to reduce support for anti-U.S. groups.

Delegitimation also requires restraint by the United States and its allies. The essence of this strategy is to highlight the horrific violence and extreme goals of the foe. If U.S. actions take center stage instead, as they will when it involves high-profile measures such as invading other countries or other dramatic uses of military force, the jihadists will draw support simply by portraying themselves as defending the Muslim community; their means and ultimate goals will be lost in the din.

Strategy Seven: Transform Terrorist-Breeding Countries

The most ambitious approach, and the most difficult, is to transform countries that "breed" terrorists. President Bush argued for this approach eloquently in a speech before the National Endowment of Democracy in 2005, describing one aspect of U.S. counterterrorism strategy as being

> to deny the militants future recruits by replacing hatred and resentment with democracy and hope across the broader Middle East. This is a difficult and long-term project, yet there's no alternative to it. Our future and the future of that region are linked. If the broader Middle East is left to grow in bitterness, if countries remain in misery, while radicals stir the resentments of millions, then that part of the world will be a source of endless conflict and mounting danger, and for our generation and the next. If the peoples of that region are permitted to choose their own destiny, and advance by their own energy and by their participation as free men and women, then the extremists will be marginalized, and the flow of violent radicalism to the rest of the world will slow, and eventually end. By standing for the hope and freedom of others, we make our own freedom more secure.[28]

As the president's remarks indicate, three broad types of transformation could conceivably affect the propensity for terrorism: democracy, economic development, and conflict resolution. The president's views have some support from scholars of terrorism. Ted Robert Gurr, for example, notes that in democracies reforms can greatly reduce support for terrorism and win over potential terrorist recruits.[29]

The most widely discussed view is spreading democracy. Because individuals have legitimate and peaceful means of seeking political change, they do not need to embrace violence. The sclerotic rule of the al-Saud, the brutality of the Mubarak government, and other grievances can all be redressed through ballots, not bullets.

Economic reform offers a different solution. Here, the presumed motivation of the terrorist is not a lack of outlets for politics but rather the corruption and lack of opportunities in his society. By giving people jobs, and more broadly hope that they can improve their condition, their level of anger will diminish. The British government, for example, poured money and jobs into Catholic parts of Northern Ireland in 1970s and 1980s. Over time, Catholic anger at the years of discrimination they faced faded. Even more important, Downing Street's claim to be an honest broker between Catholics and Protestants became more credible.

A third transformational approach is to try to resolve underlying conflicts that produce violence that acts as magnets for jihadists who, over time, transform a local grievance into part of the global struggle. The Israeli-Palestinian dispute, Russia's war in Chechnya, and the India-Pakistan fight over Kashmir are the three leading local conflicts that have captured the attention of the Muslim world. (An Iraqi civil war occurring after a U.S. withdrawal would join the list.) By resolving these conflicts, jihadists would have fewer wars to use to advertise the perceived repression of the Muslim community. Perhaps equally important, there would be fewer places for young Muslims to learn to fight, leaving them disaffected, perhaps, but much less dangerous.

The greatest attraction of these ambitious approaches is that they offer long-term solutions to the terrorism problem. Killing and capturing al-Qa'ida leaders, building defenses, or encouraging jihadist groups to attack elsewhere all at best push back the problem. But if some of the grievances that lead to terrorism can be addressed, the supply of money and recruits might dry up. Northern Ireland offers perhaps the best example. Credible British offers of political power to Irish nationalists made the use of violence increasingly seem unnecessary. Over time, and it took decades, the

IRA leadership recognized that they had more to gain by working with a democratic system.

The disadvantages largely lie in the areas of feasibility and costs. There is no recipe for making a democracy. In addition to honest elections and the protection of minority rights, common building blocks of democracy include the rule of law, a free press, civic organizations such as unions and professional organizations, and a sense of trust among citizens. In a country such as Algeria, all of these are lacking. As the United States has discovered in Iraq and Afghanistan, it can influence the process, but much of the real work must be done by locals, many of whom are at best halfhearted democrats. And at times a tight U.S. embrace discredits would-be democrats in the eyes of anti-U.S. nationalists. At the same time, anti-U.S. critics would only blame Washington more for its inevitable shortcomings and for allowing regimes like Mubarak's to stay in power.

The diplomatic costs can also be staggering. To push reform forward or to resolve bitter disputes like Kashmir, the United States must constantly push, chastise, and bribe its allies. For truly transformative change, the United States is often asking existing allies like the al-Saud to risk surrendering power, something most regimes are loath to do.

Nor will these efforts surely produce success. Britain and Spain are robust democracies, but jihadists have perpetrated horrific attacks in these countries. In much of the Arab world, the loosening of state power that is necessary for democracy may allow violent radicals to operate more freely. In addition, as elections in the Palestinian territories in 2006 show, the wrong people—Islamist terrorists—may win the elections. Because of U.S. unpopularity in much of the Muslim world, regimes that reflect popular opinion are likely to be more anti-American in their foreign policies.

Thinking Strategically about Strategy

The best approach is to work with allies to fight terrorism in the hope of containing the terrorists. In the long term, the terrorists' own weaknesses will come to the fore—something we should encourage by working hard to delegitimize them as well. Defenses can be improved, but there are limits to what is realistic, and many defensive measures are useless, wasted, or can even make things worse. The best defensive measures involve improving domestic intelligence and ensuring the support of the U.S. Muslim community rather than trying to harden every potential terrorist target. Diversion is possible in a few cases, particularly if the United States withdraws or draws down from Iraq. However, in general diversion is hard to implement, risky in the long term as the jihadists may simply become stronger, and costly given that many of the countries that would suffer (Israel, India, etc.) are close U.S. allies—and diversion is immoral to boot. I am skeptical of crushing the adversaries ourselves, as it is simply too massive a task given the global nature of our foes and is more likely to backfire and anger key allies. Despite their allure, massive efforts to democratize the world or transform their economies are also risky. Indeed, as I later argue, such efforts may have beneficial effects well beyond counterterrorism, but they may often backfire when it comes to winning over potential radicals or gaining support on counterterrorism from area governments.

There are five "fronts" in this war for this combination of strategies:

1. tracking down terrorists to arrest them and disrupt their activities;
2. killing terrorists whom we cannot arrest or whose arrest offers little intelligence benefit;
3. preventing attacks on American soil and, at the same time, mitigating the psychological costs of terrorism—but doing so at an acceptable cost;
4. pushing reform, both political and administrative, but only in a way that does not destabilize key states;
5. making bin Ladinism and associated ideologies less attractive.

The key to winning all five of these fronts is not only ensuring a strong effort at home but also choosing the right allies. In addition, we need to stop spillover from the war in Iraq—a war that has proven a disaster for the struggle against jihadist terrorism but whose abandonment also creates new problems for counterterrorism.

3

Tracking Down and Disrupting Terrorists

Why can't we catch Osama bin Ladin?
If we could flush Saddam Hussein out of his hiding place in Iraq, why not bin Ladin? On the surface, finding and capturing him seem simple. Osama bin Ladin is probably hiding along the Afghan-Pakistani border. A "snatch" operation by our troops, working together with Afghans and Pakistanis, should be relatively straightforward.

Tracking down and *arresting* senior terrorists like bin Ladin is particularly important because, contrary to popular mythology, killing terrorists is not the ideal way to fight them. Killing can become necessary, and is satisfying in a visceral way. But a dead terrorist carries his secrets to his grave. The plot may go on in his absence, and his comrades can continue to fight without fear of disruption. A captured terrorist, on the other hand, can provide information on active plots and his comrades or at least cause his compatriots to change plans in reaction to the potential compromise in their activities. Still, capturing terrorists is easier said than done. It requires understanding terrorist vulnerabilities as well as a sophisticated and massive intelligence effort. Indeed, intelligence is the core of counterterrorism. All the other instruments, such as military force or homeland defense measures, are useless (or often counterproductive) without superb intelligence. Nor can this effort be separated from broader U.S. foreign policy concerns, as U.S. allies or even shady friends such as Pakistan and Yemen are often the keys to success.

Understanding the importance of, and the difficulties inherent in, tracking and capturing terrorists can be gleaned from the chase after Khalid Shaykh Mohammad. Though his capture was a victory for the United States, the story and the problems he posed for U.S. intelligence paint a telling portrait of the triumphs and the failures of intelligence services.

On March 1, 2003, after years of an intense international manhunt, Pakistani security services found Mohammad—or "KSM," as he was known in intelligence circles—in an al-Qa'ida safe house in Rawalpindi. One of the high points in the war on terrorism was a newspaper photo of a bedraggled and disoriented KSM facing his captors. KSM was more than just the mastermind of 9/11. He also was linked to the first World Trade Center attack in 1993. He was closely associated with a failed 1995 plot to bomb twelve commercial airliners over the Pacific ("Operation Bojinka"). He was perhaps connected to the 1998 embassy attacks in Nairobi and Dar-es-Salaam that killed 224 people. He was involved in the 2000 bombing of the USS *Cole* that killed 17 sailors. And he was part of the attack on a Tunisian synagogue that killed 21 people, most of whom were German tourists.[1] He later confessed to a role in a total of twenty-nine attacks.[2] As he admitted later, "I was responsible for the 9/11 operation, from A to Z."[3]

But his notoriety largely derives from his role in 9/11. KSM initially proposed a far more ambitious plot than the one implemented on September 11. If his far-reaching plan had transpired, he would have hijacked ten additional aircraft that would have struck multiple targets: tall buildings in California and Washington State, nuclear power plants, and CIA and FBI headquarters. In a grandiose finale to his horrific plan, KSM envisioned himself landing the final plane and delivering a rousing speech to the world.[4] Grandiosity aside, KSM was a pragmatic organizer and a skilled technician. Not only did he conceive and orchestrate sophisticated plots, he also encouraged al-Qa'ida to develop more fiendish capabilities (such as radioactive "dirty bombs"), and he helped seed organizations in Southeast Asia that later became prominent in their own right. KSM envisioned unprecedented destruction. Had he not been caught, he would have tried to implement his malevolent plans.

The capture of KSM not only removed a dangerous dreamer from al-Qa'ida's ranks but also provided an intelligence bonanza for the United States. Mohammad was a senior terrorist with links to almost every aspect of al-Qa'ida. His arrest led authorities to terrorists' cell phones and computers. His personal phone book alone yielded a total of six thousand phone numbers, which authorities used as a guidebook to al-Qa'ida. These phone numbers helped intelligence officials break up rings in Saudi Arabia, Switzerland, Qatar, and Indonesia.[5]

Yet despite his heinous track record, little was known about KSM before the 1995 "Bojinka" operation, a plot to destroy 11 U.S.-bound airliners as well as to kill Pope John Paul II. For the most part he lived openly in the Persian Gulf, traveling around Europe, Asia, and the Middle East. When the U.S. intelligence community subsequently uncovered his link to "Bojinka," they also traced him to the 1993 World Trade Center attack. Ramzi Yousef, the man who masterminded the 1993 attack, was KSM's nephew. KSM tried to help Yousef with the plot, and had given a small donation to one of the conspirators. But his link remained unknown for several years. In 1996, when federal prosecutors discovered his involvement, they indicted him secretly.

KSM was a citizen of the world. His family originally came from Baluchistan, a lawless tribal area along the Iranian-Pakistani border, but KSM himself grew up in Kuwait. Like many leading international terrorists from the Middle East, KSM attended university abroad—in his case, in North Carolina, where he studied mechanical engineering. No one is sure exactly when he became radicalized. But soon after graduating in 1986, he joined the anti-Soviet jihad, first training in Pakistan, then fighting in Afghanistan until the Soviets withdrew and Afghanistan descended into civil war. In 1992, KSM fought yet again, this time in Bosnia. In 1994 he plotted attacks in the Philippines. During these years, KSM also found time to travel to Sudan, Yemen, Malaysia, and Brazil.[6] Finally he moved his family to Qatar, where he held a position in the Ministry of Electricity and Water.

When KSM's links to the Bojinka operation became clear, the hunt began in earnest. The CIA learned that he was hiding in Qatar, working for the government. But what to do? In early 1996 the military developed a plan to seize KSM, but it was rejected because the United States would in essence be invading a key ally in the Persian Gulf—a perception made worse because the military plans involved hundreds (or, by some accounts, thousands) of troops.[7] Instead, the United States tried a more passive route. Patrick Theros, the American ambassador, and Louis Freeh, the FBI director, approached the Qatari government directly, asking for help. While the Qataris hemmed and hawed, KSM—almost certainly tipped off by sympathetic officials—escaped to Afghanistan, only a few months before the slippery bin Ladin himself fled there from Sudan.[8]

In the years between his escape from Qatar and 9/11, KSM was determined to cut as wide a swath of destruction as possible. After the 1998 embassy bombings convinced him that bin Ladin was serious about striking the United States, KSM formally began to work with al-Qa'ida.[9] Somewhere in late 1998 or early 1999 he began to plan the 9/11 attacks, which he had first proposed to bin Ladin in 1996. The daunting scope of the 9/11 operation did not deter KSM from planning additional strikes. At the same time, he planned additional attacks in the United States, he sent operatives to Malaysia, and he considered attacks against Israel and Southeast Asia.[10] Only after he surfaced on the scope of the U.S. radar screen, several months after 9/11, did his role as its chief architect steadily become clearer. Given the vast scope of his activities, KSM maintained a remarkably low profile, which made him particularly difficult to capture. To evade detection, he used dozens of different aliases. As a senior FBI official noted, KSM "was under everybody's radar. . . . He's the guy nobody ever heard of. The others had egos. He didn't."[11]

The 9/11 attacks led to massive roundups of al-Qa'ida members and sympathizers around the world. Even more important, the Taliban suddenly collapsed under assault by U.S. forces and Afghan opponents of the Taliban, and the government of Pervez Musharraf in Pakistan went from being an indirect supporter of jihadists to a counterterrorism partner of the United States, albeit a lukewarm one. As a result, senior terrorists such as Abu Zubaydah, a leading recruiter and planner for al-Qa'ida, fell into U.S. hands. But once again KSM proved a wily terrorist who had left Afghanistan without a trace.

His trail became hot once again in the spring of 2002, when the German police picked up a call to Karachi from Christian Ganczarski, a suspected radical in Germany. The Germans believed that Ganczarski, a Polish-born convert to Islam, was linked to al-Qa'ida. In 2002, shortly before a suicide bomber attacked a mosque in Tunisia that killed 21 people (mostly German tourists), the bomber called Ganczarski. Ganczarski, in turn, contacted KSM. But Ganczarski was cautious and did not actually speak on the phone—the call itself was meant to be the signal.[12] The Germans traced the call to a SwissCom cell phone, but they did not know who was on the other end. Working with the French, who have lower standards of evidence for terrorism investigations than Germany, Ganczarski was arrested in Paris.

German authorities worked with the SwissCom cell phone company and learned that many al-Qa'ida members were using the same Subscriber Identity Module (SIM) cards. Ironically, in an effort to maintain their operational security, al-Qa'ida bought many cards from this company because the company did not require purchasers to provide their names. Officials began monitoring this particular type of SIM cards and traced KSM to Karachi via signals intelligence (SIGINT), but the information was not precise enough to know exactly where in the city he was living. Because more than 10 million people live in Karachi, the hunt was far from over.

Once KSM had been tracked to Karachi, human intelligence and assistance from the Pakistani government became essential. With their cooperation, officials pieced together evidence that eventually led to his capture. In one police raid on a suspected al-Qa'ida hideout in Rawalpindi in 2002, police found two of KSM's children, Omar and Abdullah, ages seven and nine, respectively.

Other detainees provided information that led to the capture of Ramzi bin al-Shibh, another major terrorist linked to 9/11. A subsequent raid that capitalized on this information yielded an e-mail with an address of another house in Rawalpindi—the house where KSM was found. The hunt was over. KSM's capture resulted from persistence, international cooperation, and the careful compilation of numerous intelligence fragments.[13]

How Do Intelligence and Law Enforcement Agencies Track Terrorists?

A massive manhunt caught Khalid Shaykh Mohammad. His apprehension—and the maddening, on-again, off-again search for him for almost a decade—offer a window into the confusing and challenging world of counterterrorism intelligence. Unlike the Hollywood image of spy movies, success did not depend on a mole planted in the highest reaches of the organization. Instead, the arrest of KSM illustrates the need for carefully assembling disparate pieces of information—obtained with methods ranging from prisoner interrogation to high-tech devices—followed by quick action on that information before it becomes stale. It underlines the essential nature of host government cooperation and the ability of intelligence agents to exploit even the slightest errors that terrorists might make.

Intelligence officers tried a wide variety of methods to learn about KSM's activities before they captured him. The first break came after a random fire in the apartment of the Bojinka plotters in the Philippines. When police investigated, they discovered an explosives lab. Even the less-than-efficient Filipino police realized this fire was the result of more than a random explosion. The information pointed the first finger at KSM.

After 9/11, more information about KSM came from debriefings of arrested or captured al-Qa'ida members. Such debriefings are a form of "human intelligence" (HUMINT), information obtained directly from detainees.

Sergeant Chris Mackey, a U.S. Army interrogator, wrote a book with journalist Greg Miller that outlined a range of techniques used on the detainees. In contrast to old Cold War techniques that were effective with Soviet soldiers, the direct line of questioning usually failed. Instead, interrogators' questions capitalized on the detainees' feelings of loneliness and hopelessness. An especially effective technique was one that convinced detainees that interrogators already knew all the essential details regarding their case. Agents made a concerted effort to gather information from one detainee, which they used to extract additional information from another. This technique proved surprisingly effective despite the initial effort. Sometimes interrogators resorted to the classic "good cop, bad cop" technique, where one person provided comfort while another threatened the prisoner. Female interrogators found that working to allay a prisoner's fears with a cigarette or a friendly remark often led the prisoner to see the interrogator as friendly and, over time, be more willing to reveal information. All interrogators also found it necessary to offer an incentive for cooperation as well as threats.[14]

Armed with new information about KSM, investigators now began to employ high-tech methods to locate and apprehend him. Once detainee reports put KSM on everyone's front burner, SIGINT is what made a cold trail hot. The SIGINT tip-off of Ganczarski's phone enabled intelligence officials to follow the trail of a relatively minor operator to his overseer in Karachi. From there, human intelligence once again played a vital role in KSM's capture. A Pakistani intelligence informant supposedly provided the tip for the significant raid that produced information on KSM's whereabouts (former CIA director George Tenet claimed that KSM's arrest was due to a "CIA spy").[15]

In the end KSM was betrayed by someone with access to his movements, someone who knew his ultimate location. This person passed the information on to Pakistani authorities,[16] perhaps lured by the $25 million reward placed on KSM's head. A letter reportedly from Ayman al-Zawahiri, al-Qa'ida's number two, attributed KSM's capture to his incaution when "someone claims to carry an important letter or contributions,"[17] suggesting that KSM let his guard down to receive communications or money—two necessities of terrorist groups. Zawahiri's statement suggests that somehow

U.S. or Pakistani intelligence exploited the moment when KSM's need for money and communication drew him out in the open. French scholar of Islam Gilles Kepel contends that KSM was caught because he wanted to gain access to al-Jazeera and that U.S. and Pakistani intelligence agents trailed an Egyptian journalist who works for the station.[18]

Most important and least understood is the role of foreign intelligence services in counterterrorism. Michael Sheehan, a former special coordinator for counterterrorism in the State Department, argues that "the most important counterterrorism activity since the fall of the Taliban has been the close cooperation of the CIA with foreign intelligence services."[19] As Sheehan points out, local intelligence services are the ones that operate the networks of informants who provide the information that, when put together by American intelligence services, provides a comprehensive picture of the adversary.

Although U.S. officials understandably want to emphasize the role various U.S. intelligence services played, the capture of KSM would have been impossible without massive foreign help. The Germans took the first step when they linked the SIM cards to the attack in Tunisia. Eventually the SIGINT operations involved more than a dozen countries, with the Swiss in the lead.[20] From there Pakistan began to play a key role, both in gathering intelligence and in providing the manpower to raid suspected safe houses.

As the pursuit of KSM suggests, terrorists' mistakes offer opportunities that counterterrorism officials can exploit. When terrorists leave their safe haven, which they must do to conduct their activities effectively, they risk exposure. Terrorist masterminds like KSM must raise money, train and instruct recruits, publicize the organization's exploits, and otherwise involve themselves in the day-to-day activities of the organization. They must travel, and even though they do so using false names, as KSM did (he had twenty-seven known aliases!), they take the chance of revealing their whereabouts. Once they are out in the open, they come in contact with a range of individuals, some of whom may betray them for the right price or out of animus. Others may do so inadvertently, as did

Ganczarski, not realizing that counterterrorism agents are trailing them as they scurry about reporting to their superiors. Terrorists face a conundrum: communications open them to exposure, yet they cannot operate in a vacuum. If KSM cannot communicate with group members, he cannot lead them. It becomes essential that agents monitor these communications whenever possible so they can identify and track individuals before an attack.

Unfortunately, most opportunities for counterterrorism officials arise after the attacks take place, not before. When they try to gather evidence against a suspect before an event, they often do not know where to look. Clues that once evaded officials seem obvious after a violent incident. Because investigators are unaware that the suspect is part of a terrorist organization, his loose talk or his sloppy documents attract little attention. So terrorists are better able to effectively keep their heads down and avoid close scrutiny. But once blood is drawn, government agents, particularly local ones, may descend, literally in the thousands. Security videotapes of the target area are examined, all individuals under suspicion are questioned, and all communications are scrutinized. Terrorists can still escape the net, but it is far more difficult once they have surfaced.

During the pursuit of KSM, the United States coordinated and led the process of analysis and multinational information-sharing. For the raid in Pakistan, the United States admitted to helping with "intelligence and forensics" but probably did much more. Indeed, the White House labeled the capture a "joint operation." Later reports even indicated that FBI agents joined the Pakistanis in the raid itself while allowing the Pakistanis the honor of the actual capture.[21] The United States continues to serve in that role today: it works with locals to put the pieces together and directs various governments around the world to gather additional information and, when the puzzle is complete enough, arrest the terrorists.

The process that ranged from intelligence-gathering to final capture was far from simple. Though investigators found KSM, they had to follow one false lead after another before they finally got lucky. The number of cold trails was staggering. Investigators traced webs of phone calls and e-mails from suspected terrorists. These communications included not only ones from their fellows in terrorism but also family members, friends, and a random assortment of other individuals, who might have ranged from a landlord to a pizza delivery company. When possible investigators monitored his e-mail searching for important operational communications, they followed his roommates and business associates, many of whom had no involvement in KSM's activities.

When KSM turned up in Rawalpindi, it raised eyebrows in counterterrorism circles. Rawalpindi is the home of Pakistan's army and intelligence services—a bit like finding a top terrorist living near the Pentagon or CIA headquarters. As one Western official told journalist Peter Bergen, "What the fuck was this guy doing just down the road from GHQ [Army headquarters]?"[22]

The Challenge of Terrorism

KSM was an exceptional terrorist, yet the challenges involved in capturing him were by no means unusual. Indeed, the difficulty reflects many of the broader problems that security officials have with regard to intelligence on terrorism. A terrorist's greatest asset is not his ferocity, dedication, or skill; it is his obscurity. This obscurity makes this problem of identification daunting for investigators. If U.S. or friendly intelligence services already know an individual is linked to terrorist groups, monitoring his communications is relatively straightforward. However, if the terrorist is not already in the sights of government agencies, it is far more difficult to distinguish pertinent conversations or e-mails from mountains of conventional traffic. Until he strikes, the police and intelligence serves are often not looking for him. To all appearances he may lead a normal life as a diligent employee and a good husband and father. Despite popular myths that terrorists are typically deranged or criminal in their habits, most terrorists are in fact similar to their fellow citizens, aside from their political dedication and commitment to violent action.[23]

Another problem for intelligence services is the ability of terrorists to blend in with their neighbors. As Paul Pillar, the former deputy chief of the CIA's Counterterrorist Center, argues:

The basic problem that terrorism poses for intelligence is as simple as it is chilling. A group of conspirators conceives a plot. Only the few conspirators know of their intentions, although they might get help from others. They mention nothing about their plot to anyone they cannot absolutely trust. They communicate nothing about their plans in a form that can be intercepted. . . . They live and move normally and inconspicuously, and any preparations that cannot be done behind closed doors they do as part of those movements. The problem: How do we learn of the plot?[24]

If anything, this understates the risk. As Pillar contends, "The target for intelligence is not just proven terrorists; it is anyone who *might* commit terrorism in the future."[25] As a British parliamentary report on the July 7, 2005, London bus and subway bombings indicates, the bombers' "identities were unknown to the Security service and there was no appreciation of their subsequent significance."[26] Resources went to what were perceived of as higher-priority targets.

Although the Bush administration and U.S. intelligence services are constantly maligned for not finding bin Ladin despite a manhunt that has lasted over five years, the complexity of this effort is immense, even for highly sophisticated counterterrorist officials. Bin Ladin is probably hiding in remote parts of Pakistan, an area that has historically resisted infiltration attempts, as the British colonial powers discovered when forces of the Raj were repeatedly ousted from the region. Even today, the Islamabad government cannot penetrate the fierce local tribes who are bin Ladin's allies. If they suspected that the U.S. forces or the Pakistani government troops planned to move against him, they would inform him immediately and he would slip away once again. Because bin Ladin does not need to be in constant contact with subordinates, he can easily issue a video or a speech at a time and a location of his choosing without detection.

If tracking down bin Ladin still seems easy, consider the U.S. experience with Eric Rudolph, the 1996 Atlanta Summer Olympics bomber. Rudolph endorsed a range of Christian Identity tenets that glorified racism and other reactionary views in the name of God.

Rudolph had a particular hatred for "the homosexual agenda" and abortion practitioners. In addition to Rudolph's bombing in the 1996 Atlanta Summer Olympics that killed two people, he also bombed two abortion clinics and a gay nightclub. Despite being on the FBI's most wanted list and having on his head a $1 million bounty for information, Rudolph successfully hid in the Appalachian wilderness for five years. The FBI and local police blanketed the area, but he eluded them with his superb knowledge of terrain and probably with the assistance of local Christian Identity adherents or sympathizers who saw him as a hero.

If it took five years to find Rudolph in the United States, consider the difficulty of finding a terrorist in a foreign country where investigators face language barriers and a hostile population. Added to the mix is the problem an investigator faces when he attempts to find a person before he or she commits a terrorist act. The terrorist is for all practical purposes often invisible until the damage is done. Because terrorist obscurity is so difficult to penetrate, counterterrorism officials face obstacles unknown to their peers. Intelligence officials tracking a tangible threat—Iran's nuclear program, for example—can draw up a list of intelligence targets from the start (though actual operations remain difficult). They can in theory monitor whether indigenous scientists are working in labs or whether the Iranians are importing foreign experts. Key officials involved in the nuclear program are widely known to reporters, to say nothing of foreign governments. Iran's supreme leader often issues pronouncement regarding Iran's nuclear plans, and the officials tasked with running the nuclear program are known to all. This knowledge does not make tracking the nuclear program easy, but at least intelligence officials know where to begin.

Most known terrorist groups fall into the intelligence category of "hard targets." Their members are difficult to identify, their actions are difficult to anticipate, and their organizations are difficult to infiltrate. It is a Darwinian process: the organizations that cannot learn operational security do not survive long. Only 50 percent of terrorist groups survive a year, and only 5 percent survive a decade; those that endure generally are skilled at minimizing their exposure to government law enforcement and intelligence agencies.[27]

KSM is not a typical terrorist. His daring and imagination are unusual for terrorists. Though he captured our attention with violence and bravura, most terrorists are likely to employ more conservative methods and weapons. Traditional means of attack include car bombs, hostage-taking, or explosives buried in garbage cans. A simple but increasingly popular method is for a terrorist to wrap himself in explosives, make a farewell video, and blow himself up at a designated target. His technique is easy, straightforward, and often successful. He becomes a suicide bomber. Terrorists prefer uncomplicated techniques to flashier, more intricate attacks that might fail. Small radical organizations that compete among themselves for members usually won't risk using a spectacular weapon. Failure is humiliating.

Typically, terrorist groups are composed of small cells where ties of kinship and neighborhood are forged into a strong ideological commitment. Hizballah's terrorist wing, for example, is dominated by several Lebanese clans, such as the Musawis, the Shehadehs, and the Hamiyehs. Outsiders, even Lebanese, are not welcome.[28] The successful terrorist groups also limit the number of people in each cell to ensure that the organization continue its activities even if a member is arrested. For the same reason, many individuals in one cell do not know the identity of their comrades in other cells.

Frequently, terrorists blend into sympathetic—or intimidated—local communities that are not willing to cooperate with security services. The locals are reluctant to share information with law enforcement officials hunting the terrorists. On the contrary, they are likely to pass on "suspicious" law enforcement activities to the terrorists. These communities provide havens for terrorists, enabling them to blend in with the overall population.

At the same time that investigators are attempting to penetrate local populations, they are employing SIGINT to monitor communications. Repeated leaks have created the sense that the United States and other intelligence services can intercept almost any phone call. But the best terrorists closely guard their communications. If anything, many terrorist groups have an exaggerated sense of U.S. communications capabilities. As a result, messengers and face-to-face meetings become the preferred means of exchanging the most sensitive information. When terrorists do use the phone, many of the more clever ones speak in code.

Deception and denial compound the problem of surprise. To counter government intelligence-gathering, skilled adversaries encrypt their data, limit the dissemination of sensitive information, and use any means at their disposal that would inhibit signals and human intelligence. In Israel, Palestinian suicide bombers disguised themselves as students, and even as Hasidim, in their efforts to avoid suspicion from Israel's vigilant public.[29] Terrorists also scheme to mislead government intelligence agencies.[30] They can fabricate attack plans or invent names of operatives to throw agents off the track.

Critics of the CIA and other agencies for an intelligence failure on September 11 fail to understand the complexity of the problem. They do not appreciate how difficult the intelligence challenge becomes when agents make the leap from predicting plans to disrupting plans. Before September 11, the CIA did a superb job of strategic warning that an attack was imminent. But that warning did little to thwart the specific plot. The CIA knew the identity of the foe, the scale of its ambitions, and the degree of its lethality. And they communicated this information in a timely manner. After the August 7, 1998, embassy bombings, al-Qa'ida warnings became a top priority in the intelligence community. Even weak pieces of intelligence set off alarms. As journalist Steve Coll contends, "It was a vast, pulsing, self-perpetuating, highly sensitive network on continuous alert."[31] By 2001, the system was on high alert, and any policymaker (or member of the general public) who cared to look could see the CIA's concern. In February 2001, Director of Central Intelligence (DCI) George Tenet testified publicly that bin Ladin and his organization posed "the most immediate and serious threat" to the United States—a clear example of strategic warning.[32] In a dramatic moment during the 9/11 Commission investigation, then national security adviser Condoleezza Rice reluctantly admitted that the title of an intelligence report dated slightly over a month before the attacks was: "Bin Laden determined to attack inside the United States."

That this warning did little good should not be shocking. Knowing that a terrorist organization is going to attack is only part of the puzzle. Prior knowledge of an attack allows policymakers to adjust their resource allocations, increase domestic scrutiny, and work more with foreign partners. Yet even if officials had been able to implement these steps, they may not have averted the attacks. We still do not know where terrorists will strike and how. Only after the attack will it seem obvious.

Thus, the harder and more important challenge is predicting where an attack will occur—"tactical warning," in the jargon. Tactical warning is part of a broader intelligence challenge known as the "signal-to-noise" ratio. Roberta Wohlstetter's *Pearl Harbor: Warning and Decision*, one of the first and best looks at the question of surprise attack, famously found that the "noise" of irrelevant information drowned out the "signal" of a looming threat for analysts looking at the question of where Japan might attack. Only in hindsight was the true signal clear.[33] As Wohlstetter contends, "In short, we failed to anticipate Pearl Harbor not for want of relevant materials, but because of a plethora of irrelevant ones."[34]

Governments tracking large terrorist movements face similar problems. They may know that certain operatives have spent more time in a particular town or that others have scrutinized specific targets. The group's manifesto may talk about the need to strike at the "military-industrial complex" or "symbols of global arrogance." Intercepted phone calls may reveal group conversations about finding explosives like those used in a truck bomb. But these snippets of information do not disclose whether that group is planning another type of attack. The Russian government thought that Chechen terrorists might seize a large public building and sent out investigative teams to guard against that. However, the government thought such a building would be a theater or a cinema, not a public school as turned out to be the case when terrorists seized a school in Beslan.

This lack of specific information is a constant headache to counterterrorism officials. Investigations of attacks before September 11 emphasized that tactical warning was lacking even though strategic warning was sound. In 1985, the "Report of the Secretary of State's Advisory Panel on Overseas Security" (the "Inman Report") examined the bombings of the U.S. embassy and marine barracks in

Lebanon and concluded, "If determined, well-trained and funded teams are seeking to do damage, they will eventually succeed." The inquiries into the 1996 Khobar Towers attack and that of the 1998 embassy bombings both found that strategic warning was sound even as tactical warning was lacking.[35] In 1999, the "Report of the Accountability Review Boards on the Embassy Bombings in Nairobi and Dar es Salaam" (better known as the "Crowe Commission") contended that "[W]e cannot count on having such intelligence to warn us of such attacks."[36] The bottom line: we will continue to be surprised by terrorist attacks, even when we know a group is out to get us.

Al-Qa'ida: The Ultimate Intelligence Challenge

Al-Qa'ida presents problems that go well beyond most terrorist groups. To evade detection, al-Qa'ida operatives use "denial"—that is, using all means possible to avoid discovery, even if it means changing their appearance. For example, the instructions of the *Jihad Manual* circulated by al-Qa'ida focused on blending in with local communities and ensuring that the overall organization is not disrupted. To avoid raising suspicion from security forces, they are instructed not to look "Islamic." In addition, they "compartmentalize" information. One member might know what kind of weapon would be used for an attack, but he wouldn't know where or when the attack would occur. Members are told not to write secret information in letters and not to reveal their true names, even to other members. Bin Ladin himself avoided using cell phones[37] and employed only trusted Arabs as bodyguards.

Because al-Qa'ida is more skilled in the art of secrecy than other terrorist groups, the signal-to-noise problem is immense. A great deal of "chatter" is heard but little is useful. Al-Qa'ida probably disseminates disinformation, although this is relatively rare among terrorist groups. The *Jihad Manual* calls for exploiting telephone lines that are known to be monitored by providing "the enemy" with misleading information.[38] These techniques served as major obstacles to preventing attacks.

Al-Qa'ida is especially sensitive to the SIGINT capabilities of Western governments. The *Jihad Manual* warns its members about the downside of communications. It clearly notes that "communications is the mainstay of the movement for rapid accomplishment. However, it is a double-edged sword: it can be to our advantage if we use it well and it can be a knife dug into our back if we do not consider and take the necessary security measures."[39] This is the communications dilemma for terrorists in a nutshell.

Governments fighting terrorists can create a spiral of success. Arrests of a few figures (even quite junior ones) can quickly generate exploitable intelligence on more senior leaders, whose arrests, in turn, yield an intelligence bonanza that leads to the arrest or death of much of the remainder of the group—a killing blow. In 1996, Egyptian Islamic Jihad suffered such a massive blow when Egyptian security forces arrested hundreds of operatives. The result of this massive security failure was the collapse of the group's network within Egypt—ironically, a major source of why bin Ladin's number two, Ayman al-Zawahiri, "went global" and joined bin Ladin.

The Greek terrorist organization 17 November (N17) collapsed in that manner. N17 took its name after the date in 1973 when the Greek military government, in a bloody battle, crushed students who had seized the Athens Polytechnic and called for democracy. In its many manifestos, 17 November trumpeted both socialism and nationalism. The organization saw force as the only path to victory, rejecting social reform, democratic politics, and other elements of the strong left-wing movement in Greece that had emerged after the seven-year period of military rule ended in 1974. It opposed the left and right parties of the Greek government and attacked a range of targets its members believed were linked to capitalism, imperialism, and the state. N17 also championed an array of nationalist goals, such as ending Greece's membership in the North Atlantic Treaty Organization (NATO) and expelling Turkey from Cyprus.[40] From 1975 to 2002, N17 was responsible for more than a hundred attacks, including at least twenty-three murders that included U.S. and other Western officials, prominent businessmen, and Greek politicians of the right and moderate left.

N17 managed to evade the police until one operative, Savas Xiros, bungled a bomb attack in June 2002. Afterward the organization quickly collapsed. In Xiros's apartment, police found documents that led to eighteen other suspects, including N17's core members—all of whom were arrested.[41] The organization that had terrorized Greece for more than twenty-five years was crushed in months.

Slaying al-Qa'ida with such a killing blow is impossible because of its global nature. A common estimate is that the organization has a presence in over sixty countries. At best, an al-Qa'ida cell or set of cells can be disrupted through arrests, and at times killings. The organization can, however, reconstitute the fallen cells using other operatives to rebuild what they've lost. In 1997, the U.S. and Kenyan governments worked closely together in a series of raids to expel or arrest al-Qa'ida figures in Kenya.[42] One year later, remnants of the cell, working with other members flown in from Afghanistan, blew up the U.S. embassy in Kenya. Like a many-headed hydra, these cells regenerate themselves.

This global presence also makes it difficult to get close to the leaders, who are privy to the details of various plots. Before 9/11, al-Qa'ida's leadership in Afghanistan was largely inviolable. One counterterrorism official noted that it was impossible to address the source of the problem when al-Qa'ida had a sanctuary. At best the intelligence community could go after the various cells and plots launched from Afghanistan, but this was like "trying to chop down a tree by picking the fruit."[43] Today, of course, this problem is lessened. Even so, al-Qa'ida enjoys a high and growing degree of autonomy in various ungoverned areas, such as the remote tribal regions of Pakistan.

The organization may also plan operations in one country and conduct them in another. A plot in Yemen may be hatched in Saudi Arabia, while a plot in France may be orchestrated from Tunisia: keeping one's own house in order no longer guarantees immunity. The bloody attacks in Jordan on November 10, 2005, that killed more than fifty people, including a particularly gruesome strike on a wedding party, were planned and executed by al-Qa'ida members operating out of Iraq. Even Jordan's exceptionally skilled security services could not prevent the massacre. The 9/11 attack is probably the best example. Afghanistan, Germany, Saudi Arabia, the United Arab Emirates, Malaysia, and of course the United States also were important places where al-Qa'ida plotted, recruited, or raised money as well as conducted the attacks.

What confounds investigators' ability to rein in al-Qa'ida is the very makeup of the organization. Al-Qa'ida seeks out members who are calm and experienced. They value these attributes as seriously as ideological commitment. The *Jihad Manual* is quite specific: "[The member] should have a calm personality that allows him to endure psychological trauma such as those involving bloodshed, murder, arrest, imprisonment, and reverse psychological trauma such as killing one or all of his Organization's comrades."[44] Indeed, al-Qa'ida's founding document notes that a requirement to enter al-Qa'ida was someone who has "good manners" and is "listening and obedient."[45]

In contrast to many terrorist groups, al-Qa'ida also understands the role of counterintelligence. Its members make every attempt to thwart their adversary's attempts to gain intelligence, and they are often successful at blocking them. Its manuals warn that the CIA seeks out operatives who have grown disenchanted or who lead a lavish lifestyle that makes them open to blackmail or financial incentives. Its operatives regularly review lessons learned in order to improve their chances of success for future attacks.[46] This enables the organization to recuperate quickly from a disaster or from successful government countermeasures.

Infiltrating a terrorist organization as sophisticated and secretive as al-Qa'ida is exceptionally difficult. By the late 1990s such a penetration was a priority for the CIA.[47] Once again, the 9/11 plot, the largest in the organization's history, is a case in point. In 2001, CIA analysts tracked possible al-Qa'ida plots in Europe, Africa, and the Middle East. The CIA was roundly criticized for missing the significance of several weak threads of intelligence related to attacks with airlines. But these reports came amid literally thousands of reports dealing with car bombs, assassinations, and other proven dangers that might occur worldwide. The U.S. homeland was also of concern, but the threat was lost in the data swamp of information related to overseas attacks. These overseas threats, moreover, were not always pure noise but rather were signals of other attacks. Al-Qa'ida was indeed plotting attacks in Europe and the Middle East, as later events would prove.

Tracking the "Global Jihad"

The "global jihad" is comprised of a much larger group of individuals than al-Qa'ida. The global jihad and al-Qa'ida are frequently conflated, when in reality they are separate organizations—or, more accurately in the case of the global jihad, a separate set of organizations and individuals. Though the global jihadists share parts of al-Qa'ida's agenda, they are not under its aegis. From an intelligence point of view, the individuals involved in the global jihad are in some ways easier to track than the traditional al-Qa'ida core. But in other ways, because of its large size and diffuse nature, the group is just as difficult to follow and disrupt. However, many of these jihadists are unknown to law enforcement and intelligence officials until after they act—and by then it is too late.

In contrast to al-Qa'ida's experienced core of professionals, among the local jihadists there is greater variation in training, discipline, experience, and overall skill. The hard-won experience that the al-Qa'ida core has gained over the years is lacking in the eager but green local recruits. For example, the first attempt to topple the World Trade Center, in 1993, which went from tragedy to farce, is often attributed to al-Qa'ida, when it was actually a group of jihadists working together without bin Ladin's guidance. After the bomb packed in a rented van exploded, one of the bombers returned to the rental car company and tried to get his deposit back by claiming the van was stolen. The FBI promptly arrested him, leading to the discovery of the rest of the cell. Such inexperience is true for regional cells that support al-Qa'ida's goals as well. Abu Mohammad al-Maqdisi, the former leader of a cell in Jordan whose members included the now infamous Abu Musab al-Zarqawi, lamented that cells and operatives in Jordan were constantly being arrested because of "organizational weakness and fatal security negligence."[48]

Unfortunately, offsetting the inept performance of the jihadists is their obscurity. As then director of National Intelligence John Negroponte testified, "Such unaffiliated individuals, groups and cells represent a different threat than that of a defined organization. They are harder to spot and represent a serious intelligence challenge." Until joining the local jihadist group, they had done nothing that would bring them to the attention of law enforcement officials. Some might be known as petty criminals or as hangers-on around military types, but even in these cases the governments in question would not devote scarce resources to monitoring their activities. Instead they would focus on those who, on the surface, would appear more dangerous. Shehzad Tanweer, one of the London transit suicide bombers, appeared harmless and highly assimilated, a stereotypical Brit. He was a passionate cricket fan, and his parents even ran a fish-and-chips shop. Neighbors described him as "a very nice lad" and noted that "he was always smiling." Nothing obvious in his background would lead law enforcement officials to see him as a possible threat unless they already had information on his clandestine activities.

Once the crime has been committed, however, investigators can track down the terrorist cell. Thus, within a month after the March 11, 2004, subway attacks in Madrid, the Spanish government first rounded up the perpetrators, and then the alleged mastermind, who was captured in Italy in June. One leader remained elusive, but by then much of the network had been quickly crushed.

Law enforcement and domestic intelligence services also can disrupt terrorists before they strike, but the challenge is far harder. Here the key is to have superb informant networks in suspect communities (e.g., congregants at a radical mosque from which several known militants have emerged). In addition, agents provocateurs can be used to smoke out threats. However, democracies in particular are in a bind, as civil liberty protections inhibit them from spying on their own citizens without some evidence to suggest criminal activity, putting pressure on uninvolved family members to gain information, or otherwise emulating the techniques that dictatorships around the world have used successfully to penetrate terrorist networks.

Though the jihadist leadership operates on a local or a regional level, its aims are global as well as local and regional in scale. In January 2006, Spanish police broke up a cell that was, among other activities, sending fighters to Iraq. The cell drew on recruits not only from Spain but also from North Africa. It worked with additional cells in France, Belgium, the Netherlands, Syria, and Algeria and maintained ties to violent Moroccan and Algerian groups.[49] Unfortunately, the consequence of the jihadists' widespread activities often results in less international cooperation against the local groups than against the global menace of al-Qa'ida. The Moroccan Islamic Call Group threatens Morocco directly, and its operatives also have been linked to attacks in Spain. But the network that helps sustain it has branches throughout Europe, even in countries such as Belgium and the Netherlands, which face little immediate danger from the group. Disrupting the Moroccan terrorists' recruitment network and logistics base thus requires the assistance of governments that lack the same incentive for cooperation. From their point of view, the Moroccan terrorists are Morocco's problems—until they abet or commit a terrorist attack somewhere outside Morocco.

Terrorist Vulnerabilities

Anticipating and disrupting terrorist attacks are perhaps the most difficult challenges for intelligence professionals. But the picture is not entirely bleak. The good news is that terrorists can become vulnerable, either as individuals or when they act together as a group. Counterterrorism capitalizes on these mistakes by obtaining information and ultimately by arresting, killing, or intimidating would-be terrorists.

Like most human beings, terrorists have weaknesses that clever governments can exploit. Police and intelligence officials can take advantage of ardent young zealots who become disillusioned, corrupt, or simply older. A British counterterrorism official relates that Britain's domestic intelligence service, MI-5, tries to approach suspected terrorists at key turning points in their lives, such as marriage or the birth of children. Once terrorists assume these responsibilities, they become, like people everywhere, much less willing to take risks and become far more concerned about spending their lives in jail. Being a husband or a father—paying the rent, watching their children grow up—become much more important than the cause. British intelligence officials approach individuals at about age thirty, a time when individuals grow more cautious.

This tactic is even used by terrorists themselves. The disbanding of "Black September," the lethal Palestinian terrorist organization responsible for the 1972 Munich Olympics operation, among others, suggests the power of this personal approach. Although much attention has been given to Israel's "Grapes of Wrath" Operation, which hunted down many of the individuals involved in the Munich plot, the Black September Organization itself was far larger and involved in many more operations than just the Olympics plot. Seeking respectability, the more mainstream figures in Fatah, the father of Black September, sought to disband the group. But how to convince such ardent believers to change course? These men, in Palestinian eyes, were the best of the best and were devoted to Israel's violent destruction. Terrorism expert Bruce Hoffman found that the Palestinians disbanded Black September by marrying members off. Fatah held a mixer in Beirut and invited young, attractive Palestinian women to meet the terrorists—many of whom were heroes in the eyes of ordinary Palestinians. To this natural attraction they added financial bonuses—an apartment and a job in a nonviolent capacity. Couples who quickly produced a baby got an additional bonus.

Faced with this mix of romance and stability, the activists lost their fire. From time to time the PLO would test them, asking them to undertake a nonviolent PLO mission abroad. The former diehards now refused to travel, fearing that they might be arrested, leaving their families fatherless.[50]

Even when living underground, many terrorists still want to see their families. Israel killed Hamas leader Abd al-Rantisi, for example, when he broke his usual cautious routine and visited his home.[51] Similarly, KSM lived with two young sons, Omar and Abdullah, which made it hard for him to slip from place to place to elude his pursuers.

Over time, the stress of this lifestyle wears down terrorists. They become eager to leave the group. Explaining Hamas's decision to endorse a cease-fire in 2005 even when the group had clearly failed to achieve its goals through violence, Avi Dichter, a former head of Shin Bet, Israel's domestic intelligence service, contends that "Senior Hamas leaders decided they were tired of seeing the sun only in pictures."[52] Smart governments take advantage of terrorists' love of family. British authorities allowed hard-core IRA terrorists who were aging to leave prison and go home for short holidays. Once home, they saw their attractive wives and elderly parents (and children who did not know their fathers). While their experience was still fresh, British security forces would step in and offer the terrorists an expedited release. At the very least, this arrangement required that the terrorists renounce violence permanently.[53] It may also have required passing along information to the authorities.

When terrorists forsake families to remain underground, they give up more than hearth and home. They also relinquish their basic human need for companionship and sex. The group becomes the terrorists' world, and as a result they may lose touch with their constituents, the very people who support them. Terrorists may find lovers or visit prostitutes, both of which present opportunities for government security officials to blackmail them.

Another source of information comes from people who seek access to government favors. These petitioners become a huge source of potential recruits. Because Israel controls the rewards of a modern state, it can use this to force people to provide it with information. Israel regularly recruits Palestinians who seek a job in Israel, who want a visa to study in the United States or another country, or who need to take a child to a doctor on the Israeli side of the lines. Other Middle Eastern governments not bound by the rule of law can put pressure on individuals' families to inform on their fellows by threatening jail, by taking away a business permit, by denying access to school, and so on. At times they can even convince an individual to join a group as a plant for the government.

Although less blatant than Middle Eastern governments, the United States can use similar tools when trying to gain information from U.S. residents, particularly if they are not citizens. Frequently law enforcement officials can use a family member involved in petty crime or a visa violation as leverage with a relative whom they want to recruit. Intelligence officials routinely note that the ability to work with immigration officials gives them a tremendous advantage when trying to convince individuals to cooperate with them.

Another way to undermine a terrorist organization is for security forces to recruit one or more members to become informants. Whether or not the official is successful, the very act of recruitment—"pitching" them—can sow distrust within the organization. Members may fear that an individual has been compromised simply because he has been "pitched." Security forces believe that many plots are called off because intelligence and police agencies convince the terrorists that the government knows more than it actually does.

Detainees themselves become important sources of information. Captured terrorists know vital facts about the identities of their network's leader or document forger or funders. Questioning terrorists can be problematic. Groups such as al-Qa'ida carefully prepare their members for interrogation. They assure members that if they are captured, the group will take care of their families. Still, once in prison, authorities can manipulate the terrorists' environment by limiting access to books and to exercise privileges. Small changes in the environment such as a change in a cellmate can loom huge for a prisoner. The very act of survival in prison is difficult for many terrorists. As Dichter said to me during an interview, "Prison brings out people's weaknesses." Taking cigarettes away from a smoker or isolating a sociable person are simple but devastating techniques that can make individuals more pliant. Even if they won't talk, they are often captured with their Palm Pilots, their cell phones, and their computers, all of which can generate huge amounts of information, including many people whom the person called or e-mailed.

Just as individual group members are vulnerable, the group as a whole also has its own weaknesses. Terrorism, particularly when it involves full-time professionals, is a time-consuming and resource-intensive business. Many assume that is not the case because, with a few exceptions, the actual cost of attack is modest. One hashish deal paid for the Madrid commuter train bombings, and the first World Trade Center bomb cost perhaps $300 for the rental truck and bomb materials. But individuals within an established group must either be paid or find jobs. If members work, they will devote less time to the group in question. Many groups pay the families of those killed in the service of the cause; it turns the group from a source of loss to the family (they lose the economic activities of a young man) to a source of gain. Israel claims that the Saudi government paid families of Palestinian suicide bombers $5,000, making them rich by the standards of the poverty-stricken Gaza Strip.[54] Prior to 9/11, al-Qa'ida members received a salary and benefits, including paid vacations, disability, and subsidized furniture though it is unclear if they still do.[55] Such rewards are an incentive for individuals to stay with the group: al-Qa'ida's local rivals often do not pay as well, and the individuals in question often have few skills that would let them earn a similar living if they abandoned jihad.

If terrorists are paid, however, costs begin to mount and leaders find themselves running a business. Like successful aid organizations and charities, group members must then spend a considerable amount of time raising money. Leaders give talks, advertise selectively, woo rich donors, and otherwise try to develop a steady source of income. Bin Ladin, for example, financed al-Qa'ida for many years primarily through the financial support of wealthy donors in the Persian Gulf. Because of this financial dependence, the donors' opinions about the target and the means of attack became important to the group. These donors pushed the group away from attacks on children like the Beslan atrocity, or indiscriminate violence, such as that practiced by the GIA in Algeria in the mid-1990s.

If local groups cannot raise money from donors, they may instead finance themselves through crime. Ahmed Ressam, who was arrested when he crossed from Canada to the United States in an ill-planned attempt to bomb Los Angeles International Airport near the 2000 millennium celebrations, financed much of his activities in Canada through drug trafficking. A life of crime has its own problems. Potential terrorists may suddenly appear on the police radar screen for credit card fraud or narcotics trafficking, rather than political activity or planned violence.

Whether terrorists obtain money through donors or through crime, business records can leave a paper trail. Once an organization begins paying people, they risk exposure. If found, these records can be a treasure trove for investigators, revealing group members' names and relative ranks in the organization. Almost forty years ago Italy's Red Brigades faced this problem when they decided to pay their full-time activists. The leaders determined that the average wage of a Fiat auto company worker as the appropriate level.[56] As with any organization, some disgruntled members resented the pay scale. Italian intelligence exploited this. Similarly, Jamal al-Fadl, the first major defector from al-Qa'ida to the United States, turned against bin Ladin in part because as a Sudanese he resented making less money than the Egyptians in the organization.

Another paper trail may be left when the group needs documents. While some groups may have their own in-house forgers, others regularly turn to criminal types for assistance. But reliance on criminals is risky: groups often can get the documents they need, but the criminals will happily sell them out, either to protect themselves or for the right price. Yet these services are essential. Possession of the wrong documents can lead to arrest. Former director of Central Intelligence William Webster noted that during the Gulf War the Iraqi intelligence officers used sequentially numbered passports. As a result, once several officers were arrested, the rest were easily discovered and detained.

The group becomes most vulnerable, however, when they begin to communicate their plans with one another and with outsiders.[57] KSM himself noted, "When four people know the details of an operation, it is dangerous; when two people know, it is good; when just one person knows, it is better."[58] KSM's location was narrowed when Garczarski phoned him, even if Garczarski didn't speak to him directly. Placing the call was enough. At some point individuals need to tell operatives where, when, and how to strike, and the operatives must report back to the leadership on their progress. Less dramatic but no less important, communications entail group efforts to recruit, raise money, train people, and maintain the group in general. This need for interaction means that terrorists leave the best hiding places, such as the mountains of Afghanistan or the vast wilds of Yemen, for urban areas where they can be tracked down by counterterrorism forces.

When terrorists begin to communicate, they are susceptible to signals intelligence—an area where the United States excels. At that point, security services may intercept e-mail, place wiretaps on phones, monitor cellular communications, or otherwise take advantage of vulnerabilities in communications technologies. The *Washington Post* reports that 80 to 90 percent of the valuable information gleaned from terrorism networks comes from SIGINT.[59] KSM, for example, needed to communicate to implement his terrorist plans. So he risked leaving his safe hiding place in the countryside for Karachi, to be in the center of operations. Karachi is a major hub in Pakistan, with flights connecting the city to every continent. U.S. law enforcement officials claim that KSM simultaneously talked on one cell phone and sent text messages on another—a skill heretofore limited largely to American teenagers.[60] KSM reportedly used not only cell phones but also e-mails, couriers, and shortwave radio.[61] Without these phones he could not have orchestrated the various plots around the world. But the many SIM cards he used for his various cell phones and his easily accessible location eventually proved his undoing.

Groups recognize U.S. SIGINT capabilities and adapt by eschewing modern communication forms such as phones and e-mails in favor of messengers, a method that is at best a mixed blessing for the terrorists. Messengers are far slower and less efficient than e-mail and cell phones. It is like relying on the Pony Express in the age of technology. Most of the modern world is dependent on the telephone and e-mail for their business and personal life. Groups unable to use these tools suffer as a result. While messengers may decrease the use of SIGINT to collect information, they become a great potential source of human intelligence if caught. Once captured, they are easy to "turn" and can become immensely valuable as sources.

Each new messenger, each new member, each new phone call, each new collaboration increases the risk of the group's exposure.

Amnesty programs, often derided as being "soft" to terrorists, also are challenging for groups. Amnesties can encourage individuals to defect from the group, and when they do so, the price is usually to inform on their former colleagues. Equally important, the group has to spend far more time policing its ranks and compart-menting information more, to guard against the risk that someone will defect. The Algerian government claims that its repentance program produced thousands of recruits, which devastated several radical groups there.

How to Do It Better

The global jihad wants an international war targeting much of the world. Countries dedicated to preventing terrorist attacks around the globe must view the preservation and enhancement of intelli-gence flow as top priorities. *All* of the high-value terrorists the United States holds were captured by or in cooperation with foreign security services. If America attempts an independent operation, be it a controversial attempt to recruit a foreign government official in Indonesia or a targeted killing operation in Pakistan, it must weigh any possible gains against the potential loss of government intelli-gence cooperation. Angering the government, even if justified for the operation in question, jeopardizes the long-term cooperation on which ultimate success depends.

Thus we should be skeptical of calls to solve the problem of counterterrorism intelligence by increasing U.S. unilateral pene-trations of terrorist groups. While always desirable, such penetra-tions are exceptionally difficult for U.S. intelligence and usually better done by U.S. allies. Risking allies' long-term cooperation must be done only under exceptional circumstances.

Nor can intelligence-gathering be divorced from the issue of winning popular support. If allied governments are not popular (or sufficiently feared), they will not be able to gather the necessary intelligence from their populace. Local residents may see terrorists as heroes—more as Robin Hoods than as criminals to be arrested. In Pakistan's tribal areas, bin Ladin remains far more popular than the United States, with local leaders clearly reluctant to provide information on his whereabouts.

When U.S. policy becomes isolated from that of its allies, the United States will find it far harder to maintain local cooperation, even when it is in the locals' interest to do so. Similarly, people around the world are not likely to divorce their general view of U.S. policy from their particular feelings about anti-U.S. terrorism.

The intelligence community also must make getting bin Ladin a priority. The *New York Times* reports that in late 2005 the CIA disbanded Alec Station, the unit that focused on hunting bin Ladin and his key lieutenants.[62] This was foolish at the time and even more mistaken today. The al-Qa'ida core remains active and is getting stronger. Moreover, bin Ladin's continued survival gives him a form of symbolic victory and helps keep his fractious movement together.

Covert action also is necessary in tribal parts of Pakistan. U.S. intelligence should work with tribal elements that oppose the jihadists and otherwise try to build a local coalition against bin Ladin's forces. Such an effort will be difficult, as bin Ladin is popular and suspicion of the United States high. Forcing bin Ladin to focus on local threats rather than being able to enjoy complete security, however, will deplete his organization's resources and make it harder for him to focus on striking the U.S. homeland and other difficult targets.

4

Killing Terrorists

S alah Shehada was a marked man. For two years the senior Hamas leader had directed terrorist attacks against Israel. According to one Israeli security expert, he orchestrated 52 attacks that killed 220 Israeli civilians and 16 soldiers.[1] Shehada's time ran out on July 22, 2002, when an Israeli F-16 used a 2,000-pound bomb to obliterate his apartment building. Also killed in the blast were 14 civilians, including Shehada's daughter and 8 other children.

The moral complications of the Shehada killings were matched by their political complexities. Before deciding to kill Shehada, Israeli officials first went to the Palestinian Authority (PA) and demanded his arrest. Despite repeated requests, the PA refused. Israeli officials next sought to arrest him themselves. But arrest was problematic because Shehada lived in the middle of Gaza City, and any Israeli raid would have met with resistance from local Hamas fighters. A full-blown skirmish would endanger the Israelis sent in to arrest him, and risk killing civilians in the cross-fire. In the midst of the fighting, Shehada would escape.

Israeli officials decided to kill him. A primary Israeli rule, however, forbids deliberately killing noncombatants. Moshe Ya'alon, then the chief of staff of the Israeli Defense Forces, claims that Israel repeatedly avoided striking Shehada during earlier sightings because he was with his daughter. Rather than kill his daughter, Israeli officials called off eight different operations. In the end, they decided to kill Shehada even if his wife was with him, claiming that she was heavily involved in Shehada's activities and thus a legitimate target. But they ruled out killing him if any children were present.

The process of gathering intelligence for the operation was formidable. The Israelis used spies and scouts who observed Shehada's comings and goings. But before the operation could begin, two problems had to be solved. First, the target had to be confirmed. Second, the people traveling with Shehada had to be identified. Though intelligence could confirm that the target was present, they could not identify who else was with him. Was Shehada meeting with fellow terrorists or at dinner with his family? Was he driving to a terrorist meeting or to a wedding? A primary question for the Israelis was whether Shehada was traveling with children.

Then Israel's domestic intelligence service, Shin Bet, learned that on a particular day, Shehada would be in an apartment building with no innocents nearby. Because the intelligence did not reveal exactly where in the building Shehada was, Israeli officials rejected the use of a missile, fearing it would not kill him. They decided finally to use a massive bomb that caused extensive damage. It led to the collapse of the five-story building that housed Shehada and damaged several nearby buildings. Many innocent civilians, including children, were killed. After all the aborted attempts, the intelligence was, in the end, flawed. Shehada was present, but so, too, were his wife and daughter. Tragically, the surrounding buildings also had been occupied, not vacant. Although Israeli intelligence had tracked Shehada's movements assiduously, their assessments were disastrously incorrect. Israeli officials knew that the bomb would damage neighboring buildings but assumed they were empty. They were also wrong in assuming that Shehada's daughter would be away from home.

The political reaction to the attacks was overwhelmingly negative. Not surprisingly, Hamas declared it a massacre, and distributed a leaflet saying it would fight until "Jews see their own body parts in every restaurant, every park, every bus and every street."[2] Hundreds of thousands of Palestinians turned out to mourn the victims of the Israeli attack. World leaders also condemned it, and even the

Bush White House—usually very sympathetic to Israel's actions—
declared the strike "heavy-handed."

Afterward, Israel temporarily became more careful in its targeting of terrorists, but that caution soon proved deadly for them. Two
months after Shehada's death, Israeli intelligence learned that all of
Hamas's senior leaders—"the dream team," as some Israeli officials
called it—were meeting in one location. Determined to strike but
leery of causing more civilian deaths, Israel used a small bomb in its
attack. Predictably, the explosion did not kill the leaders. Some were
killed six months later, but in the interim Hamas conducted more
terrorist attacks. Former head of Shin Bet Avi Dichter lamented to
me, "How many Israelis died as a result of this failed killing?"

The question of whether to kill terrorists directly is not limited
to Israel. It became paramount when the United States attempted to
target bin Ladin before 9/11. In December 1998, CIA operatives
located bin Ladin in the Afghan city of Kandahar. The U.S. government had long prepared for this moment and was ready to launch
cruise missiles to kill the terrorist leader. But policymakers vacil-
lated, fearing that the attack would lead to the killing of innocent
women and children. In the end, no strike was launched. Again, in
February 1999, CIA assets had pinpointed Osama bin Ladin's
location in a hunting camp in a desert south of Kandahar. The
U.S. military was prepared to strike with cruise missiles. Once more,
policymakers wavered. This time they feared that the strike would
also kill members of the United Arab Emirates royal family who
were camped near (or possibly with) bin Ladin. Again, they failed to
launch.

These missed opportunities typified a caution with regard to the
use of force under both the Clinton and early George W. Bush
administrations. Until September 11, the U.S. government refused
to send special operations forces into Afghanistan. Officials issued
cumbersome directions to the CIA about assassinating bin Ladin.
And these officials hung back from working with the Taliban's
enemies against bin Ladin. Even now, many commentators eschew
political assassination as a means of fighting terrorism. Citing the
moral implications of assassination, they instead espouse more traditional means of destroying the enemy. But after September 11, the

scale shifted toward tolerating assassination. After the appalling carnage of that day, many politicians believe this reluctance to strike is unforgivable. They claim that many lives might have been saved if only the United States had been more aggressive in using force.

Killing terrorists is necessary because not all terrorists can be arrested, and even some of those who can be arrested have little if any intelligence value yet will attack if left alone. Many (though not all!) are highly committed, and even the threat of arrest or execution will not deter them from striking. In short, we must kill them before they kill us. But this simple statement masks a complex reality. Killing and the use of military force can often backfire, angering the very communities and countries whose help we most need to track and disrupt terrorists. In addition, the intelligence and logistical requirements for killing operations are considerable, and if not met, can lead to devastating mistakes.

The Rewards and the Costs of Targeted Killings

The example of Salah Shehada shows how military forces can fight terrorism by conducting strikes on terrorists themselves—what is often referred to as targeted killings. B'tselem, an Israeli human rights organization, says that since the second intifada began in September 2000, until September 2005, Israeli security forces have killed 191 Palestinians deliberately through targeted killings. An additional 109 innocents (or others not deliberately targeted) died in the process. The year 2003 was the peak year, with 91 killings.[3]

Although the scope of U.S. targeted killings is far more narrow than the Israeli operations, targeted killings are an important part of U.S. counterterrorism today. On November 3, 2002, the United States killed Abu Ali al-Harethi, a senior al-Qa'ida operative who was one of the masterminds of the October 12, 2000, attack on the USS *Cole*. An unmanned, remote-controlled drone fired a Hellfire missile at Harethi's vehicle, killing him along with five other operatives in a remote part of Yemen. In 2001 the United States conducted similar operations that killed Mohammad Atef, al-Qa'ida's military leader in Afghanistan, and in 2005 they killed Abu Hamza Rabia, a senior al-Qa'ida figure in Pakistan, echoing the Israeli strike on Shehada. On January 13, 2006, another unmanned drone fired at a Pakistani village where Ayman al-Zawahiri, al-Qa'ida's number two, was thought to be hiding. The strike killed more than a dozen people, some of whom may have been al-Qa'ida and others who were not part of the organization. But it did not kill Zawahiri.

The Israeli experience suggests that targeted killings can indeed disrupt terrorist attacks. When the second intifada grew in scope, Israel stepped up its targeted killings of Hamas and other terrorist group leaders. The Israeli campaign soon took its toll, and Palestinian terrorism became far less lethal. B'tselem reports that through the end of October 2005 only 34 Israeli civilians died at the hands of Palestinians, down from 68 in 2004, 129 in 2003, 172 in 2002, and 151 in 2001; figures for Israeli soldiers also show a comparable decline.[4] Shattered by their losses, the terrorist groups became far less capable of conducting effective operations. The Israeli killings infuriate terrorists and, as many critics point out, only increase their desire to kill. Nevertheless, the killings have greatly decreased the number of lethal attacks in Israel. Israeli officials claim that they stop 80 to 90 percent of terrorist attempts.

With the Israelis hovering over them and their leadership decimated, the terrorists had less time to plan successful attacks. Even the attacks that were successful grew less destructive. The number of Hamas attacks grew steadily as the intifada progressed, growing from 19 in 2001 to 34 in 2002, 46 in 2003, 202 in 2004, and 179 in 2005 (with most of the attacks occurring in the first half of the year, before the tentative cease-fire took hold). Critics of targeted killings anticipated that the number of attacks would grow considerably after the targeted killings began. But even though the number of attacks grew, the number of Israeli deaths plunged, suggesting that the attacks themselves became far less deadly. Though the numbers rose from 3.9 deaths per attack in 2001 to 5.4 in 2002, its highest point, the rate began to fall in 2003, plunging from 0.98 death per attack that year to 0.33 death per attack in 2004 and falling further, to 0.23 death per attack in 2005.

The statistics speak for themselves. When the terrorists' cells are decimated by the loss of key members, the attacks do not cease altogether but become far less effective. Contrary to popular myth, the number of skilled terrorists is often quite limited. Instigators of terror such as bombmakers, trainers, document forgers, recruiters, and leaders are scarce in number. They require months if not years to hone their skills and gain expertise. If they can be eliminated, the organization as a whole will be disrupted. The movement may still have willing recruits, but it will no longer function well.

If a targeted killing is to be effective, the pace of the attack must be swift. In the 1980s and 1990s, when the Israelis attacked Hizballah, they did so at a slow, almost desultory pace. They killed a number of Hizballah leaders, but these deaths did not slow the number of attacks. Because the Israeli strikes were infrequent, most Hizballah leaders did not worry about hiding. So Hizballah had the leisure to ensure that the replacements were fully trained. In contrast, Hamas and other Palestinian groups found it difficult to replenish their skilled members. Attacks against al-Qa'ida, on the other hand, have struck only a limited number of leaders. Though the United States has been unable to stop attacks through targeted killings, arrests of key al-Qa'ida figures have devastated its core.

In addition to eliminating key facilitators and leaders, targeted killings force surviving terrorists to spend their time on the run rather than on operations. To avoid Israeli strikes, Hamas members must constantly change locations. Their hiding places must be kept secret even from their cohorts, lest they be discovered. Given this level of secrecy, it becomes difficult if not impossible for leaders to communicate with one another. Unable to issue orders to their followers, their activity wanes. The terrorists cannot see their parents or children without risk of dying. Over time the stress begins to take its toll. Those who stray from their hiding places pay the price. The head of Hamas, Abd al-Rantisi, for example, was killed when he broke his usual cautious routine and visited his home.[5]

Leaders in hiding find it difficult to lead. After Israel killed Shaykh Yasin, Hamas appointed Rantisi as his successor. Israel promptly killed him. Hamas then announced that it had appointed a new leader but would not name him publicly, a necessary step for the leader's survival perhaps, but hardly a way to inspire followers, let alone win new recruits.

Again and again Palestinian groups call for Israelis to end their practice of targeted killings, which suggests that the Palestinians deeply feel its effects. Before his death, Rantisi conceded that the killings of Hamas leaders made operations more difficult for its operatives.[6] As Hamas expert Khaled Hroub contends, "On the ground, there is no question that Hamas has been seriously weakened by the decimation of its ranks through assassination and arrest."[7] Indeed, Hamas declared that it would unilaterally accept a "period of calm" in 2005 because of the losses in its senior cadre.

Still, you can't kill everyone. When affiliates and would-be members are included in its numbers, al-Qa'ida is a large organization. The United States and its allies might be able to kill hundreds of terrorist leaders, but given the group's ability to replenish fallen comrades, these killings will not make the terrorist problem disappear.

Israeli security forces freely admit that arrests are a far better alternative to targeted killings. When Israel retook the West Bank's cities in 2003, soldiers preferred to arrest terrorists rather than kill them. Once captured, detainees become a vital source of intelligence. In detention, security forces interrogate the suspect, who can disclose nascent plots and reveal operatives' identities. One arrest can generate a cycle that will devastate a group. Killing a suspect does indeed prevent a terrorist from striking, but dead men tell no tales.

Targeting terrorists, however, is a serious intelligence challenge. Those who are on the wanted list can easily blend in with the native people. Israel overcame these barriers by maintaining a robust intelligence network in Palestinian areas. Equally important, Israel developed a remarkably efficient system of information-sharing, whereby information collected by domestic intelligence services was quickly passed to the Israeli Air Force and other "shooters" for processing. Finally, Israel had an entire apparatus of sensors, attack helicopters, strike aircraft, and other forces at the ready to act quickly on perishable information. The result was a near-constant Israeli surveillance and strike presence over Palestinian areas. As Dichter noted, "When a Palestinian child draws a picture of the sky, he doesn't draw it without a helicopter."[8]

Acquiring this intelligence requires exceptional effort. Israel found that as many as two hundred people were involved in some of their operations. These included a pilot, sources on the ground, individuals assessing potential collateral damage, and people monitoring a vehicle as it moves. Ehud Ya'ari, an Israeli journalist, noted, "Each one is a little war, with an operations room."[9] Without the capacity for rapid action, the intelligence is useless. If the intelligence is laboriously cross-checked and the decision is debated until the strike forces are put in place, the process could take several days. During that process, the moment for action will have come and gone. In 1998 and 1999, the Clinton administration often tried to cross-check information on bin Ladin's whereabouts before it gave the order to kill him, a decision much criticized in hindsight. When the initial information was finally confirmed, it was outdated.

Vital to the Israeli intelligence and military effort was a political process that allowed for rapid action. Israel went through several steps to ensure that those on the targeted-killing list belonged there. The process began with intelligence officials who proposed names; the names went all the way up the command chain to the top, where the deputy and head of Shin Bet signed off. Those on the lists included senior terrorists or, in a few cases, individuals who were just about to launch a suicide attack. During the process, the military also reviewed all the information and made sure that the senior leaders approved. From there the names went to the minister of defense and, if he approved, to the prime minister. For particularly important or controversial targets (e.g., Hamas founder Shaykh Ahmad Yasin), the cabinet also was briefed.

Yet even if targeted killings are effective in preventing terrorist attacks, the results can have negative consequences. In Israel and the United States, the killings are extremely controversial because there is no judicial oversight. Though legal advisers are consulted during the process, they are not involved in making the final decisions. Michael Sfard, an Israeli lawyer who has challenged the killings before Israel's Supreme Court, declared, "Today we execute people without trial. It's so simple. That's what we're doing. No one shows evidence to anyone."[10]

Another negative outcome is the retaliation that killings pro-voke. In the 1980s, Hizballah increased suicide attacks on Israeli forces after Israel's targeted killings.[11] Some experts also believe that the 1992 and 1994 bombings in Argentina against Jewish and Israeli targets that killed twenty-nine and eighty-five people, respec-tively, were retaliations against Israel's targeted killing of a Hizbal-lah leader and the kidnapping of another. Hizballah scholar Clive Jones contends that the targeted killings crossed "a Rubicon of restraint that had been tacitly acknowledged by both sides."[12]

When Palestinian violence heated up during the 1990s, Israel revived the use of targeted killings. In 1995 Israel killed the head of Palestinian Islamic Jihad (PIJ), Fathi Shikaki, which disrupted the organization for several years. In 1996 Israel detonated a bomb in Yehia Ayyash's cell phone, killing the archterrorist who was known as "the Engineer" because of his skill in building bombs. In re-sponse, Hamas launched several attacks against Israeli buses and other targets. That spree discredited Shimon Peres's more dovish Labor-led government and led to the election of Benjamin Netan-yahu, who viewed the Oslo Process with skepticism, and a general hardening of Israel's attitude toward peace talks with the Palestin-ians. In 1997 Mossad agents tried to poison Shaykh Khalid Mash'al, a senior Hamas leader, in Jordan. The plot failed, and the agents were captured. A furious King Hussein, one of Israel's few friends in the Arab world, forced Israel to supply Mash'al with the antidote and to release Hamas's venerated political leader Shaykh Yasin in exchange for the return of the agents.

Not surprisingly, Mohammad Dahlan, a senior Palestinian secu-rity official, contends that "whoever signed off on killing a leader among Hamas or any other leader on the Palestinian side should turn the page and should sign off on killing 16 Israelis."[13] On July 31, 2003, Hamas bombed a student cafeteria at Hebrew University in Jerusalem, supposedly to avenge the killing of Shehada.

Not all terrorist groups operate at full killing potential. But after the Musawi and Ayyash killings in the mid-1990s, Israel learned that terrorists can raise the stakes in horrific ways.

The terrorists' ability to increase violence grew less during the second intifada. As the uprising grew in scope and Israeli military operations commenced, groups such as PIJ and Hamas were operating at full strength. Despite the bloodthirsty rhetoric that followed the killings of Shehada and later Yasin, the Palestinians were not able to kill more Israelis in response. The same comparison may hold true for al-Qa'ida. If al-Qa'ida had the capacity to do more harm to the United States, it would.

There is one important difference between the United States and Israel that should shape our thinking on the use of targeted killings. Israel's enemies operate in governments hostile to the country or in areas where there is no effective political control (and in the Gaza Strip, which is a combination of the two problems). In contrast, most of the anti-U.S. terrorists live in and operate from countries friendly to the United States. One theater is Western Europe, and another is made up of Muslim countries such as Afghanistan, Egypt, and Saudi Arabia. All are U.S. allies. Thus the rule has been and should be that the United States works through the allied government. Because the host country controls intelligence and operations, the United States does not often deviate from this rule.

The logistical challenges for the United States grow accordingly. The intelligence challenge for Israel is massive, and it operates in a very small geographic area where it has a superb intelligence network and considerable control over the lives of the local inhabitants (compare the tiny Gaza Strip to, say, the Afghan-Pakistani tribal area). The United States, in contrast, must operate globally. It often lacks the intelligence and cannot concentrate its precision strike capabilities in all the regions in which al-Qa'ida operates.

Another damaging consequence of targeted killings is the diplomatic cost. Israel's attacks were roundly condemned when they began, and the killing of perceived political leaders such as Yasin invoked particular criticism from EU and Muslim world leaders. Even the Bush administration criticized several Israeli killings as excessive and implemented a token punishment of restrictions on helicopter spare parts. Because most of the Western world sees targeted killings as illegal, the United States, too, must recognize that killings, particularly if they inadvertently kill innocents, will damage the reputation of the United States.

Adding to these drawbacks and difficulties is a fundamental and damning moral dilemma: targeted killing leads to the death of innocents. Israel's record was remarkably impressive in targeting the guilty party. But it was not perfect. Mossad operatives killed Ahmed Bouchiki, a Moroccan waiter, in Lillehammer, Norway, in 1973, mistaking him for a leader of Black September, the organization that took credit for the Munich Olympics atrocities. In fact, Bouchiki had no connection to terrorism. They killed an innocent man. Later, Norway and Canada discovered that the Israeli agents used fake Canadian passports to mask their identity and strenuously objected: it's a common spy trick but a diplomatic no-no.

Even the most carefully plotted killing can result in the death of innocents. Errors in intelligence, identification, or even aim (when it comes to missiles) are all, over time, inevitable. The costs of such mistakes go beyond the loss of innocent lives by delegitimizing the counterterrorism campaign. We cannot condemn terrorists for taking innocent lives, and then kill innocents with our counterterrorism operations. Some Israelis have expressed unequivocal condemnations of the policy as a result, and others, such as the dovish member of Parliament Yossi Beilin, have argued that targeted killings should only be used to prevent a "ticking bomb" from going off.

When innocents die, the United States looks both incompetent and brutal, a perception that increases support for terrorists. Many in the Middle East believe that the United States has developed a plan to dominate the region. They also believe in the near-infallibility of American precision weapons, so if a strike is not precise and children are killed, many in the Middle East assume it must have been the original intent.

The alternatives to targeted killings, however, are not passivity, but other means that often entail considerable civilian suffering. Thousands of Palestinians, the majority of them civilians, have died in the second intifada. Israel, for example, often imposed travel bans on or even cut off travel from radical hotbeds in the West Bank and Gaza. When people cannot travel, normal economic life is disrupted. Food and potable water become scarce. Sick people cannot see doctors, and students cannot go to class. In the long term, cutting off Palestinian areas to prevent terrorist travel has impoverished the

Palestinian lands.[14] Unemployment has skyrocketed while foreign investment has plummeted. Although innocents die from targeted killings, far fewer do so than from these more common counter-terrorism measures.

Political assassination is a conundrum. On one hand, if officials hesitate to use it, they lose the opportunity to disrupt major terrorism attacks. On the other hand, if they conduct an attack and kill innocents, they become objects of moral censure. The key, then, is not to wholly dismiss political assassination but to use it judiciously.

Retaliatory Strikes

The use of force for counterterrorism goes well beyond targeted killings. In 1986 the United States bombed Libya because of the country's use of terrorism. In 1993 the United States struck Iraq in response to its attempted assassination of former president George H. W. Bush. And in 1998, the United States attacked Afghanistan and Sudan after al-Qa'ida bombed U.S. embassies in Kenya and Tanzania.[15] The Afghanistan attack was meant to kill bin Ladin, but the others were small, general, retaliatory strikes against "state sponsors."

The United States is not the only country that employs limited uses of force in response to terrorism. Egypt attacked Sudan in 1995 after Sudanese-based Egyptian terrorists tried to kill President Mubarak in Ethiopia. Turkey used the threat of invasion to compel Syria to end its backing of the Kurdish Workers' Party. India has long threatened military retaliation for Pakistan's support of Kashmiri groups. Throughout its history, Israel has conducted military strikes against Egypt, Syria, Jordan, Lebanon, and Tunisia. Israel has launched attacks directly against Palestinian targets, Lebanese Hizballah, and the Lebanese government, and they have struck regimes that back Palestinian terrorist groups.

This tactic appears to be mostly counterproductive. Most governments view capitulation in the aftermath of such a military attack as an unconscionable admission of weakness, particularly when the strike affects only a few people. For the Taliban to have surrendered bin Ladin after the 1998 U.S. strikes on Afghanistan, for example, would have demonstrated to a highly nationalistic people that the regime caved in in the face of outside pressure. In the months before the U.S. strike, the Taliban had indicated that it might be willing to surrender bin Ladin or at least curtail his activities. But the day after the bombing, the Taliban's leader, Mullah Omar, declared, "Even if all the countries in the world unite, we would defend Osama by our blood."[16]

The U.S. bombing of Libya in 1986 known as Operation El Dorado Canyon illustrates many of the difficulties of decapitation strikes in the name of counterterrorism. The 1986 raid was designed to punish Libya for past attacks, such as the La Belle Discotheque in Berlin, to deter Libyan leader Muammar Qaddafi from supporting terrorism, to destroy the Libyan infrastructure for supporting terrorism, and to demonstrate U.S. resolve. U.S. leaders also hoped the strikes would encourage antiregime coup plotters. Although the strikes were impressive from a logistical and technical point of view, Libyan infrastructure was not damaged significantly, and many targets were missed. Qaddafi's hold on power was not shaken. There was no coup, and the infrastructure for supporting terrorism remained intact. If anything, Qaddafi's power at home and his stature in much of the world grew.[17] Few European states or other allies openly supported the attacks, and many made clear they thought the United States was overreacting.

Most importantly, while defenders of the raid insist it "sent a message" to Qaddafi, in reality it appears to have backfired. Violence surged after the attacks. Immediately after the bombing, the British ambassador's house in Lebanon was attacked because Britain allowed several of the U.S. airplanes that participated in the attack basing and overflight rights, and several other Americans and British in Lebanon were killed by a group with links to the Abu Nidal Organization, which was then in Qaddafi's employ. The Central Intelligence Agency also reported that Libya "bought" Peter Kilburn, an American hostage in Lebanon, and executed him. Libya later bombed Pan Am 103 in 1988, killing 270 people. In addition, in 1989 Libya again challenged the U.S. Navy, despite having repeatedly lost aircraft in past confrontations.[18] Nor was the United States the only Libyan target. In 1989, Libya also bombed

UTA 772, killing all 170 people on board, in response to France's support for the Habre regime in Chad.

These problems multiply when force is used directly against terrorists. In contrast to conventional militaries, terrorist groups themselves have few assets worth destroying. Training camps are rudimentary, and the weapons systems involved are small and easy to replace. Tarnak Farms, bin Ladin's massive training camp in Afghanistan, consisted mainly of rocks and dirt with a few primitive housing facilities.[19] Even worse, terrorists take flight after an attack and melt into the civilian population. If they are pursued, there is a strong likelihood of significant civilian casualties, especially if air strikes are employed. Not surprisingly, some terrorists deliberately put their facilities near hospitals and schools, targets that are off-limits for civilized nations. Even worse, the terrorists often retaliate. When Israel attacked Lebanon in the 1990s, Hizballah shelled Israeli settlements near the borders.

Perhaps most important, military strikes can make a terrorist group stronger. The 1998 U.S. strikes against al-Qa'ida camps in Afghanistan transformed al-Qa'ida from a regional group to a nationally known terrorist organization. The strikes killed Arab, Afghan, Pakistani, and Kashmiri militants, but failed to kill bin Ladin himself or other senior leaders.[20] Not only did the strikes miss their target, they also became a strategic disaster. Bin Ladin became a hero, and the young anti-U.S. Islamists outside of Afghanistan lionized him. As Maulana Sami al-Haq, a senior Pakistani religious leader, told Peter Bergen, a journalist and expert on al-Qa'ida, the U.S. strikes transformed bin Ladin into "a symbol for the whole Islamic world. . . . He's a hero to us, but it is America who first made him a hero."[21] After the attacks, al-Qa'ida became a stronger organization. With its newly found prestige, the organization greatly expanded its fund-raising and recruiting. The Taliban, reluctant to be labeled as a U.S. and Saudi stooge, felt newly committed to protecting their guest. The bombing also led to turbulence in the region. Pakistan in particular experienced anti-U.S. street demonstrations. Pakistan's weak civilian government tried to appease enraged Islamists, promising to speed the introduction of Islamic law.[22]

Force legitimates terrorists. It demonstrates that defiance works: the world's superpower sees men in caves as dangerous foes. Bruce Hoffman, one of the world's leading terrorism experts, argues that terrorists win by not losing. If terrorists are not destroyed by the military strike, in essence they "win" the encounter. Simply out-witting the United States to fight another day is proof of their vitality and U.S. weakness.

The Politics of Killing

Both the Clinton and George W. Bush administrations were criti-cized for not responding to the al-Qa'ida attack on the warship USS *Cole* on October 12, 2000, which killed seventeen sailors. It has become conventional wisdom that when the United States decided to do nothing, al-Qa'ida was encouraged to escalate attacks against the United States. The reasoning goes that bin Ladin must have then assumed that if he successfully attacked a U.S. warship, he could also execute deadly strikes in the U.S. homeland.

Would retaliation for the *Cole* bombing have prevented the 9/11 attacks?

The United States could have bombed camps in Afghanistan and perhaps killed a few of the thousands of jihadists. But first the United States weighed the possibility that an attack might worsen the insta-bility in Pakistan, which was already tense from the near-war in India over Kargil and the subsequent military coup one year earlier. If they missed, the strike would have demonstrated that the United States could neither kill him nor inflict serious damage on al-Qa'ida. Meanwhile, al-Qa'ida would emerge from the attack as David fight-ing Goliath, a small group facing down the giant United States.

Bin Ladin eagerly awaited a military response from the *Cole* attack, and he was, in fact, disappointed when one did not come. The 9/11 plot itself was already well under way.

Marshaling popular support to act decisively before casualties mount is very difficult. In 2000, with America caught up in the heat of a presidential race, the political will for invading Afghanistan was lacking. The attack on the *Cole* received little media attention. Before 9/11, no Republicans or Democrats called for serious military action. International support was even weaker. Former national security adviser Sandy Berger noted that in Afghanistan, even "our closest allies would not support us."[23] It took the carnage of 9/11 to make war politically feasible.

Justice and politics demand a response to terrorist attacks. The public wants the villain punished, and uses of force offer immediate rewards for politicians. After all, the greatest impact of terrorism is psychological: one of its goals is to undermine confidence in government. Israeli politicians have found targeted killings immensely rewarding for a public hungry for revenge. More generally, force satisfies a public demand to "do something" in the face of continued violence.

Although it is easy to dismiss these responses as crass politics rather than good policy, it makes some sense to counter an essentially psychological attack with a viscerally satisfying one.

Still, military strikes invoked as a sign of "getting tough" are often the exact response the terrorists intended to provoke. While symbolic retaliatory strikes are operationally easy for the military, they are poor counterterrorism instruments. Politicians have an obligation to make the public understand that even though a retaliatory strike is flashy and offers instant gratification, it is also ineffective as a long-term instrument. Despite the challenge, explaining these options should be a primary political goal for elected officials, even if it means lifting the veil of secrecy on these issues.

Public debate builds rather than destroys consensus. Mistakes in the use of force are inevitable. A Hellfire missile will at some point kill the wrong person, or perhaps the right person and his innocent child. (The U.S. bombs that killed Abu Musab al-Zarqawi, who was a leader of Iraq's foreign jihadists, on July 7, 2006, also reportedly killed two children under five.)[24] U.S.-trained paramilitary forces will brutalize innocents or disrupt democratic elections. If these risks are acknowledged early, and politicians from all camps join together, then an occasional error will not shake the public consensus behind the policy. A debate mounted around policy is preferable to one framed in the aftermath of a gruesome error. An informed public will better understand the risks and difficulties of using force and become more tolerant of inevitable mistakes.

For in the end a discriminate use of targeted killing remains necessary, and U.S. leaders must prepare the public for the mistakes that will inevitably occur. When the government that hosts the terrorists is unwilling or unable to arrest them, U.S. options outside of killing are poor. A U.S.-directed capture attempt is still preferable for the intelligence benefits, but this is operationally far harder than killing the terrorist. Taking targeted killings off the table would at times leave a dangerous killer unmolested while he plans attack after attack. Because intelligence and delivery means are fallible, however, the United States should use targeted killings only for high-value targets and when it has a high degree of confidence in the intelligence. (As discussed in chapter 8, aiding allied counterinsurgency efforts is another important military role.)

Planning for Operations in Pakistan

The United States and its allies must also prepare for military operations in tribal parts of Pakistan, where the al-Qa'ida core is reconstituting itself. For now, the best option is to push the Musharraf government to more aggressively go after terrorists operating from tribal regions. But Islamabad's willingness to confront the terrorists there is uneven, and its ability to eliminate the haven also questionable. Should the haven grow and should Pakistan prove unwilling or unable to confront this, direct U.S. military action may be necessary.

As the Iraq experience demonstrates, this should be a last resort. The tribal forces would fight back, and they would be joined by many Pakistanis who might otherwise oppose them. Nevertheless, successfully reestablishing the haven could allow al-Qa'ida to once again conduct spectacular terrorist attacks on a regular basis.

As the need to prepare for operations in Pakistan suggests, one of the most vital military roles is the most difficult to observe: deterring states from offering al-Qa'ida a haven. The U.S. military must retain the capacity not only to go after terrorists directly, but also to topple any supportive governments. If this capacity and the U.S. will to use it are clear, the few governments that might consider directly aiding the jihadists are likely to fear U.S. wrath and prudently avoid such assistance.

5

Defending the Homeland without Overreacting

Imagine this scenario. Terrorists plan to attack the U.S. food supply. They move carefully, taking advantage of any possible security lapse. Their first step is to obtain a job in a food plant. Once employed, they contaminate ground beef and orange juice with anthrax, and ship these products to cities around the country. Hundreds of people die. Panic grips America. Other terrorists release bubonic plague (the "Black Death") into a major city's transportation and sporting hubs. Thousands more die. Yet another strike occurs on America's financial infrastructure. Terrorist hackers post credit card data on the Internet and attack the data systems of large pension funds and mutual funds, thus destroying citizens' trust in the financial system. The results of these attacks are that millions (probably billions) of dollars are lost as products are taken off the shelves, the health care system becomes overburdened, confidence in financial institutions plunges, and panic leads people to stay home.

Frightening? A B-movie plot? Though it may seem the stuff of cheap thrillers, all of these situations are taken from scenarios that the Department of Homeland Security (DHS) and other U.S. government institutions consider real possibilities, and they regularly share these fears with the public.[1] And that is a problem. While such worst-case scenarios can highlight U.S. weaknesses and lead to more robust plans, they are too often more sensational than real, and too frequently disconnected from the goals and capabilities of actual terrorist groups. The result is what scholar Leif Wenar has called a "false sense of insecurity."[2]

Deluged by nightmarish possibilities, we may miss the real threats and the real dangers.

Just as generals often plan for the previous war, policymakers often focus on preventing another 9/11 without understanding that the threat has morphed. We have weakened al-Qa'ida and made it much harder to attack the United States in such spectacular fashion. Local angry jihadists, often untrained, pose the biggest current threat to the U.S. homeland, but their capabilities and target sets are distinct from those of bin Ladin and his organization.

It is tempting to say that too much preparation never hurts and that a steady drumbeat of fear is necessary to prepare for what is, in the end, a dangerous movement. After all, who wouldn't drive a car that was "too safe" or eat a diet that was "too healthy"? But excess preparation is costly. At the very least, it can waste tens or hundreds of billions of dollars that could be better spent on fighting terrorists abroad, or, for that matter, on domestic concerns. More dollars could be spent on providing health care coverage, cleaning up environmental toxins, funding cancer research, subsidizing automobile safety, or on any of a number of other potentially life-saving policy priorities (or, if you prefer, on a tax cut). Aside from the dollars saved, unnecessary preparation can impede trade and discourage tourism. Many terrorist preparation measures carry a considerable human and civil liberties cost. Strict immigration controls discourage foreigners from studying in and visiting our country, which in turn increase hostility to the U.S. government, perhaps even enhancing the potential for anti-U.S. terrorism.

Exacerbating this problem is the current debate on homeland security, which focuses on an extremely high level of preparation that rarely takes cost into account. We regularly hear the ominous statistic that we inspect only a tiny percentage of containers coming into the United States. But the cost of inspecting every container runs in the tens of billions of dollars, if not higher, and would effectively shut down many imports to the United States. Imagine, for example, the ruinous waste of foreign produce rotting in containers, waiting to be inspected.

U.S. homeland security efforts often create fear rather than fight it, thus helping the terrorists achieve their objectives. Doom-saying over the risk of possible low-casualty chemical attacks, for example, will only heighten the psychological effects of these weapons.

At the moment, the threat to the United States is real but not existential—al-Qa'ida will not destroy the United States. Unfortunately, too many analyses emphasize the worst possible case, and too few consider the very real limits of our adversaries and their political objectives. A close examination of potential terrorist targets reveals a discrete set of targets that deserve the lion's share of security focus. Of primary concern in determining where and what to defend is to consider the nature of the would-be terrorists, many of whom are unskilled but also dangerous. We must also guard against a solution that would be enormously counterproductive: taking measures that would alienate Muslim Americans and create a problem where none exists today.

The Costs of Too Much Defense

An excess of defense can be too much of a good thing, with costs both human and financial. Intrusive surveillance erodes civil liberties. Tourists, immigrants, and students pay a particularly heavy price. David Cole, a legal expert and critic of the Bush administration, notes that most of the government's domestic counterterrorism measures have been targeted at foreign nationals, not Americans: "While there has been much talk about the need to sacrifice liberty for a greater sense of security, in practice we have selectively sacrificed *non-citizens*' liberties while retaining basic protections for citizens."[3]

Foreign nationals from selected, mostly Muslim, countries face tougher visa requirements. Waiting times are much longer. They are more likely to be questioned as they enter the country. If they are allowed to enter, they must undergo elaborate steps to provide their whereabouts at all times. Once they are settled in the United States, they are far more vulnerable to deportation for associating with suspected individuals or groups.[4] One program requires that males entering the United States from selected countries must be fingerprinted and photographed every year; nineteen of those twenty-five countries are Arab. Not surprisingly, tourist and business visas issued to travelers coming from the Persian Gulf fell 70 percent from 2000 to 2004. The number of Egyptians who came to the United States fell by more than 50 percent during that time.[5]

We may be protected against our enemies in the Arab world, but we're not creating any more friends there.

In the name of counterterrorism, the Bush administration also has increased domestic monitoring. The USA PATRIOT Act allows the FBI increased independence in monitoring suspected terrorists. The FBI, however, still must answer to a court of law, which acts as a guardian of civil liberties. More problematic is the *New York Times* report stating that the Bush administration has used the National Security Agency to monitor phone calls and gather together vast numbers of phone records, all without judicial oversight.

Even if there were no incursions on civil liberties, excess defense incurs staggering financial costs. Since 9/11, spending on homeland security has gone up perhaps 200 percent. The government has not tallied the total cost of homeland defense, but estimates of different parts of the equation are suggestive. In fiscal year 2006, the DHS budget ran to the tune of $41 billion.[6] Training and deploying air marshals cost $1.5 billion, a significant cost for a threat that diminished considerably after airlines began locking cockpit doors. Los Angeles International Airport has to spend an extra $100,000 per day for additional security when the alert goes from yellow to orange. Increase that sum for alerts at other major airports and for more orange days, and the numbers rise steadily.[7]

Much state and local spending is done without a formal risk analysis that looks not only at the consequences of a successful attack, but also at the likelihood of the attack occurring in the first place.[8] Because the concept of national defense has not been narrowed, any expense can be justified. Small-town movie theaters are apparently on al-Qa'ida's hit list. Homeland security "pork" is also considerable. In the years after 9/11 Grand Forks County, North Dakota, received $1.5 million for disaster-response equipment.

North Pole, Alaska, received $500,000 for homeland security rescue and communications equipment.[9] Enterprising bureaucrats and legislators also use the counterterrorism label to justify their pet programs, ranging from antipoverty (so terrorists don't take advantage of despair and anger) to gun control and even to prescription drug benefits (citing the "terror" you would feel if you did not have access to your medication).[10]

The costs of the domestic programs we fail to fund are even higher. The government has invested massive resources in anthrax vaccines and programs. Yet the influenza virus causes many more deaths and, unlike anthrax, is contagious.

When spending priorities change, limited resources within the homeland security community also shift. After 9/11, the FBI decreased spending on drug trafficking by 60 percent. The FBI and federal authorities focus less on gangs and on domestic terrorist groups (such as white supremacists), even though drugs and gangs have not become any less serious a problem.[11]

The Nature of the Threat to the Homeland

The question then is how to determine which threats are immediate and possible and which threats are remote and improbable. A list of real and potential targets can be established if there is a better understanding of the threat. At first glance, it seems that defenses must be massive. Because attacking the United States remains a priority for al-Qa'ida, no stone can remain overturned. As FBI director Robert Mueller III noted in 2005, "al-Qa'ida continues to adapt and move forward with its desire to attack the United States using any means at its disposal. Their intent to attack us at home remains—and their resolve to destroy America has never faltered."[12] But intent is not the same as capability. For more than five years now, al-Qa'ida has tried to repeat its murderous feats of 9/11—and it has failed. The ten-foot-tall jihadist monster that menaced us on 9/11 is weaker than we supposed, and much of this weakness stems from successful U.S. counterterrorism.

As outlined in chapter 1, the jihadist threat to the homeland can be broken down into three categories: local and organized jihadist groups; individuals or cells that bin Ladin inspires; and the al-Qa'ida core or other organizations based overseas. The threat from organized groups in the U.S. homeland can be dealt with summarily; at the moment, there is almost no danger. After 9/11, a range of experts feared that the nineteen hijackers represented only a few of the vipers from a seething nest of jihadists operating in the United States. Subsequent attacks in Indonesia, where the al-Qa'ida threat was previously assumed to be limited, reinforced this concern. Many feared that an already organized group with many tentacles in the United States would strike. Throughout the Muslim world and even in Europe, organized groups of al-Qa'ida–linked radicals tied to local insurgencies conducted attacks in Morocco, Saudi Arabia, Pakistan, India, Kenya, Egypt, and elsewhere.

The internal al-Qa'ida threat now appears to be idle, or at least limited. There is no "al-Qa'ida of America" counterpart to "al-Qa'ida of Iraq," "al-Qa'ida of Saudi Arabia," or the host of organized groups in the Arab and Muslim world that have allegiance to al-Qa'ida. The FBI has scoured the country looking for such large-scale organized groups and has come up empty-handed.

In fact, the lack of attempts on the U.S. homeland by the al-Qa'ida core since 9/11, even though jihadist attacks have continued at a considerable pace around the globe, has astonished experts. Richard Reid, the "shoe bomber," is one obvious exception, but even there the attack paled in comparison to the sophistication and scope of the 9/11 attacks. Reid himself borders on being mentally unbalanced. Unlike 9/11, the plot was conceived and executed in months rather than years.

The U.S. counterterrorism campaign against the al-Qa'ida core explains the paucity of subsequent attacks. Al-Qa'ida fled after it was ousted from Afghanistan. Because its members were on the run, they were forced to change their tactics. Instead of operating independently, they relied more on local groups (the "al-Qa'ida of Saudi Arabia"–type organizations), and because they no longer could plot, orchestrate, and conduct attacks as they did repeatedly before 9/11, they began to function only as an inspiration to these local groups. Planning complex operations and planting operatives in the United States—with no local groups integrated into the global network to provide logistical support—have grown more difficult. Remember that the 9/11 attacks took years to plan, and that the plot included key individuals in countries such as Germany, Afghanistan, Saudi Arabia, the United Arab Emirates, and Malaysia.

Today, al-Qa'ida's core will find it difficult to implement a global plot. With their operations under siege throughout the world, they have no remaining safe haven in which to plan, as they once did in Afghanistan. A similar attempt today might be disrupted at any or all of the locations in which they used to function. Not only have they lost their former refuge, but they also lost several of their key leaders. Many of al-Qaida's captured lieutenants revealed to U.S. and allied intelligence officials details of incipient plots. The organization cannot take years for its plots to reach fruition without a high risk of discovery.

Alarmingly, the core appears to be regenerating, thus greatly increasing the danger to the U.S. homeland. The plot broken up in August 2006 to bomb as many as ten airlines over the Atlantic is a sign that al-Qa'ida remains committed to plotting spectaculars and retains some capacity to do so. Yet the use of the United Kingdom as a staging area suggests that it is still easier to attack the United States from "over there" than from here. As the organization solidifies its position in parts of Pakistan, its ability to plan spectaculars can only grow.

That said, a far more immediate concern for homeland security exists: individuals or small groups acting on their own. Like the London or Madrid bombers, domestic terrorists can construct homemade bombs and explode them on U.S. subways or in bus terminals. Bin Ladin might be a hero to these people, but they would have received their limited expertise from the Internet or from criminal networks, not from training camps in Afghanistan. Nor are they tied to a large domestic group. They remain invisible to the FBI and other security officials because of their obscurity.

The FBI claims that there are about a thousand al-Qa'ida sympathizers in the United States and that it has three hundred extremists under surveillance. Clark Kent Ervin, a former DHS official, believes these numbers are low.[13] Examples include Iyman Faris, who plotted to knock down the Brooklyn Bridge; the "Lackawanna

Six," who attended training camps in Afghanistan; a Toledo "cell" of three individuals who sought to kill U.S. soldiers in Iraq; seven men in Miami who planned to attack the Sears Tower, among other sites; Shahawar Matin Siraj, a Pakistani immigrant who is charged with plotting to bomb a subway station in New York in 2004;[14] Ehsanul Islam Sadequee, an American of Bangladeshi descent living in Georgia who, along with a Pakistani-American friend, discussed attacking oil refineries and military bases;[15] and Earnest James Ujaama, a Seattle-born man who was convicted of providing goods and services to the Taliban.

At first blush, a look at the long list of individuals arrested and charged with crimes related to terrorism suggests a high level of threat. But several cautions are in order. All of these individuals are alleged to have been involved in an attack, but few of the plans came close to fruition. Most of the plotters were talking only about possibilities. Many were charged with "material support" for terrorism rather than an act itself. This extremely broad charge includes a range of assistance vital to terrorist organizations, but it is quite different from implication in a full-fledged plot. Few had any direct links to al-Qa'ida.

A New York Times analysis in September 2006 found that of those indicted from terrorism-related investigations, almost two thirds were charged with crimes unrelated to terrorism, such as fraud or violation of immigration status. Of those indicted on federal terrorism charges, most were in the talking stages or were vague at best.[16]

An important exception may be the case of four men who in 2005 plotted an assortment of attacks that may have included three California National Guard facilities, the Israeli consulate in Los Angeles, the El Al Israeli Airlines ticket counter, and several synagogues. Luckily, one of the terrorists dropped his cell phone during a run-of-the-mill robbery of a gas station. When police searched one suspect's home, jihadist literature and a list of possible attack sites were found, though it is unclear if a specific target had already been selected. No direct link to bin Ladin was found.[17] Three of the four were converts to Islam, born in the United States. Some of the plotters had close ties to Jamiyya Ul Islam Is Saheeh, "The Assembly of Authentic Islam," an organization that actively attempts to convert prisoners to Islam.

In general, those charged with links to terrorism were low-skilled. Investigating officials described Toledo cell members as "inept" and "clumsy." They never came close to participating in the fighting in Iraq that they wished to join. Faris initially planned to cut through the many mammoth cables of the Brooklyn Bridge with a blowtorch, an incredibly lengthy and almost impossible scheme. Many of those arrested had at best a faint idea of what they would strike and how they would do it; their knowledge did not keep pace with their enthusiasm.

Though plans may be quixotic and the planners inept, terrorists still have the ability to kill many people. They can panic citizens by firing away in a shopping mall at Christmastime, as the snipers Lee Boyd Malvo and John Allen Muhammad did during October 2002 in the D.C. area. But compared to 9/11 or some of the more ominous threat scenarios that the DHS is preparing for, the actual numbers killed or the damage inflicted would be limited.

Another important curb on domestic terrorism is the limited support for al-Qa'ida types of organizations among the U.S. Muslim and Arab populations, both native and immigrant. In contrast to the United Kingdom or France, not to mention Muslim states such as Indonesia or Pakistan, there is little support for Islamism in general in the United States, let alone its violent fringe. There is another difference between these countries and the United States. Many of these nascent U.S. attackers were converts to Islam, whose radicalism was nurtured in American prisons. The California and Miami plotters, for example, were part of radical black Muslim groups, while the notorious José Padilla converted to Islam in prison. FBI director Mueller has warned that converts in prison might be fodder for the jihadist cause—a caution amply borne out by the experiences of European countries and the California cell.[18]

In determining priorities for homeland defense, the government should recognize the limited skills of the jihadists and their lack of appeal within the United States. Even before 9/11, al-Qa'ida had trouble finding operatives who could function in the United States.[19] Added to the mix is the consideration of where terrorists are most likely to strike. An attack on the U.S. data storage infrastructure would inflict enormous economic harm, but terrorists almost never attack such targets because they have no symbolic value to their would-be constituents back home. Similarly, planning for a massive agroterrorism event would be wasteful if al-Qa'ida or its affiliates have no intention of laying waste to the U.S. corn crop. The United States has spent billions on port security, yet no terrorist group has ever devised a serious attack plan for such a strike.

Too often, analysts focus on theoretical vulnerabilities rather than on plausible threats.

As homeland security expert Jeremy Shapiro has noted about such scenarios, "Each type of attack is convincingly demonstrated to be possible, but there is often little effort to discern whether there is any particular actor in the world who has both the desire and the capacity to actually carry them out."[20] In short, when thinking about homeland defense, the United States needs to understand the worldview of the adversary.

Let's start with the al-Qa'ida core. Historically they have focused on symbols of U.S. military, political, and economic might. From al-Qa'ida's point of view, the devastation of the Twin Towers and the successful attack on the Pentagon were the pinnacles of success. Other targets considered for 9/11 included the Sears Tower, the Capitol, the White House, and a foreign embassy, as well as a nuclear power plant.[21] Bin Ladin and his senior lieutenants also have tried to go after civil aviation targets. In the summer of 2006, core members plotted to blow up multiple airplanes flying between the United Kingdom and the United States. Richard Reid sought to blow himself up on American Airlines Flight 63, a transatlantic flight from Paris to Miami in December 2001. Two years earlier, with bin Ladin's support, Ahmed Ressam planned to attack Los Angeles International Airport, though, unlike Reid's, his plot never came close to fruition.

A less ambitious but similar logic motivates locals inspired by al-Qa'ida. They, too, want their claim to immortality, but in accordance with their limited capability, they aim for smaller targets. Rather than strike the Pentagon or a military base, they may try to kill soldiers who are riding to work or drinking in a bar. Instead of planning an attack on the Capitol, they might go after a local federal building or military recruiting office. Public transportation still could be a target. But instead of striking closely guarded airports or airplanes, they might attack buses or subways, as their brothers in Europe and the Middle East have done. Symbolism trumps scale.

Looking at the list of targets of individuals arrested on terrorism charges in the United States since 9/11 is suggestive. Civil aviation remains a major target of even unskilled groups: some plan airport attacks, others seek to use surface-to-air missiles, but they all want to target airplanes and airports. Still others embrace al-Qa'ida's goal of supporting jihadist insurgents and have sought to join anti-U.S. fighters in Iraq or Lebanon.

Locals, however, are not simply less capable clones of the al-Qa'ida core. In particular, social issues often come to the fore for the locals. In Europe, local radicals have attacked filmmakers and intellectuals. The California cell members plotted against "soft" Jewish targets such as synagogues, and military and Israeli targets.

Also of tremendous concern are nuclear plants and fissile material, which have appeared on the jihadist list of targets. Any attack on either plants or material could wreak massive human and psychological damage in the United States. Al-Qa'ida leaders have repeatedly expressed a desire to acquire nuclear weapons and, in the past, have tried to do so. Khalid Shaykh Mohammad, the 9/11 mastermind, initially placed a nuclear power plant on his target list, as did a cell in the Netherlands.

Terrorist attacks are not only an attempt to impose maximum harm upon the United States. They also are intended to inspire and impress potential followers. When selecting their targets, jihadists prefer to impress Islamists, and particularly other militants, over Americans. An attack that devastates a dam along a river in the Midwest may be costly for Americans, but it has far less appeal than an attack on a national icon.

Prioritize Defenses

National leadership is an obvious target (and one that is already well defended). Our priority should be individuals known around the world: the president and the vice president, the secretaries of state and defense, the attorney general, the heads of the FBI and the CIA, the director of national intelligence, and the commanders of the U.S. Central and European commands. The secretary of the treasury, on the other hand, is vital in the U.S. system, but his death is not eagerly sought by militants around the world. The same logic applies to federal buildings recognized around the world. The White House, the Capitol, the Supreme Court building, and the Statue of Liberty are prime terrorist targets and should have strong defenses. The Department of Agriculture should not.

Military bases also are targets. Attacks on U.S. military forces are a feather in al-Qa'ida's cap because they avoid the opprobrium that comes with attacks on civilians. It is hard to argue that the finest military in the world is defenseless and that those who attack it are cowards. Even if the damage is limited, attacks on military bases earn status and glory for al-Qa'ida. Attacking them is heroic in jihadists' eyes; success is just a bonus.

Other targets, such as nuclear and chemical plants and dams, warrant a prominent place on the defense list because of the possibility of mass casualties. Even if they are lower on the jihadists' target list, they deserve extra scrutiny. Fortunately, the FBI already monitors these sites carefully.[22] In addition, many safeguards are in place in these vulnerable spots, not because of a terrorist threat but because of the possibility of accident and the capriciousness of nature. Although a hurricane or a fire is quite different from a truck bomb, these systems have redundant safeguards, and if serious problems arise, the systems shut down. Nevertheless, because of the possibility of mass destruction, these targets deserve to remain on the list.

Nuclear and infectious biological weapons rank high as risks despite the low likelihood of terrorist attacks in the near term. But what about chemical and radiological weapons? In the hands of highly skilled users, these weapons could, except in the rarest circumstances, kill dozens at most. Still, the psychological effect of releasing chemical or radiological weapons would be devastating. Thus they merit a twofold approach: they deserve considerable scrutiny from intelligence and homeland defense officials, and a public emphasis on the limited danger they pose.

Defenses should be concentrated on cities that have an international profile, such as Washington, D.C., New York, and Los Angeles. Rural areas or less iconic cities are not as vulnerable; attacks in the hinterlands mean far less to the jihadists' Muslim audiences overseas. Yet in recent years, Wyoming received $35.30 per capita in homeland security grants and North Dakota $28.70, versus $4.70 for California and $5.10 for New York; the ratios should be reversed.[23]

An important question to ask is "What are we not defending?" If the answer is that we want to defend all plausible targets, we will fail. Our efforts will be overstretched, poorly coordinated, and inordinately expensive. In most low-priority cases, the standard defenses already in place for crime and accidents would suffice.

In fact, danger can arise from too many safeguards. Political scientist Scott Sagan points out that increasing the number of guards at every nuclear power plant seems like an obvious step. But this greatly increases the chances that an "inside man" will either attack the facility himself or help others in doing so—potentially a far more dangerous problem than a terrorist assault on the facility.[24]

If we overextend our defense networks to include all low-tech targets, we will reach the point where defenses will simply break down—a problem that many proponents of endless spending on homeland defense seem to miss. Former DHS official Ervin warns that terrorists could attack shopping malls, movie theaters, restaurants, nightclubs, and similar soft targets and, in so doing, "terrorize the entire nation."[25] Perhaps. But at the same time, Ervin notes that terrorism is "like water, it seeks, finds, and takes the path of least resistance."[26] Ironically, such a statement also argues *against* protection. The second-deadliest terrorist attack in history occurred in 1978: almost four hundred people in Iran died when an arsonist set a movie theater on fire. It was a horrific crime but one that was low-tech and almost impossible to prevent. Presumably one could have armed guards at every restaurant, nightclub, gas station, or, for that matter, anyplace where people congregate. Even if all public places were protected, the terrorists could simply shoot the guards and proceed with their attack. The key is to separate the targets that matter more from those that matter less.

Whether we try to defend all targets or not, some attacks will occur. If the passengers and crew aboard American Airlines Flight 63 had been a little less alert (or if Richard Reid, the "shoe bomber," had been a little less stupid), there would have been many dead Americans. At some point the attackers will be either exceptionally skilled, as they were on 9/11, or simply lucky, and Americans will die.

Most of the likely attacks—say, a bombing of the Metro in Washington, D.C., or an attack on an Israeli ticket counter at Los Angeles International Airport—are tragic, but they do not signal an end to civilization. Claims by Ervin and many others that the United States is highly vulnerable and that such an attack could change our way of life ignore the evidence of 9/11 itself. Those attacks destroyed an unprotected national symbol and caused an entire nation of people to change their view of the world. Despite this, life in the rest of the country and, for that matter, Manhattan and Washington, went on.

Less lethal attacks against a population now alert to terrorism will not have anything like that kind of impact.

Domestic Intelligence Needs

In some countries—Britain, France, and Israel, for example—the Home Ministry or the Ministry of the Interior collects intelligence on their own citizens and on the suspect activities taking place on their own soil. These countries regard internal threats as seriously as they do external ones.

The United States, too, has a domestic intelligence agency: the Federal Bureau of Investigation (FBI). But neither the FBI nor U.S. citizens recognize it as such. The FBI has historically been primarily a law enforcement agency; the intelligence function is of low priority and constrained. The 9/11 attacks, however, revealed serious faults within the organization. As an intelligence agency, it was broken. The FBI not only failed to intercept the plotters, but more tellingly did not appreciate the danger the country faced. In contrast to the CIA, which in the years before 9/11 constantly warned policymakers about the danger bin Ladin posed and developed new programs to pursue him, the FBI stood still. Before September 11, the FBI was not properly structured or oriented for counterterrorism or, more broadly, for intelligence work. This failure occurred in part because of the FBI's emphasis on law enforcement, but also because as information about al-Qa'ida grew, the organization failed to understand and respond.

Before September 11, the FBI frequently failed to collect information relevant to counterterrorism. For example, when Abdul Hakim Murad was interviewed in connection with his participation with Khalid Shaykh Mohammad's plot to bomb as many as twelve airplanes over the Pacific in 1995, the FBI did not devote attention to his possible plans to crash an airplane into CIA headquarters—a harbinger of the September 11 plot. Nor did the FBI place opportunities for intelligence collection in context. They failed to link suspicious flight-training activity in Arizona or the arrest of an Islamic extremist such as Zacarias Moussaoui in Minnesota to the heightened national threat level. The FBI neither trained its operatives sufficiently in intelligence collection nor provided intelligence officers with sufficient resources, particularly with regard to surveillance and translation.[27]

Frequently the FBI did not disseminate what limited information it did collect, either within or outside of the FBI. The FBI's antediluvian computer system and case-file approach to holding information meant that important details were not regularly passed from the field to headquarters or to other FBI agents and analysts working on similar problems. The FBI did not see itself as part of the national security apparatus and did not share information with the national security community.[28]

As a result, the FBI did not inform policymakers of the jihadist threat at home. Two former White House officials working on counterterrorism wrote about learning FBI information from trial transcripts of al-Qa'ida suspects. "In many instances, we discovered information so critical that we were amazed that the relevant agencies did not inform us of it while we were at the NSC."[29] It is not surprising that policymakers, agencies, and analysts outside the FBI never learned of this information; most of the FBI did not know of it either.

Nor did the FBI conduct strategic analysis. Richard Clarke, President George W. Bush's and President Clinton's chief counter-terrorism adviser, depicts the FBI as plodding and hidebound, comfortable in its ignorance of al-Qa'ida. The office created to conduct strategic analysis atrophied. Only two FBI analysts looked at bin Ladin threat information.[30]

As an organization, the bureau's culture and organization fostered these problems. Before September 11, the FBI was primarily a law enforcement agency, and it was probably the world's best. But law enforcement focuses on prosecuting a case, not on understanding its broad network. Law enforcement emphasizes gathering specific evidence, not collecting and sharing relevant information. Given this organizational ethos, it is not surprising that terrorism was viewed as a criminal matter and treated accordingly. FBI leaders emphasized finding the perpetrators of the last attack rather than preventing the next one.[31]

The FBI's organizational structure reflected this narrow approach and made it worse. The decentralized FBI field office structure allowed offices to set their own priorities, few of which focused on terrorism or al-Qa'ida. The fifty-six FBI field offices in the United States were all independent fiefdoms, with local priorities taking precedence.[32]

The FBI also faced countless restrictions—and close political scrutiny—on its counterterrorism functions. For example, in 1996 right-wing conservatives joined liberal civil libertarians to block legislation that would allow multipoint wiretaps, which are useful for tracking terrorists who change phones or use multiple phones. In addition to restricting the tools available to the FBI, the pressure from these strange bedfellows made the FBI exceptionally sensitive to investigating religious-based terrorism in the United States.[33] Congressional investigations into deaths at Ruby Ridge and Waco further increased FBI sensitivity. In general the FBI preferred to err on the side of respect for civil liberties, setting a high bar for surveillance.

In the more than five years since 9/11, Director Mueller has made extensive efforts to transform the FBI from a law enforcement organization into an entity more focused on preventing attacks and gathering intelligence. John Gannon, a career intelligence official who has held senior positions in both the FBI and the CIA, and who is often quite critical of the FBI today, described Mueller as a "director of legendary energy, dedication, and integrity."[34] Resources devoted to counterterrorism are now considerable, and the FBI has made major institutional changes to centralize its work on counterterrorism to prevent some of the problems that plagued it before 9/11. The organization now has more than 120 joint terrorism task forces, more than double the number it had on 9/11.

As a result, the FBI has successfully stopped several potential plots before they became truly dangerous. Because of aggressive FBI investigations, the Miami cell, whose aspirations were deadly, never came close to carrying out an attack. The California cell came closer to success. In this case a mishap during a robbery led alert local officers to notify federal investigators when they discovered jihadist literature—a linkage that before 9/11 they might not have made.

Despite this good news, serious shortcomings remain. A report by the National Academy of Public Administration found that the bureau still has significant problems in how it recruits, hires, and develops its leaders.[35] Language capabilities, while improving, are still deficient.[36] Gannon declared that "we still do not have a domestic intelligence service that can collect effectively against the terrorist threat to the homeland or provide authoritative analysis of that threat."[37] Part of the problem is that law enforcement concerns continue to outweigh those of intelligence: the FBI still thinks in terms of cases, and the organization still focuses on prosecution over prevention.

The analytic side still has grave problems. It is a mistake to depend on intelligence to predict specific attacks. Nevertheless, intelligence should enable policymakers to recognize the overall level of the danger, which would then permit them to allocate resources toward that end. Because the FBI does not regularly produce a domestic threat assessment, U.S. policymakers still do not have a comprehensive view of the current threat (or lack thereof) and how it is evolving. Nor do the "first responders"—state and local officials—have access to FBI information. The new actors in homeland security, those who are first on the scene in an emergency, are out of the loop.

Because of these problems, the intelligence function should be severed from other FBI operations, either by creating a separate agency that focuses exclusively on domestic intelligence, or by placing the domestic intelligence function within the DHS. Creating a separate agency makes more sense on paper, but American suspicions of the very idea of "domestic intelligence," even if the new agency's powers were the same as those already given to the FBI, might make this a political nonstarter. But the DHS, Gannon notes, already has a mandate to reach out to the private sector and other areas outside the government. Moreover, because the DHS is not a law enforcement agency, it does not convey a sense of menace to American citizens.

In any event, the DHS should increase regional intelligence,[38] which is an essential link in transmitting information up the chain of command. If, for example, the DHS discovers the presence or the absence of infrastructure vulnerabilities, or if it unearths information about a potentially hostile group of individuals, it can then pass this information on to officials at the national and local levels.

Ensuring a functioning domestic intelligence system must be a national priority. If we fail to gather accurate intelligence, we will not allocate resources properly, and the result will be both a tremendous waste of resources and glaring gaps in intelligence. Most important, we will miss opportunities to disrupt plots before they reach fruition.

American Muslims: The Key to Victory

Most of the effort in homeland defense has involved extending borders beyond our shores by trying to stop problems overseas, be they container security in overseas ports, attacking the al-Qa'ida haven in Afghanistan, or going after cells in Europe. When our partners can use their regulatory and security capabilities to improve our security, the result is financially and practically advantageous for us. Moreover, pushing other countries to take measures to protect U.S. security involves few threats to civil liberties and little overall sacrifice from the American people.[39]

However, fighting the war on terror exclusively beyond American borders ignores perhaps the most important future danger of terrorism: that the number of jihadist sympathizers in the United States might grow and that some might turn actively against their government and society. The European experience demonstrates problems that can arise if resident Muslims are discontent. The deadly bombings in Madrid and London were conducted by individuals who had long lived in Spain and the United Kingdom, respectively, and were radicalized there. The European attacks and the pattern of plots against the United States suggest that we should take all measures to ensure the support of the American Muslim community. This should include not only Muslims of Arab origin, but also converts to Islam. Because prisons are breeding grounds for terrorist activity, the government should pay special attention to those who convert in prison.

Of the 6 million Muslim Americans, roughly one third are of South Asian ancestry, one quarter are of Arab origin, and 10 percent are African American. The remaining one third come from other countries. Approximately two thirds of American Muslims were born outside the United States.[40] Americans frequently assume that all Arabs in the United States are Muslim, when in reality the Arab American community is approximately two thirds Christian and one third Muslim. Many Christian Arabs oppose many aspects of U.S. policy in the Middle East, but they are not realistic recruits for the jihadist movement.[41]

Unlike Europe, the Muslim community in the United States is not a fertile ground for radicalism. The 9/11 attacks were carried out by infiltrators from abroad, not homegrown terrorists. Many American Muslims are educated professionals who are well integrated into American society. Often they have higher average incomes than do non-Muslims.[42] Polls taken shortly after 9/11 indicated that the vast majority of American Muslims see U.S. efforts after 9/11 as directed against terrorism, not Islam.[43] The various plots uncovered since 9/11 have all involved small, disconnected groups and individuals rather than a larger, countrywide network. Several appear to have been discovered with information volunteered from the local Muslim community. Unlike Europe, there is little divide between

Muslims and non-Muslims. Polls conducted in 2006 show that Americans associate far fewer negative images of Muslims than do Europeans who also were polled.[44]

But American Muslim suspicions of the government are growing. Polls in 2004 showed that half of America's Muslim community indicate they know someone who had experienced discrimination since the attacks, though only 40 percent felt they had experienced it personally.[45] Since 9/11, Arab Americans have reported a greater fear of the police and immigration authorities. A 2005 survey of Muslim youth activists found that 70 percent felt the American public had "significant hostility" toward Muslims.[46] This is not paranoia on the part of young Muslims. Negative ethnic and religious comments directed toward Muslims have become more frequent since 9/11, as have acts of intimidation, such as vandalism of mosques. A December 2004 survey found that almost half of Americans believe the civil liberties of Muslims should be restricted.[47]

Because of measures taken to interview Arab Americans and to fingerprint and photograph immigrant men, this community believes they are being unfairly harassed. Efforts to monitor nongovernmental organizations that may have links to terrorist groups have drawn criticism for interfering with Muslims' religious obligation to contribute to charity. Complaints about the USA PATRIOT Act are particularly common, though this is often shorthand for a host of procedural and legislative changes that have occurred since 9/11.

The lower bar for suspicious activity has also created suspicion within the Arab American community. The Justice Department has prosecuted many cases of groups that supposedly raised money for terrorist causes. But because most of these cases had no merit and collapsed during the trial process, many Muslim Americans believe that the government was persecuting the community.[48]

These perceptions have made it difficult for police to increase trust between the community and local authorities. As one police officer lamented, "Suppose I get a call about suspicious activity. I have to respond, even if it's based on prejudice. If I show up, the Arab American feels he is being profiled and trusts the police less.

If I don't show up, I get an angry call or complaint that I am not doing my job. It's a lose-lose situation."[49] These suspicions can severely hamper counterterrorism efforts. In the worst-case scenario, they could inspire Muslims to turn violent. But more likely and more important, the Muslim American communities might present an obstacle rather than an asset to domestic intelligence. As one police officer noted, "We can't afford to alienate them. Otherwise, we cut off our sources of information."[50]

For now, the problem is limited, but it is essential that it does not become worse. As one expert told me, the key is "not to anger a largely content group of people." The Bush administration has taken some impressive measures to encourage a sense of belonging. Shortly after the 9/11 attacks, President Bush joined with Muslim ambassadors for an *iftar* dinner during Ramadan, traditionally a festive time to celebrate the end of the day's fasting, and subsequently met with American Muslim leaders. Yet at the same time, the Bush administration did not distance itself from political allies in the U.S. evangelical community who made hateful statements about Islam. Similarly, senior members of the administration did not censure others in the administration who at times made disrespectful comments.[51]

Ensuring broad assimilation is necessary. The 2005 youth activist survey of Muslim youth revealed that almost half felt a sense of conflict between their identity as Muslims and their identity as Americans.[52] This percentage is far less than it is in Europe, even given the fact that these youth activists care more about their religion than average Muslim youths. Still, the numbers are high enough to cause concern.

To improve ties to the community, several obvious steps should be taken. These range from promoting cultural awareness in the FBI and police to being more available to community leaders who wish to communicate their concerns. Police and the FBI should also strive to work with community leaders, particularly the leaders of the religious community.

Before new counterterrorism measures are announced, we should consider how these measures will be perceived in the Muslim community. When possible, measures should be designed in consultation with local communities and implemented with their cooperation. Short-term and tactical benefits such as increased fingerprinting of immigrants must be weighed carefully. In the end, a supportive and loyal Muslim American community is far more valuable for counterterrorism than any particular piece of intelligence or law enforcement tool.

Freedom from Fear

An important but often ignored part of homeland security is perception management. As John Mueller contends, "The costs of terrorism commonly come much more from hasty, ill-considered, and over-wrought reactions (or overreactions) to it than from anything terrorists have done."[53] After 9/11, Americans flew less and took fewer vacations, which led to massive job losses in the aviation and tourism industries. As Mueller further notes, the anthrax attacks that killed five people in 2001 have cost the U.S. Postal Service $5 billion: $1 billion per death.

Politicians—and, for that matter, many terrorism analysts— tend to exaggerate the overall level of threat. Thus, in response to an attack, they can provoke panic among the population. Media coverage of terrorism exacerbates this response by suggesting that terrorism is more widespread than it actually is and by dramatizing the effects in a way that is not done with hazards such as smoking, heart disease, or car accidents. The resulting panic leads people to make poor decisions. Not understanding the appropriate level of risk, they cancel holidays, they mistrust strangers, and they drive long distances instead of flying in planes.

If Americans truly understood the risk they faced, they would know that the biggest danger is not from the actual attack but from the terrorists' potential to foster insurgencies and undermine governance, particularly in vulnerable states. Most terrorist attacks kill few people. Nevertheless, people do not calculate these odds when deciding whether to travel by plane, ride the subway, or visit the Statue of Liberty. Thus, because of attacks such as 9/11, fewer people fly, even though they are far, far more likely to die on the highways than in the air. One reasonable estimate by Michael Sivak and Michael J. Flannagan is that driving is sixty-five times as risky as flying.[54]

How Americans Are Likely to Die[55]

How Americans Might Die	Lifetime Odds (1 in ___)
Heart disease	1 in 5
Cancer	1 in 7
Motor-vehicle accident	1 in 100
Suicide	1 in 121
Firearm assault	1 in 325
Drowning in your bathtub	1 in 10,455
Being struck by lightning	1 in 83,930
Dog attack	1 in 147,717

Terrorism expert Brian Jenkins finds that in recent years, including 2001, an American's chance of dying in a terrorist attack is only one in half a million—a figure that goes to one in a million if the period is extended from 1997 to 2006.[56] Over a lifetime, the odds of dying from terrorism thus are close to being (literally) "struck by lightning." Even if one assumes that there are more 9/11s in the future and the figures rise considerably, the risk is still far less than highway fatalities or murder, to say nothing of cancer or heart disease.[57]

Yet there are several reasons why we should care more about deaths from terrorism than about ones from accidents. Terrorism, in contrast to lightning strikes and car accidents, is committed by murderers. If they are not stopped, they will kill more; if they are stopped, fewer will die. Terrorism thus might snowball or decline in response to government action.

Most important for Americans to remember is that terrorism is specifically aimed at undermining a population's faith in the ability of a government to protect its people. The deaths of twenty or even twenty thousand people do not necessarily cause a government to collapse. Confidence in government rose after 9/11, just as it does in many wars. The perception of government failure is a far greater threat than the deaths of individuals and must be treated as such.

In the United States the biggest risks are psychological, political, and economic. But because of the high level of fear, politicians sometimes overreact to terrorism, and even fan the flames of fear for political gain. Instead, government agencies such as the Department of Homeland Security should counter these fears by reinforcing the true odds of dying from a terrorist attack. To avoid frightening people, public alerts should be used sparingly. Since 9/11, alerts have been issued in response to intelligence chatter, such as threats suggesting attack on transatlantic flights or during major sports and political events. Each alert creates panic, yet each desensitizes the public if it is not eventually linked to a concrete danger.

Ironically, by tying the war on terrorism to the war in Iraq, the Bush administration has worsened the perception management issue. The setbacks the United States has suffered in Iraq have created the perception that the homeland is at grave risk.

A particularly important perception that should be countered is the threat from chemical, radiological, and noninfectious biological weapons such as anthrax. Typically these weapons kill far fewer people than do explosives. Yet as the anthrax attacks in 2001 demonstrated, they can instill fear throughout the country. A constant message that reinforces the limited damage of these weapons would offset their psychological power.

As they fight misperceptions on the risk of terrorism, U.S. leaders also should focus on building societal resilience. Much of the debate on the proper response to a terrorist attack focuses on prevention and recovery. Although these are vital issues, even more important for victory is reducing the chain-reaction effects of a terrorist strike. If a terrorist attack does occur, Americans must be encouraged not to retreat. Instead, they should go about their business as usual and strengthen their ties with their neighbors. Though we may sometimes live *with* fear, we should not live *in* fear.

Vital to this is educating the public on a realistic goal for victory. A complete end to terrorist attacks can be the ultimate objective, but policymakers must ask a question, one more difficult to resolve: What level of violence necessitates fundamental changes in U.S. foreign policy? The deaths of small numbers of Americans, overseas or at home, must be weighed against other U.S. goals, such as nonproliferation. The greater the risk, the more counterterrorism should come to the fore, but if policymakers use zero casualties as the metric for success, they may jeopardize other foreign policy goals or spend hundreds of billions in a futile attempt to eradicate a tactic that has been used for thousands of years.

A case in point is Israel, a country that has experienced a number of terrorist attacks. During the second intifada, which began in 2000, Israel suffered from a deadly terrorist campaign by various Palestinian groups. While the constant attacks disheartened Israelis, the government paid particular attention to shoring up public morale. This involved high-profile measures to strike back, such as killing Palestinian leaders, as well as ambitious defense projects, such as the security barrier. But equally important were the less dramatic steps. Bomb sites were quickly cleaned up and repaired, to create the impression that life goes on. Politicians of all stripes encouraged Israelis to be resilient rather than to panic. These measures did not remove the fear Israelis felt, but they prevented that fear from dominating the public mind.

Such steps do not kill or imprison terrorists, but they do make terrorism far less damaging.

Finally, the focus on "homeland defense" should not neglect that offense is vital to any successful defense. Keeping al-Qa'ida and its affiliates under siege around the world makes them less able to infiltrate terrorists into the United States. Most important, the United States must keep pressure on the al-Qa'ida core and prevent it from using its base in Pakistan as it did the Taliban's Afghanistan. If bin Ladin and his lieutenants can again plot freely, more 9/11s are only a matter of time.

6

Fighting Terrorism with Democracy?

In January 2006, U.S. leaders thought they had achieved a major policy goal in their effort to transform the Middle East into a region less prone to radicalism. The corrupt and sclerotic Fatah movement, led by Yasir Arafat until his death in 2004, dominated Palestinian politics. The United States had long pushed for free and fair elections as a way to install a more legitimate and honest government. The 2006 elections in the Palestinian territories, it was hoped, would usher in a more responsive government that would be more willing to pursue peace with Israel and better govern at home.

But the terrorists won.

Instead of moderate and pro-Western reformers receiving a mandate for peace, the radical terrorist movement Hamas gained a surprise victory. Frustrated by the corruption, incompetence, and overall poor record of secular parties, Palestinians turned out in droves to usher Hamas into power. The terrorist organization had considerable stature because Palestinians saw it as standing up to Israel with its regular and bloody attacks and because it was deemed less corrupt and more able to provide competent social services.

U.S. policymakers, however, have uncritically embraced democratization in the name of counterterrorism. At his second inauguration,

157

President Bush issued an eloquent call for America to spread the blessings of liberty: "For as long as whole regions of the world simmer in resentment and tyranny—prone to ideologies that feed hatred and excuse murder—violence will gather, and multiply in destructive power, and cross the most defended borders, and raise a mortal threat."

Senior Bush administration officials have echoed this theme— that "the force of human freedom" can defeat such a threat. Even many Democrats share the president's lofty rhetoric.

Given the absence of weapons of mass destruction or links between Saddam Hussein's regime and terrorists, spreading democracy to Iraq has become the major justification for America's war and continued occupation of Iraq. The attempt to broaden democracy worldwide, however, includes more than just Iraq. The United States spent approximately $200 million in fiscal year 2006 on promoting democracy throughout the Middle East, excluding Iraq.[1] The Bush administration has tried to foster democratic forces in authoritarian enemies such as Iran and Syria, and in allies such as Saudi Arabia, Yemen, and Egypt.[2]

However laudable the goal, many Middle East and terrorism specialists are skeptical of the president's use of democracy as a tool for fighting terrorism. President Bush's former top counterterrorism official Richard Clarke scoffed, "It is not the lack of democracy that produced jihadist movements, nor will the creation of democracies quell them."[3] Middle East specialist F. Gregory Gause III argues forcefully that there is no security rationale for promoting democracy: the presence of democracy does not reduce terrorism or decrease popular support for extremism (though it would likely increase the number of anti-U.S. regimes in the Middle East).[4]

Progress toward democracy in Iraq, Palestine, Lebanon, and even Saudi Arabia makes this debate more than a rhetorical issue. Democratization is occurring—at times promoted by the United States, at times without any significant outside intervention. And in Iraq, Lebanon, and Palestine, democratization has been accompanied by chaos, giving terrorists more space to operate and empowering their political wings, which increases their public legitimacy and overt influence. Unfortunately, neither side in this debate appears to understand the nuanced and conflicted relationship between democracy and terrorism.

The answer is neither to embrace democracy uncritically nor to reject it completely. Democracy does have benefits for counterterrorism, but the process of democratization can often make the terrorism problem worse. Because democracy offers many benefits beyond counterterrorism, democracy still is worth promoting, but this should not be done uncritically—particularly in countries such as Saudi Arabia, vital for successful counterterrorism. Rather, policymakers should recognize when and where the promotion of democracy should be eagerly pursued and when it should be put on the back burner.

The Case for Democratization

At a most basic level, terrorists take up arms because they cannot shape government policy to address their grievances. Give them a voice, and they have no need for violence. Democratic governments also are more likely to have open economic systems and the rule of law, spurring economic growth. In a democracy, over time, high-quality jobs are likely to be more plentiful. Ideally, corruption will diminish, and a meritocracy will arise.

A genuine offer to let terrorist leaders participate in politics might not convince them to change course by itself, but their constituents, hopeful that talks might lead to a productive peace, may become less supportive of violence. This increases pressure on the group to hold off on violence for fear of losing recruits, money, and overall sympathy.[5] Engagement also can strengthen the hand of more moderate elements of a terrorist group, increasing the chances of successful negotiation. For example, the U.S. dialogue with Sinn Féin and Provisional IRA spokesman Gerry Adams that began in 1994 contributed to the Provisional IRA cease-fire decision later in that year. Adams grew in popularity at the expense of those in the Provisional IRA's senior ranks who favored continued violence.[6]

Though political participation does not always soften the group's violent stance, it may create divisions among its members. When peace talks lead to an offer of concessions, fractures arise within a movement, especially if some members oppose compromise. When members' goals are not uniform, terrorist groups that once enjoyed widespread support become vulnerable to fissures.

Excluding splinter groups from the political process carries risks. Terrorism is not static: a refusal to include a particular group in the political process may strengthen extremists by showing that nonviolent means offer no hope. Hamas and other Islamists, for example, historically gained more support when peace talks were foundering.[7]

Critics of democratization rightly point out that the jihadist leaders were never outcasts. Bin Ladin himself is a scion of a staggeringly wealthy Saudi family, and his principal deputy, Ayman al-Zawahiri, comes from an extremely distinguished Egyptian family; neither man experienced poverty or political isolation. Many, if not all, of the international terrorist attacks on the United States have involved operatives who lived in democratic Western European countries such as Germany or Britain. These countries also suffer from homegrown terrorism.

Jihadists have, in fact, repeatedly denounced the idea of democracy, claiming that it replaces God's laws with laws of man. After all, lawgivers could legalize homosexuality, give women equal status and rights, forge a lasting peace with Israel, or otherwise violate what the jihadists see as God's guidance. But democracy still could have an impact. Even if democracy would not influence bin Ladin and his followers, it can isolate them by changing their popular image from Robin Hoods to thugs. As befits a people who know the true face of tyranny, the Arab world is highly supportive of the idea of democracy. A survey in the UN-backed 2003 *Arab Human Development Report* reports that more than 60 percent declare that "democracy is the best form of government," a result higher than in Western Europe or North America.[8] Democratization would thus place the jihadists on the defensive. Their opposition to a truly democratic system would expose one of the least popular points in their agenda. Families that now offer the jihadists their sons or their money would instead help the police and security services. Terrorists would have to expend much of their time and effort ensuring the silence of the people around them.

Another important consideration is the popularity of Islamist political parties. Because they would undoubtedly do well in elections, the divide between peaceful and violent Islamists would presumably widen. Thus the success of moderates at the polls would undermine the jihadists' claim that violence is necessary to bring about a just society. Jihadists, therefore, would turn their vitriol on their peaceful counterparts. Moderate Islamists, understanding that they are likely to be targets of violence, would have a strong incentive to marginalize their violent counterparts and would know full well that these attacks could provide a pretext for regimes to abort democratization. For the United States, the intelligence advantage of acquiring Islamists as allies would be immense. Because the Islamists would know who within their tightly knit communities is violent, they could identify them to the authorities. For all this to work, however, the moderates' success at the polls needs to translate into concrete policy accomplishments when in power. If they fail due to regime restrictions or their own incompetence, radicals will ridicule them and the democratic process, pointing to their poor track record as "proof" that violence is the only solution.

Elections also would separate more moderate Islamists from extreme *salafis*. Many salafis are extremely suspicious of politics, viewing the process as inherently corrupting. As the inevitable exigencies of power weigh down Islamist politicians, this critique would become even more widespread: some supposed Islamists would prove to be corrupt, while others would get sidetracked by the goal of preserving power. In Iran today, traditional religious scholars are often scathing about what they see as the corruption and compromises of clerics who have joined the political process. In their eyes, politics and religion must be separated to preserve the sanctity of the faith.

Once the democratic system is in place, the process can over time reinforce moderation over radicalism. In part this moderation occurs because the political system pays off: the groups obtain positions of power and can enact real changes without violence. In addition, if radical Islamists participate in the governing process, they will be forced to moderate their stance due to the mundane realities of governing. Political Islam expert Ray Takeyh contends, "Many radical groups find that once they are part of the governing order, the imperative of getting re-elected leads many to actually abandon their disruptive and costly utopian schemes in search of more practical solutions."[9] Movements such as Morocco's Justice and Development Party and Jordan's Islamic Action Front are increasingly characterized by pragmatism. In power, Turkey's Justice and Development Party has proved quite pragmatic. The commonplace realities of governance became its focus, not backing radicalism. Analyst Amr Hamzawy contends, "Instead of clinging to fantasies of theocratic states, Islamist movements in these countries now see the wisdom of competing peacefully for shares of political power and working within existing institutions to promote gradual democratic openings."[10]

Like pragmatic politicians, radicals are judged not only by their ultimate aspirations but also by the quality of trash removal and the level of corruption. Indeed, power may result in discrediting mainstream Islamists in favor of more secular alternatives. As Islam specialist Graham Fuller notes, Islamists have powerful critiques of their countries' problems but have few practical solutions to offer.[11]

Regardless of whether and how much these benefits would materialize in countries such as Egypt and Pakistan, an argument can be made that the United States would win simply by changing public perceptions. Currently the United States can rightly be accused of supporting despots of different stripes, from Uzbekistan to Saudi Arabia to Morocco. Not surprisingly, when the president of the United States is photographed shaking hands with Egyptian president Mubarak, who, despite his title, is a classic strongman, the world assumes that the United States is a foe of democracy. In justifying anti-U.S. violence, bin Ladin himself regularly cites such support in his decrees.

Again, this approach is likely to have a stronger impact among the outer circle of the radical movement and ordinary Muslims than on the jihadists themselves. The jihadist list of grievances is long, and U.S. support for brutal regimes is only one small part of their complaints. But U.S. support for better governance may diminish the level of anger among potential sympathizers.

Hard Realities

Yet the case against democracy promotion as a counterterrorism instrument is strong. One of the most powerful criticisms is that there is no inherent link between the presence of democracy and the absence of terrorism; indeed, several studies suggest that democracies are more vulnerable to terrorism than are autocratic governments. Two scholars of terrorism, Leonard Weinberg and William Eubank, compare democratic rule with authoritarian regimes and contend that "stable democracy and terrorism go together."[12] Since their founding, India and Israel are two democratic countries that have suffered from terrorism by an array of enemies.

The danger is even more considerable for countries transitioning to democracy. Mature democracies such as Sweden and Germany may be peaceful and have established means for airing and redressing citizens' grievances, but terrorists can find opportunities in countries where the institutions of democracy have not yet coalesced. Insurgencies, which are often tied to terrorist groups, are more likely to break out among countries with weak governments.[13] Because new democracies are fragile, they become more vulnerable to insurgency and unrest. Turmoil often ensues early on, when the senior political leadership attempts to purge the police and security services, while old rivals watch eagerly for opportunities to reestablish themselves. A pillar of the ancient regime, fear, may have been toppled, but the ideas of equal citizenship and the rule of law still have shallow roots. In such circumstances, limited violence can easily bubble over. Violence from the Basque separatist group ETA, for example, surged as Spain underwent a transition from fascism to democracy in the late 1970s, in part because the security services were reorganized as a necessary component of democratization.[14]

The problem goes beyond weakness. The democratization process itself is likely to create new grievances. Even in the absence of objective grievances, the process of democratization creates political winners and disgruntled losers: for one group to win, another has to be ousted. In Afghanistan, for example, the Pashtun community, which once held near-absolute control under the Taliban, became less dominant after the movement fell from power. In Iraq, the Sunni Arab tribes who enjoyed Saddam's largesse suddenly found themselves purged from the armed forces and senior government ranks, with their former victims now holding power. Not surprisingly, terrorists found fertile sources of recruits in these communities.

But as Weinberg and Eubank's work suggests, success also has its perils. Democracies can be feeding grounds for terrorists even when the state is functioning well. In free states, targets are widespread and usually poorly defended. And because democratic legal systems impose restraints on the security services, it is difficult for them to monitor and disrupt terrorist plots. Unlike Egypt, the government of Germany cannot round up thousands of suspects simply to find the few dozen who might be supporting terrorism.

Radicals also exploit democracy's embrace of free speech and free assembly. Until the bombings in London in July 2005, the British capital was home to Islamist militants of all stripes. The governments of Saudi Arabia, Algeria, Egypt, France, and Israel all complained to the British government that firebrand preachers were stirring up hatred against these governments and organizing for their overthrow.[15]

The benefits of a democratic government are even greater for the branches of the organization not directly involved in violence. Extremists can raise money in the guise of charity—for, say, the widows and orphans of the Chechen war. Preachers can lambaste the United States, Russia, India, or other countries fighting insurgencies, as long as they are careful not to directly endorse violence. The initial steps of recruitment are also protected. "Spotters" in mosques or other areas where young Muslim men hang out can identify potential recruits. Free to move about as they wish, the spotters introduce them to members of the movement, turn them against traditional Islamic teachings, and otherwise start to transform them into extremists. They can help launch them on a journey to Iraq, Pakistan, or other parts of the world where they can become yet more radicalized and formally embrace violence.

Even the economic advancement that may accompany democracy—so often touted as the main prerequisite of democracy—can be risky. Though it may seem counterintuitive, the decline in poverty enables recruits to join terrorist organizations. A common myth about terrorism links violence to poverty and a lack of learning. Studies of terrorists in the Gaza Strip, however, have found that many terrorists are well educated and hold jobs—this in a region where the majority of young men are unemployed. Peter Bergen and Swati Pandey found that the masterminds of some of the worst anti-Western terrorist attacks in the past fifteen years all had university degrees, and of the total seventy-nine involved, more than half had attended college—slightly more than the American average.[16] A British government report found that *both* well-educated British Muslims and underachievers (often criminals) were at risk of extremism.[17]

One only has to look at domestic politics to see the reasons for this phenomenon. People who enter politics typically have some degree of education. The truly poor usually worry more about their next meal than educating their children and engaging in sustained political activity.

The dirty little not-so-secret of U.S. counterterrorism is the benefit it derives from its partners' lack of democracy. An ally without civil liberties concerns can arrest thousands of "the usual suspects" in the hope of ferreting out the dozen or so who may be culpable. The United States can ask Egypt to eavesdrop on, detain, or otherwise gain information on a suspect and even take him off the street. To do the same thing with Germany requires a much higher standard of evidence—commendable from a human rights point of view, but costly for counterterrorism.

In its use of renditions, the United States has exploited—how else can one say?—the lower standards of its allies. Typically a rendition occurs when the local government, in cooperation with U.S. officials, bundles a suspect on a plane and sends him to a third country, where charges stand against him. In contrast to an extradition, the suspect does not go through the legal system of the country where he is arrested. More rarely, U.S. officials or their agents may pull a suspect off the street without the cooperation of the host government.

Counterterrorism officials find renditions attractive because they get terrorists off the street. In 1998, the *Wall Street Journal* reported that CIA officers and the Albanian police closed down an Egyptian Islamic Jihad cell that planned to bomb the U.S. embassy in Tirana. The suspects were sent to Egypt, where two were executed, and others jailed. Their interrogations also led to the arrests of numerous affiliates, dealing a crushing blow to the organization.[18] Renditions also are sources of information even when they do not lead to a lengthy imprisonment. Security forces can ask suspects questions, examine their documents, and otherwise gather information that might be relevant to past or future attacks.

Counterterrorism officials find such renditions attractive because of the high bar U.S. law sets for convicting suspected terrorists. Intelligence agencies often cannot meet the legal standard that requires proof "beyond a reasonable doubt." Often the only available intelligence is hearsay, rumor, and circumstantial evidence—information that can be maddeningly imprecise, incomplete, and at times contradictory. Many U.S. allies in the Middle East have a far lower standard of evidence and can bend their rules in response to a U.S. request.

A number of countries used for renditions, such as Egypt, Jordan, Morocco, and particularly Syria, brutally mistreat prisoners.

Though the U.S. government demands that foreign governments promise not to use torture, officials have little control over suspects once they leave U.S. custody; one CIA officer called these promises a "farce."[19]

The pragmatic use of authoritarian regimes creates a fundamental tension in U.S. policy, particularly as the United States tries to sell itself as a benevolent friend of the Arab and Muslim worlds. The United States needs a stable Middle East to ensure its interests. As Abdelwahab El-Affendi notes, "the United States is presently trying to walk a tight-rope between engaging the populace in public diplomacy dialogue while still doing business with the regimes it has openly identified as their oppressors; officials want to have their despotic cake and eat it too."[20]

Though the United States might espouse democratic goals in the Middle East, the actual outcome of free and open elections might not be in its favor. Citizens could freely elect an anti-U.S. Islamist political party.

Democracy might divide radical and moderate Islamists, but even the moderate Islamists could easily oppose U.S. foreign policy goals. As Gause contends, "The problem with promoting democracy in the Arab world is not that Arabs do not like democracy; it is that Washington probably would not like the governments Arab democracy would produce."[21] For example, the same *Arab Human Development Report* that describes the strong support for democracy in the Arab world also notes that fewer than 20 percent of those polled favor gender equality in the workplace.[22]

Some Islamist groups advocate a very conservative social agenda. In foreign policy they oppose what they see as "imperialism," championing struggles against Russia, China, Israel, India, and other supposed oppressors.[23] The "democratic" result of an Islamist victory in Egypt, for example, might be a decrease in women's rights, a harsher stand against Israel, or more criticism of the U.S. position in Iraq. At the very least, such a government would be less inclined to cooperate with the CIA in hunting suspected terrorists. At most, it might expel the U.S. military from the bases it uses in Egypt and actively support groups such as Hamas that use terrorism against Israel.

Many of these Islamist parties may also prove to be fair-weather democrats. Once in office some of these groups may reject democratization or embrace philosophers who, like the jihadists, are hostile to the idea of putting man's law above God's.[24] The theory that the realities of power will moderate radicals and force them to focus on filling potholes rather than preaching hate is just that—a theory. It may be true, but while we know that exclusion radicalizes Islamists, we do not know that inclusion gentles them.[25]

Make no mistake: the Islamists would do well if free elections swept the Middle East. In Palestine and Iraq, candidates linked to the terrorist group Hamas and pro-Iran militants have emerged victorious from elections. Islamists have done well in elections in Morocco, Egypt, Yemen, Bahrain, and Saudi Arabia and probably would have won outright were it not for tight regime control over the results. To keep their hold on power, regimes have used many tricks, including limiting access to the media, bribing politicians, gerrymandering districts, passing laws that criminalize those who criticize the government, and imposing outright bans on religious parties to offset their popularity.[26]

Even if all these problems could be overcome and the price of Islamists in power proves to be worth paying, it is important to note that success, if it came, would be incremental rather than complete. Some groups may engage in the political process while continuing their brutal business as usual. When the PIRA accepted a cease-fire in September 1994, it kept its cell structure, logistics network, and pattern of brutal beatings. Even after talks had progressed for several years, it still had made no effort to shut down its infrastructure of cells or decommission any weapons, including its stockpiles of explosives such as Semtex and mortars.[27] Government efforts to split a movement and wean away the moderates may succeed, but enough hard-core members remain to guarantee that terrorism continues. Many members of the Basque separatist movement ETA's political wing Herri Batasuna responded to the Spanish government's policy of "social reinsertion" (concessions that maximized Basque cultural and political rights), but some radicals maintained control over the movement and continued violence in the name of complete independence.[28] Many members of M-19 in Colombia also turned away from bloodshed, but a violent fringe remained.[29] While far from ideal, even this limited success can reduce the scale of violence, making it easier to gather intelligence on the perpetrators.

An engaged movement itself may reject violence, but new groups may form from rejectionist remnants. The Continuity IRA and the Real IRA both rejected the PIRA's embrace of negotiations over violence and conducted several bloody attacks after the PIRA had signed the Good Friday agreements.[30] In an effort to derail promising peace talks, fringe players may actually escalate their use of violence.

The Difficulty of Promoting Democracy

Despite the increased funding for democratization programs— including support from the president himself—the United States thus far lacks a coherent strategy for democracy promotion. J. Scott Carpenter, who heads one effort to foster democracy in the Middle East, noted that "We don't know yet how best to promote democracy in the Arab Middle East. I mean we just don't know. . . . I think there are times when you throw spaghetti against the wall and see if its sticks."[31]

This lack of a strategy is not due to the idiocy of policymakers; no one has articulated a detailed way to build democracy in countries where it has little history. The academic and analytic communities have at best a limited understanding of how democracy promotion should function in countries that lack such a tradition. Many questions have yet to be resolved. What aspects of democracy are the most important? What is the proper sequence: must there be the rule of law before free elections, or the other way around? Is democracy a path out of civil strife, or must there be domestic harmony first? What means do outsiders have of influencing the spread of democracy?

A related problem of promoting democracy is that its formal components—elections, for example—are easier to create and monitor than the more amorphous elements of toleration, trust, and social cohesion. Without these components, elections frequently become a means by which a majority dominates a minority. Havoc can result if communities mobilize for fear that the new government will "democratically" disenfranchise or impoverish them. The United States has often successfully pushed for elections in divided societies ranging from Kosovo to Iraq but has had much less success in creating the less formal conditions under which elections result in a true liberal democracy.

The formula for spreading democracy throughout totalitarian regimes has yet to be written. Sometimes even inoffensive attempts to bolster democracy can anger local regimes. The spread of democracy flies in the face of the interests of Arab rulers, most of whom are U.S. allies. The Yemeni government, which cooperates closely with the United States on counterterrorism, opposed a seemingly innocent U.S. effort to encourage different tribes to work together to stop revenge killings because it feared that if the tribes worked together they would be more effective in uniting and opposing the government.[32]

A divided country is a more easily controlled one.

Unfortunately, the daunting unpopularity of the United States in the Muslim world risks diminishing the very voices we are trying to support. The United States today has a poison touch. Reformers hoping to capture popular support thus shy away from American backing. Authoritarian regimes, including many that are close allies of the United States, cleverly play on this tension and accuse human rights activists of all stripes of being Western puppets.

The United States is caught between a rock and a hard place. It may be the best and most fair policy, but direct attempts to spread democracy can alienate allies and discredit would-be reformers and the chance of short-term success, and at the same time there is little guarantee that U.S. policies will produce success.

Not If but Where

Choosing our battles is essential. Given the complexity of democracy's impact on terrorism, the real question is not whether the United States should support democracy but when it should do so. Several principles should guide policymakers. First, Western efforts should focus on consolidating democracy in Muslim countries that are already in transition—a daunting task in itself. While success could pay substantial dividends, the ongoing process of democratization means the West is already running the risk of instability, weakness, and a hostile government, even without coming to the aid of a fledgling democracy. In short, there is less to lose and—because the process has already started, due to indigenous efforts—the hope for success is stronger.

Indonesia, the world's most populous Muslim country, is the obvious place to begin. Democratization is widening the rift between moderate Islamists and jihadists, but it is also fostering new forms of rivalry and strife.

The United States must be particularly careful to avoid repeats of Algeria in 1991 and 1992, where aborted elections that Islamists were poised to win tipped the country over into massive civil war. In the Algerian case, the military junta destroyed its own legitimacy while simultaneously "proving" that the radicals were right all along—that the gun, not the ballot box, was necessary for serious change. As a result, the radicals gained tens of thousands of recruits and perhaps millions of sympathizers at the start of their campaign. It took the carnage of war, and the radicals' extreme brutality, for them to lose this support.

Where democracy is nonexistent and democratic groups are weak, Western attention would be better spent building institutions such as the courts and police. These institutions will strengthen government counterterrorism efforts and, if democratization occurs, make strife and government weakness less likely. Pakistan is a logical place to start such an effort. U.S. pressure for elections would only destabilize the regime and inhibit vital counterterrorism cooperation without putting anything positive in its place.

Yet ever here we must recognize our own limits. U.S. efforts to build police forces and promote the rule of law have a dismal track record in Afghanistan, Iraq, and other places.

Caution should be the order of the day. Pushing democracy is in accord with American values, and it is at times desirable for policy goals beyond counterterrorism. But democracy promotion's at best uncertain effects on counterterrorism and the difficulties of spreading it from Washington should lead policymakers to use this instrument carefully and selectively.

7

The War of Ideas

Among all the images that dominate jihadist propaganda, pictures of Iraq are the most prominent. As if the brutalization of prisoners at Abu Ghraib weren't enough, in May 2006 the world learned that American troops allegedly killed twenty-four Iraqi civilians in Haditha. The victims included a five-month-old infant and a seventy-seven-year-old man in a wheelchair. In the propaganda, such atrocities mingle with pictures of U.S. leaders and soldiers, many of whom make callous comments taken out of context. Killing Iraqis is "awesome," declared a smiling U.S. marine to a CNN reporter. Juxtaposed with these reports are images of mujahideen firing rocket-propelled grenades at U.S. convoys or exchanging fire with U.S. servicemen in Fallujah. For Muslims, the message is obvious: the United States oppresses Muslims, and the mujahideen are fighting back. So what are you doing as Iraq is raped?

Iraq is not the only theme in the propaganda, simply the most prominent. The Caliphate Voice Channel relays world news with a jihadist spin, featuring a broadcaster obscured in a kaffiyeh. Web sites detail obituaries of martyrs, a list skyrocketing from suicide bombings in Iraq. Western jihadists have even produced a clumsy but effective rap video in which they complain about Israeli atrocities and boast about destroying the "Twin Towers." Video images of Western leaders such as Putin, Blair, and Rumsfeld mix

173

with Arab rulers such as the late king Fahd of Saudi Arabia and Egypt's president Hosni Mubarak. As these faces flash by, the words "kill the Crusaders" repeat, and—presumably for the kids—the vampire "Count" from *Sesame Street* morphs into Mubarak.

To counter this propaganda, the United States has expanded its public diplomacy to win support for U.S. policies. In an attempt to reach a young audience, the United States has created a rock-and-roll radio station (Radio Sawa) and a satellite news station (al-Hurra, or "the free one"). Both try to advance a more balanced picture of the news than local media outlets. The United States believes that a more nuanced news program will build a more favorable image of America. Through official trips and appear-ances on regional media such as the satellite news station al-Jazeera, U.S. officials try to explain controversial U.S. policies to skeptical audiences.

The response to the U.S. effort has been tepid. In a series of advertisements, the United States ran the "Shared Values Initiative" in Pakistan, Malaysia, Indonesia, and Kuwait through January 2003.[1] The initiative showed images of an American Muslim and his family living comfortably at home, praying openly, and otherwise enjoying America while practicing their religion freely. Other advertisements featured the Algerian-born Dr. E. Zerhouini, the head of the National Institutes of Health under George W. Bush; a schoolteacher in Ohio who openly wears the *hijab* (a head covering worn to denote modesty); and Farooq Mohammad, a firefighter in New York City. But the campaign flopped. Images of the Palestinian intifada and the testimony of poor treatment of Muslims who vis-ited or lived in America easily overshadowed the well-intentioned effort.[2]

As this comparison suggests, the jihadists are far more aggres-sive, creative, and visceral in their approach to propaganda than the United States is. If anything, the comparison understates the problem the United States faces as it tries to win the hearts and minds of the Arab street. The jihadists aggressively use whatever tools they have in their arsenal. To spread their messages, they post vivid images on the Internet, deliver fiery sermons in mosques, and spread their message of destruction through word of mouth. The result is a paradox lamented by Richard Holbrooke: "How can a man in a cave outcommunicate the world's leading communications society?"[3]

Not surprisingly, study after study finds that the United States is losing the war of ideas to the jihadists. Changing the perceptions of the Muslim world (and of Muslims living in the West) requires understanding the different audiences, both at home and abroad, that the United States and the jihadists seek to influence. When this is done, the next step is to play up jihadist atrocities and unpopular elements of their agenda; rather than building ourselves up, we must tear them down. Such a shift is conceptually simple, but it requires dramatically reorienting the content of U.S. public diplomacy efforts.

Most calls to "win the war of ideas" and "reinvigorate public diplomacy" largely consist of empty rhetoric that is divorced from what the United States can realistically accomplish. The United States can certainly do better, but policymakers must recognize that it is exceptionally hard for the United States to "win" the war of ideas unless it would make significant (and, in my opinion, often foolish) policy concessions, and even then it may make little progress. Going negative will get us farther, but this will not make the United States loved, but rather increase hatred of the jihadists.

Understanding the War of Ideas

The U.S. war of ideas is directed toward one audience: the hearts and minds of the Muslim world. Winning hearts and minds is vital. But it is better accomplished by adopting a more comprehensive and dynamic approach than creating rock-and-roll stations. The United States must not only consider its own information strategy, but also that of its adversary; the two cannot be separated. Both al-Qa'ida and the United States have many audiences they wish to influence:

1. the core al-Qa'ida and the jihadist activists;
2. potential jihadist supporters;
3. the U.S. government and citizens;
4. potential supporters of the U.S. government around the world.

To reach their core audience, al-Qa'ida camps indoctrinate train-ees on the "correct" interpretations of Islam. Focusing on potential supporters, Internet sites glorify the dead as martyrs and promo-tional videos display Russian atrocities in Chechnya and American horrors in Iraq. The videos exhort young Muslims to give their life to the cause while their elders give their money. Bin Ladin directs some of his missives to audience number three, America, the Great Satan. Finally, bin Ladin has continually sought to weaken ties between the United States and Europe by offering separate truce agreements to the Europeans if they are willing to abandon support of the United States. All four of these efforts are part of a relentless jihadist propaganda and information campaign.

For the United States, the president must make the American people feel secure against the threat of terrorism. Terrorism is a psychological weapon; if the American people have no confidence in their government, the terrorists win. The United States also must woo its incipient supporters around the world, both governments and peoples. If the United States can gain the cooperation of local governments, the jihadists can be isolated and their ability to in-fluence events reduced. A third audience consists of political Islamists and other Muslims whom the jihadists hope to recruit or influence. Most of this audience is hostile to the United States. But if these Islamists were to reject the jihadists, the extremists' hopes of sparking a broader movement diminish and the U.S. ability to gather intelligence is strengthened. Finally, the United States should seek to influence the jihadists themselves, both to create divisions in their ranks and to discourage them from additional attacks.

Bin Ladin's Information Strategy

From early on, al-Qa'ida understood that it must teach potential followers not only to fight but also to think. Al-Qa'ida's parent organization during the anti-Soviet struggle in Afghanistan, the Office of Services, took an important early stride by publishing the magazine *Al-Jihad* in 1984—a move that bin Ladin himself sponsored.[4] The inaugural issue set the tone for later themes of the jihad: the heroism of the mujahideen, the atheism and satanic nature of the foe, the glorification of martyrdom, and the necessity for every good Muslim to engage in jihad.[5] From the time of their founding, training camps linked to al-Qa'ida offered classes in history, theology, and political science in addition to military training, all with a salafist tinge. Unlike most terrorists, bin Ladin and his lieutenants wanted to shape the ideological vanguard as well as serve as its instrument.

This emphasis on shaping the ethos of the jihadist movement and the discourse in the Muslim world has grown steadily and has involved a range of communications techniques. To al-Qa'ida, propaganda is as essential as fighting. As a result, it has long maintained a practice of elevating officials responsible for propaganda to senior positions within the organization. An early spokesman was even nicknamed "Abu Reuter," after the news organization. Today al-Qa'ida continues to regard propaganda as an integral part of its organization, using sophisticated technology to further its ends. In 2005, an al-Qa'ida mouthpiece on the Internet called for volunteers who can help with video production and publishing.[6]

Al-Qa'ida professes a peculiar mixture of ancient ideology fused to cutting-edge technology. More than any other terrorist group in history, it has seized on the communications revolution systematically and creatively. Jihadist Web sites have grown exponentially in the past ten years.[7] The content of these sites includes various official or semiofficial statements from the al-Qa'ida leadership. They make available documents important to the jihad—such as manuals outlining various fighting techniques—and testimonies from martyrs who died fighting American, Russian, or other foreign troops. These technically sophisticated sites can be read in multiple languages and are user-friendly for computer neophytes.

These sites serve several purposes. Perhaps most important, they spread the ideas that al-Qa'ida champions: the need for jihad, the corruption of Muslim governments, and the evil of the United States. Proselytization follows, with appeals for recruiting men and raising money. Much as modern charities use pictures of starving children to wrench our hearts and our consciences, jihadist sites depict graphic violence against Muslims alongside jihadist victories over U.S. or Russian troops (often video feeds) to stir the blood of potential donors and recruits. The message is clear: Muslims are suffering. If you join the jihad, you can make a difference. To facilitate payment, supporters can give money via the Web. The Chechen guerrillas even have sites that accept "Paypal."[8]

These Web sites provide the nitty-gritty tools for those who want to join the fight, in effect weaving together the many threads of this movement. In one chat room, a wannabe fighter who called himself "Redemption Is Close" asked, "How do I go to Iraq?" He received his answer promptly, complete with a propaganda video and a request to download software that inhibits Internet monitoring.[9] Iraqi fighters use Web sites to announce their policy positions and their alliances.[10] In 2003, Zawahiri began calling for supporters to kill Pakistani president Pervez Musharraf. Several months later, assassins tried to kill him. Bin Ladin later began calling for strikes on Saudi Arabia's oil infrastructure. Heeding the cry, insurgents attempted to destroy Saudi oil facilities.

As the importance of the al-Qa'ida core declined and regional or local jihadists rose to the fore after 9/11, the role of the Internet emerged as a bottom-up tool for the overall movement. Would-be al-Qa'ida members post their views on the types of targets that should be attacked and the countries that should be hit. For example, once jihadists realized that 9/11 was a tremendous economic blow to the United States, they began to talk about the need for economic warfare against the United States. Similarly, jihadist Web sites pointed out that Britain, Spain, Italy, and Poland also deserve to be attacked because of their role in Iraq. Through the Web, bin Ladin and other jihadists exhorted followers to attack U.S. allies so they would drop out of the U.S.-led coalition in Iraq. A Web posting before the Madrid bombings noted that "Spain and Poland do not have a great, real interest in Iraq." They continue to say that terrorist strikes will influence the general elections in Spain and the Spanish people will push their government to withdraw—a prediction that later proved correct.[11]

That is not to say that jihadists have abandoned traditional techniques. Technology only enhances the tried-and-true methods of the jihadists. Television messages also are used to appeal to the masses. Throughout Europe and the Middle East, religious leaders continue to preach doctrines that paint the West as hostile to Islam, while praising fighters in Iraq, Chechnya, or elsewhere. These sermons alone do not cause terrorism, but they do make recruitment far easier. Terrorism expert Marc Sageman observes that before 9/11 many jihadists were recruited when a respected fighter did a tour in their area. A small network of friends and family members who organized on their own will meet the fighter at the mosque, where he inspires them to join the broader global movement.[12] For the most part, this is not a top-down al-Qa'ida–driven effort. It is driven by local efforts, which are now further augmented by the Internet.

Not only does propaganda justify and support violence, but violence also is used as a form of propaganda. This technique is not unique to al-Qa'ida: terrorists throughout the ages have used violence for "propaganda by the deed."[13] Terrorists often believe that violence not only strikes a blow against their adversary but also rouses the spirits of the masses, be they the sleeping proletariat, misguided ethnic brethren, or insufficiently pious cobelievers. Part of the purpose of 9/11 itself was just that: to demonstrate to the Muslim world that the United States could be hurt by the believers and thus to inspire them to join the cause. Al-Qa'ida and its affiliates recognize that action is a far more compelling recruiting device than words. Not surprisingly, the jihadists videotape and disseminate their attacks. Indeed, jihadists also have interwoven propaganda with their attacks. During a May 29, 2004, attack on a foreign workers' compound in Saudi Arabia, one of the terrorists called the Arabic television station al-Jazeera to do an interview in the middle of the assault.[14]

The education systems of many countries in the Muslim world also exacerbate violence. Schools, whether they are state-run or private religious-oriented madrassas, teach a curriculum that emphasizes hostility toward Israel and the United States. To be clear, these schools rarely produce skilled international terrorists. As Peter Bergen and Swati Pandey point out, the curriculum produces functional illiterates, not sophisticated terrorists.[15] Nevertheless, because these schools lionize the jihadists, they mold supportive populations that will later be receptive to hiding terrorists. These schools encourage regional jihads, such as Islamist insurgencies fighting against the Indian government in Kashmir, rendering these conflicts far more deadly than they otherwise might have been.

Bin Ladin's biggest success is that he has framed the nature of the debate. Through propaganda, he has deflected the focus from his own organization and centered it on his enemies. Web sites, videos, and sermons at the mosque spend far more time vilifying the United States and their cohorts, the "corrupt" regimes in the Muslim world, than they do deliberating the specifics of the jihadist political program. Rather than focus exclusively on his own agenda, bin Ladin has been able to generate a positive image by portraying himself and his gang as heroes who fight evildoers.

Two ideas are at the core of al-Qa'ida's message. First, they convince would-be recruits that the political and social injustices they perceive locally are actually global problems. Muslims everywhere experience the same difficulties. That is to say, the issue is not jobs in Germany or the repression of the Hashemite monarchy in Jordan; the true fault is with the United States and its policies.[16] Second, each Muslim has a duty to join the fight; this is a responsibility that cannot be avoided.

The U.S. Information Strategy and Its Weaknesses

Condoleezza Rice expressed the Bush administration's view of the importance of waging ideas when she declared in 2004, "True victory will not come merely when the terrorists are defeated by force, but when the ideology of death and hatred is overcome by the appeal of life and hope, and when lies are replaced by truth."[17] Rice articulated two purposes of public diplomacy. First, it would "dispel destructive myths about American society and American policy." At the same time, the United States would seek to "encourage the voices of moderation and tolerance and pluralism within the Muslim world."[18]

Though Americans accept the administration's message, the United States has been far less effective in convincing the other three essential audiences: potential allies (whether Muslim or non-Muslim); the broader Islamist community; and the jihadist enemy. In a 2005 Pew survey conducted among staunch American allies such as Britain and Canada, the favorable opinion of the United States of people in these countries barely cleared 50 percent. The number fell to a third or less with a favorable view of America in a survey of important potential allies in the Muslim world, such as Indonesia, Turkey, Jordan, and Pakistan. All these represent dramatic drops from the late 1990s. U.S. policies, particularly the belief that the United States acts on its own without consideration of the interests of other nations, are widely criticized.

Focusing propaganda on promoting U.S. values can play into the jihadists' hands. While the United States is proud of the role women play in every avenue of society, jihadists despise the fact that women are empowered, both politically and professionally. They believe that U.S. popular culture shamelessly promotes female sexuality. (In fact, many Americans would agree.) Spinmeisters may dispel some of the jihadists' more ludicrous conspiracy theories, but they cannot change or disguise American culture. Any debate of women's roles would make matters worse. Focusing on these issues would only further the jihadists' agenda, making them look more like defenders of traditional values than criminals.

In contrast to al-Qa'ida, we do not integrate the war of ideas into our actual policy decisions. In the highest echelons of the National Security Council or other top decision-making bodies, there is no post dedicated to winning over hearts and minds of our friends and our enemies. The closest position is undersecretary of state for public diplomacy. But this person has to compete with a wide range of diplomatic concerns within the State Department, to say nothing of the rest of the national security bureaucracy. American policy is thus shaped without consideration of how people around the world are likely to perceive it. Rather than consider worldwide reaction before a policy decision is made, diplomats try afterward to spin the issue in a way that reflects favorably on the United States. The unfortunate result is that the United States fails to take advantage of opportunities to present itself in a positive light.

Ironically, a significant U.S. problem results from one of its virtues: a transparent government. Unlike more autocratic governments, the

United States cannot talk out of both sides of its mouth. Within the global media environment and the Washington culture of openness (and leaks), the United States cannot formulate one policy and espouse another with any hope that it will pass unnoticed. As retired ambassador William Rugh contends, "Washington officials speaking publicly are thinking about an American audience rather than a foreign one."[19] Unfortunately, the global media market and the consistency of leaks make it impossible to simultaneously sell conflicting messages. The result is that statements meant for domestic audiences are played up everywhere overseas: Vice President Cheney, for example, condoned Israel's assassination of Palestinian officials in a television interview—a justified position, but one that plays poorly in the Muslim world.[20] Twenty years ago, few Muslims in pro-U.S. countries would see Cheney give such a statement, for their state-run media network would not show it. With satellite television, they can now watch the vice president in real time. The statements of U.S. evangelical leaders such as Franklin Graham, who offered the invocation at George W. Bush's first inauguration and who decried Islam as a "wicked" religion, received considerable attention as well, as did Jerry Falwell's declaration that the prophet Mohammad was "a terrorist."[21] The closeness of these leaders to the Bush administration makes it difficult for U.S. officials stationed abroad to simultaneously push the idea that the United States respects Islam.

This openness in government has proven a particular problem in the debate over public diplomacy. Through the statements of U.S. officials, Muslims have learned that the goal of the United States is to change and influence Muslims' beliefs, often in the guise of reforming Islam, rather than to change unpopular aspects of U.S. policy. The resulting messages to the Islamic world are thus seen as manipulative rather than genuine.[22]

Doing It Better

An obvious first step is to recognize that U.S. relief efforts in the Muslim world have a strategic as well as a humanitarian purpose. Responding to the 2004 tsunami's devastation in Indonesia or that of the 2005 earthquake in Pakistan wins friends and counters negative perceptions of the United States. We cannot anticipate any particular disaster, but as natural disasters occur regularly, we can plan to quickly seize upon the next one to show that America's heart is in the right place.

Another way to win over key audiences is to woo nonviolent Islamists. This goal may seem obvious, but it is exceptionally difficult to implement. We cannot assume that "you're either with us or against us." The reality is that if you are not with the United States, you are not necessarily with the jihadists. As former CIA operative Reuel Marc Gerecht contends, "Muslims who loathe these holy-war killers and want to see them extirpated from their societies can often themselves dislike, if not hate, the United States for a wide variety of reasons."[23] Some Muslims may dislike the United States because of its policies in Iraq and support for Israel; others might abhor U.S. social policies and support for area despots. All of these policies provide reasons for antipathy. Even so, it does not necessarily mean that Muslims want jihadists in their midst.

Politically, it is difficult to reach out to the nonviolent Islamist community. If the United States were to sponsor conferences, meet with religious leaders, or otherwise try to build bridges to this community, it would be met with a firestorm of suspicion from local audiences, many of whom would use the forum to spout anti-U.S. rhetoric. Efforts to shape the agenda of the meeting would degenerate into fulminations against the United States for its support of Israel and its incursion into Iraq. U.S. sponsors of these efforts then become vulnerable to the charge that we are paying our enemies or giving them a mouthpiece. Even if these meetings were moderately successful, and they did reduce suspicions and egregious misconceptions, many of the core value and policy issues would remain as barriers to communication.

Because of U.S. difficulties in direct communication with peaceful Islamists, there is another approach to improving relations, one that is vital in the war of ideas. Regimes that are geographically close to the disaffected groups can be used to segregate extreme elements. Saudi Arabia, for example, worked effectively with both state-supported religious leaders and those who in the past had been critical of the al-Saud as a way of isolating the most fanatic elements in its midst. Several leading Saudi clerics have strongly condemned terrorism.[24] Although many jihadists dismiss the more moderate religious establishment, they crave the legitimacy that these clerics can bestow. In Iraq, for example, quarreling extremists frequently turn to clerics in Saudi Arabia to validate their positions.[25]

To further isolate the radicals, the United States should reach out beyond the Islamist community to business leaders and media figures. While this community is not necessarily pro-American, they are often more secular and more cosmopolitan than the Islamists. This approach may involve bringing these people to the United States for trips and tours, thus increasing their interaction with U.S. officials. A Heritage Foundation report sensibly recommends increasing scholarships to future elites as a way of shaping the next generation.[26] Yet even if we do begin closer communication with more secular groups, we are playing catch-up: from 1995 to 2001, cultural exchanges dropped by more than a third.[27]

The United States should be realistic about the possible outcomes of such outreach efforts. Rather than expect these officials to become friendly to the United States, we should assume that at best they will be more willing to support their local governments against the jihadists, and less likely to view those who use violence as a necessary evil. If the Islamists and other elites themselves were to meet occasionally with U.S. officials or if they were to visit the United States periodically, local governments' ties to the United States would no longer be seen as a blanket endorsement of U.S. policies. But to gain more traction with these audiences, the United States would have to make policy concessions—something it so far has been loath to do and something that would often be a mistake.

Fortunately, we have an ally in this effort to woo nonviolent Islamists: the jihadists themselves. When the jihadists condemn the Islamic religious establishment, they create enemies among the Islamists. The jihadists correctly note that these preachers are often paid by the state, and lack independence, producing what the late Ayatollah Khomeini of Iran used to call "American Islam." Nevertheless, these establishment preachers remain respected in their communities, and many Muslims are resentful when extremists attack them.

Going Negative

Even more important than reaching out to nonviolent Islamists is changing the terms of the debate. Rather than focus on supposed U.S. crimes, the debate should center on the very real brutalities of the jihadists. U.S. efforts to "sell" America as friendly to Muslims have had at best a marginal effect, in large part because the ads focused attention on the United States, whose policies and values are often unpopular. Any good politician knows that it is easier to make your opponent hated than to make yourself loved. Al-Qa'ida propagandists understand this concept very well and use it against the United States. In a similar manner, American messages can target moderate Islamists by focusing on the violent excesses committed by al-Qa'ida, actions that repel the more judicious Islamists. The United States can highlight the victims of terrorism, particularly Arabs, Muslims, or children. For the moderates, no matter how noble a cause al-Qa'ida claims to represent, these victims are off-limits. Even without American encouragement, violence is repugnant to ordinary Muslims. A July 2005 survey by the Pew Global Attitudes Project found that support for "violence in defense of Islam" fell substantially in countries ranging from Indonesia to Pakistan to Morocco. Similarly, support for bin Ladin fell in most countries from high points after the 2003 war and the initial U.S. occupation in Iraq.[28] This ill will can be fertile ground for American propaganda, but unfortunately the United States is doing little to exploit its advantage.

History shows that government efforts can accelerate public aversion to violence. Britain successfully engaged in a negative campaign after the Greek terrorist group 17 November murdered their defense attaché, Stephen Saunders. For twenty-five years, 17 November had operated with impunity. The Greek security services was both reluctant to go after the terrorists and incompetent when they tried.[29] Saunders's widow, Heather, made repeated public appeals and talked about her daughters, noting that "he was the best daddy in the world" and that "not only have they killed my husband, they have destroyed me and my family."[30] This campaign won support from the Greek people, many of whom in the past felt little sympathy for the British military but did shed tears for a widow and her daughters. It also shamed the Greek government into taking more aggressive action against the group and simultaneously made it politically easier for security forces to receive training from Scotland Yard.

Private citizens also can play a role in deterring extremists. When the brother of the McCartney sisters was murdered by the Provisional IRA, they pressed their case publicly. So successful were they that the sisters convinced President Bush to meet with them rather than IRA leader Gerry Adams on St. Patrick's Day. Furthermore, their actions led Irish American champion Senator Edward Kennedy to denounce the IRA's "ongoing criminal activity." Even in Saudi Arabia, a country where popular hostility toward the United States is high, such efforts can reduce support for the jihadists. As Nawaf Obaid, a Saudi national security consultant, argues, Saudis "Like what he [bin Ladin] says about what's going on in Iraq and Afghanistan. Or about America and the Zionist conspiracy. But what he does, that's where you see the huge drop."[31]

In May 2003, a series of attacks—that continue even to this day—were waged against the government in Saudi Arabia. The Saudi government demonstrated what can be done to rouse public opinion against the extremists. At the behest of the regime, Saudi Arabia's usually bland media explicitly portrayed the gruesome impact of attacks by al-Qa'ida of the Arabian Peninsula on Muslim civilians. For example, Saudi television aired a show called "The Beautiful Virgins." The show used the 2004 attack on a compound of expatriate workers in Saudi Arabia to emphasize the brutality and corruption within al-Qa'ida's organization.[32] One Saudi paper wrote that terrorists treat their children poorly, a particularly grave accusation in Arab society. The paper cited an instance where a terrorist killed his own son when he tried to surrender to Saudi security forces.[33] In addition, Majid al-Sawat, a Saudi soccer player for the well-known al-Rashid team, traveled to Iraq to carry out a suicide bombing. On television, he later stated that he was held against his will. Sawat claimed that he went to Iraq in response to a fatwa that prohibited soccer except as used for jihad training. Senior Saudi clerics have rejected the fatwa and called for prosecuting those who issued it—a good example of rallying the religious establishment behind the regime and against the jihadists on an issue that makes jihadists look foolish.[34] The result was a wave of popular revulsion against the jihadists. The public relations disaster forced them to shift tactics from Muslim civilians, a shift that made operations much harder and demonstrates that considerable damage had been inflicted on their credibility. The negative image will, in the long term, make recruiting and fund-raising harder and ease the task for the kingdom's intelligence services.

Similar efforts to interview widows and orphans of terrorist attack victims, particularly Muslims and Arabs, highlight the human cost of terrorist attacks and enable local audiences to separate their dislike of the United States from the broader issue of support for violence. The 2005 attack in Jordan is a painful example of what can be done. Only the most extreme of the extremists would endorse targeting a wedding, even if it is in a Western hotel. Dramatizing the plight of the families of the victims and the general horror of such attacks tarnished the jihadists' image among those they most seek to impress.

Together, these efforts put the jihadists on the defensive. Rather than focusing discussion on U.S. support for Israel or intervention in Iraq, the debate revolves instead around their own violence and organizational pathologies. The regime's efforts will not convince all supporters or fence-sitters to reject the jihadists, but they do raise doubts among the Islamists and damage the image of Robin Hood that the jihadists want to project. Beyond terrorist attacks, al-Qa'ida leaders such as bin Ladin and Zawahiri have repeatedly endorsed ideas that are highly unpopular in the Middle East. We should use their own words to design advertisements that discredit them among the very audiences they seek to sway.

Washington and its allies also should play up the jihadists' aversion to traditional Islamic practices. Salafis oppose all forms of syncretism and what they see as idol worship. Jihadist salafis take this aversion one step farther and often declare more spiritual tendencies within Islam, such as Sufi movements, to be heretical. They also may desecrate graves and shrines, believing them to be objects of idol worship. In Pakistan, salafist groups often have alienated other Muslims by their extreme stands. Because folk customs are widely practiced in the Islamic world, highlighting this hostility will decrease support for the radicals.

Finally, the United States should try to drive wedges among different segments of the radical community. Zawahiri for many years was engaged in a personal and bitter power struggle for control over the Egyptian jihadist community with Shaykh Omar abd al-Rahman—the "blind shaykh." Both are terrorists who are responsible for the deaths of Americans, but the United States can use their vitriol against each other to discredit both and drive them apart. In addition to creating divisions among the jihadists, the United States should take advantage of the coercive powers of its allies to counter a key al-Qa'ida recruitment source—the radical mosques that foster hatred. Because al-Qa'ida's recruitment relies heavily on face-to-face contacts, shutting down a few key mosques in Saudi Arabia and elsewhere would have a disproportionate effect on al-Qa'ida's recruitment. The United States must identify such loci of the jihadist movement and encourage the removal of voices that advocate violence.

Initially these measures will have only a limited effect on the jihadists. Over time, however, they will affect potential sympathizers and the broader Muslim community. Recruits and funds will diminish, and communities will be more likely to lend a hand to the police than provide a hiding place for jihadists. The United States, too, will benefit: it will not convince the world, let alone hostile Muslims, to embrace America's policy and culture, but it will help prove that the jihadists are a far greater menace.

Bureaucratic Changes

To better wage the war of ideas, the United States should undertake a series of bureaucratic changes. One shift is to elevate voices for public diplomacy in parts of the government beyond the State Department. Studies by senior diplomats and the Defense Science

Board found that public diplomacy is neither coordinated system-atically within the government nor integrated into overall U.S. policy.[35] Rather than force diplomats to work with policy after it has been formulated, the policy's effects on the Muslim street should be considered before it is drafted. The bureaucracy that coordinates the U.S. message must be made stronger and given a more promi-nent role. In particular, the bureaucratic rank of such officials must be elevated. Organizations involved in public diplomacy should be organized in an entity separate from the State Department and given their own seat in the interagency process to ensure that their voices are heard early and often. Improved integration would enable the United States to consider the message it conveys before the final policy is completed.

But as public diplomacy is integrated at the national level, much of the actual ideas and implementation should be done at the local level. Embassy officials in particular are well positioned to deter-mine what messages will and will not work in their country. One size does not fit all in the Muslim or Arab world; each country has its own hot-button issues and potential opportunities. Indeed, in countries such as Pakistan, Indonesia, or Algeria, where regional differences are strong, the United States should try to shape its messages to individual ethnic and regional communities as well as to the country as a whole.

Another shift involves intelligence. Evaluating the success of the U.S. information campaign requires monitoring the activities of both sides: the potential sympathizers of the jihadists and the United States. One indicator of jihadist leanings is in the sermons of leading clerics. The tenor of their messages can determine whether they encourage extremism. Sophisticated polls that distin-guish ordinary Muslims from those who consider themselves Islam-ists also would be useful. Regional differences also should be understood, to improve the implementation of aid at the local level.

In an increasingly free media environment, the U.S.-funded media have neglected a key lesson from the Cold War experience; the result is misdirected uses of media in the Middle East. The reason why Radio Free Europe and other anti-Communist efforts succeeded was that East European citizens had no free-press alternatives. That is not the case in the Middle East, where satellite television stations aggressively compete for their viewers, and the more stolid U.S. efforts lack credibility. Satellite television stations such as al-Jazeera, Abu Dhabi Television, and al-Arabiya have revolutionized the information environment in the Middle East by providing coverage and footage on a wide variety of issues. The United States has complained about the anti-American tone of much of the coverage of stations such as al-Jazeera, without acknowledging that these stations are also intensely critical of a number of Arab regimes in the Middle East.

Rather than rely on U.S.-funded alternatives, it is better to work with these existing media outlets, even though they will not function as U.S. mouthpieces.

Public diplomacy is not a magic wand. The United States and other countries can toil for years and, in the end, make only limited progress toward improving the U.S. image in the Muslim world. Despite these limits, a supreme effort is essential. Our goal is not to be loved; it is to make the jihadists hated. A refusal to engage in this effort seriously is tantamount to surrendering the legitimacy question to the jihadists.

We must never forget that bin Ladin's propaganda successes rest on precarious foundations. He has managed to convince sizable parts of the Muslim world that the killing of innocents is acceptable and that his own noxious agenda should be supported as the alternative to U.S. dominance. By changing such perceptions, we can isolate the most extreme jihadists. We cannot change their violent ends, but we can render them, over time, a far less dangerous fringe movement.

8

Diplomacy

International cooperation is vital to the war on terrorism. The 9/11 Commission pointed out that "Practically every aspect of U.S. counterterrorism strategy relies on international cooperation."[1] Though the Bush administration has used September 11 to justify important decisions in its foreign policy, most notably the invasion of Iraq, its alliances have not changed to meet the threat of terrorist groups. This disregard is serious: lack of critical alliance partners significantly weakens our attempts to thwart terrorist attacks. Whether we bomb Taliban strongholds in Afghanistan, work with Thailand to capture local al-Qa'ida members, or press the United Arab Emirates to halt its citizens' financial support for jihadists, all efforts require assistance from allied governments.

Choosing the wrong allies can have devastating consequences. At the very least, the United States may lavish money and policy concessions on the undeserving. At the worst, neglect of a key regime could destabilize entire regions and might even encourage a jihadist takeover.

The September 11 attacks opened up new opportunities for alliances, but so far the United States has been slow to seize them.[2] The United States has improved counterterrorism cooperation with former adversaries such as Russia and strengthened relations with a host of previously neglected countries such as Djibouti and Uzbekistan.[3] That effort is not enough. In many regions of the world there are widespread suspicions of U.S. motives, especially efforts linked to the war on terrorism. As former CIA official Paul Pillar contends, "Global cooperation against terrorism is already fragile."[4]

Allies are vital for counterterrorism, but what we ask of allies today differs greatly from what we asked of them during the Cold War era. To deal with terrorism in the twenty-first century, we need to identify new allies based on new criteria. We must ask our political partners if they can provide intelligence on al-Qa'ida, if they have strong counterinsurgency capabilities, if they can sway potential state sponsors of terrorism, if they have the capacity to aid states whose police and military forces are too weak to stop terrorists, and if they can influence the Muslim world. Particularly important are countries that currently have restive Muslim populations.

For purposes of the war on terrorism, our list of key allies should have shifted. Britain, Canada, Egypt, France, Saudi Arabia, and Turkey remain high on the list of essential allies, just as they were during the Cold War and immediate post–Cold War eras. Now that the U.S. focus is on al-Qa'ida, China, Japan, and South Korea are lower on the list, though they remain important for nonterrorism issues. Today several new countries emerge. Before September 11, 2001, the countries of Afghanistan, Iraq, Jordan, Kenya, Mali, Nigeria, Somalia, and Yemen were not considered important allies. Now they join the list of countries essential to fighting terrorism. The most important new partners are India, Indonesia, and Pakistan, all of which are at the center of the struggle against terrorism.

Once alliances are in place, the United States must devote attention to improving intelligence. We can begin by sharing information with allies, gaining access to allied intelligence services, restructuring the U.S. military to focus more on helping allied counterinsurgency efforts, and reviving programs to improve the security services of other countries.

The Role of Allies in Counterterrorism

Although allies are vital to almost every aspect of U.S. counterterrorism, their most important role is providing intelligence. In contrast to most terrorist groups throughout history, al-Qa'ida's activities require cooperation that goes beyond a country or a region. Their activities require that the United States track them in literally dozens of countries in the Middle East, Europe, Asia, and Africa. It is possible that the United States might have strong independent intelligence capabilities in several of these countries, but it is highly unlikely that the United States will be strong everywhere. In particular, the United States is likely to need assistance in areas that have not in the past been traditional intelligence priorities, such as Africa and Southeast Asia.

Even if the United States has established intelligence links in the country, allies usually do a better job collecting intelligence on a local level, particularly when human intelligence is required.[5] Local officials are more proficient in their native language and culture, they can use local laws to their advantage, and they can tap into police manpower to augment surveillance.

Allies are more likely to have trained personnel who speak the particular dialects of suspected terrorists. Also, because they are steeped in their native cultures, allies may possess superior interrogation skills. In addition, with their access to suspects' families, they can increase pressure to cooperate by rewarding or threatening those whom the terrorists value most.

The states that have strong intelligence capabilities against al-Qa'ida and its affiliates correlate with states that suffer from Islamist unrest. This correlation is no coincidence: to retain power, these regimes have had to develop knowledge against their adversaries. Al-Qa'ida and its affiliates oppose many of the world's most powerful regimes. They are particularly hostile to Muslim countries that do not follow their rigid Islamist doctrine (i.e., all of them). Not surprisingly, the security services of these threatened states have extensive information regarding local jihadists as well as al-Qa'ida.[6] Because previous (and sometimes current) supporters of jihadist organizations such as Sudan and Pakistan have already amassed considerable intelligence on their former friends, they are especially valuable allies. The price they pay for working with the United States is not cheap. Often it means they must abandon the radicals and their former friends, or at least it means they risk antagonizing them by working both sides of the street.

Several countries outside the Middle East have a significant global intelligence presence that can aid in the battle against terrorism. Israel, France, and Britain are particularly prominent. All have a strong intelligence presence with regard to Islamist organizations and networks.[7]

Allies are as vital for successful counterinsurgency as they are for intelligence-gathering. Both work best with help from allies who have superior local knowledge of the region, including the population, the adversary, and the terrain—all the elements necessary for a successful campaign. The stakes are high for local governments whose survival or territorial integrity is jeopardized, so they are likely to have a larger stomach for the fight than the United States. They are willing to take—and inflict—more casualties in a conflict and expend considerable resources to ensure their success. And most important, an obvious U.S. presence would add fuel to al-Qaida's fires, discredit the government in question, and lead to a nationalistic backlash that would help rather than hinder the Islamist insurgents.

Fortunately, many allies have sought U.S. support to assist their counterinsurgency efforts. Though the United States has an interest in the defeat of jihadist-linked insurgencies, this interest is usually dwarfed by the life-or-death concerns of the host government. The United States can provide equipment that will greatly bolster their firepower and mobility. Even more important, U.S. special operations forces can offer training that would help regional militaries become more effective in combating guerrilla movements. U.S. aid programs also can increase support for the government by improving the material well-being of key areas.

Through traditional means of military and economic coercion, allies also can discourage "passive" sponsors of terrorism—states that look the other way while the organization hatches its violent plans. After the fall of the Taliban, al-Qa'ida no longer enjoyed a state sponsor. Yet al-Qa'ida remains active, largely because of its link to passive states. Local allies have means of suppressing terrorism that are far more effective than attempts by outsiders. They understand the kinds of appeals that will encourage their own publics to diminish terrorist support.[8] Allies also can fight against passive sponsors by ostracizing them diplomatically and economically. Global sanctions, as opposed to unilateral U.S. condemnation, are a far more powerful weapon that can shame the regime into cooperating.

Allies are vital in bolstering weak or failed states. They can provide training for security services, money for reconstruction, expertise to rebuild an infrastructure, and even help establish the rule of law.[9] But it is important to remember that this effort is costly and time-consuming. It may take decades for the locals to be able to assume responsibility for their own security.[10]

The coordination of these massive tasks that go beyond standard counterterrorism intelligence-sharing can best be done through international organizations such as the United Nations and the World Bank rather than through bilateral or multilateral structures. To achieve this coordination, however, the United States will have to work with key partners to make sharing a priority and to ensure action.

The presence of allies adds to the overall legitimacy of the U.S. effort overseas, which, in turn, reduces local opposition to cooperation with the United States. The very lack of allies suggests that the terrorists' cause enjoys some sympathy, which gives them a degree of legitimacy. Local support is particularly useful in parts of the world (including almost the entire Muslim world) where the United States is unpopular, and where many unilateral initiatives would be resisted simply because they bear the U.S. stamp.

When allies cooperate with the United States in fighting terrorism, their support also bestows legitimacy at home, a particularly important benefit, as many of the means of counterterrorism are not widely accepted. International support can bolster the arguments of U.S. leaders and convince domestic audiences that the government's objectives and tactics are justified. Political support is vital for controversial counterterrorism tools such as preventive detentions, targeted killings, and extraordinary renditions—practices that are not typical of domestic law enforcement or standard wartime operations. In France, domestic support for a strong counterterrorism program eroded in the aftermath of the war in Algeria when the French public deemed many counterterrorism methods illegitimate.[11]

Particularly important countries that the United States should pursue as local allies are those that jihadists might control. Afghanistan under the Taliban and Sudan under the influence of Turabi demonstrate how dangerous a jihadist-led state can be. In both instances, the regime backed a variety of terrorist groups (including al-Qa'ida) and supported Islamist insurgencies on their border. Fortunately, both Sudan and Afghanistan were exceptionally weak states. Control of a country rich in natural resources, such as Saudi Arabia, would be exponentially more dangerous because jihadists would have far more money and far more dangerous weapons with which to pursue their goals. For that reason, control of a country such as Saudi Arabia is one of al-Qa'ida's top objectives.

Also vulnerable to jihadist threats are Indonesia, Iraq, Nigeria, and Pakistan. Indonesia faces a skilled Islamist terrorist group, the Jemaah Islamiyya, an organization that has carried out several terrorist attacks against the regime and foreign targets. Its most notable attack was the October 2002 bombing of a Bali discotheque that killed 202 people, many of them Australian tourists.[12] Indonesia remains a potential hotbed of unrest, with myriad ethnic and sectarian problems. Jihadists could exploit any of these problems to foment unrest and increase their influence.

In Iraq, the current insurgencies against the U.S.-backed Iraqi government stem from a host of problems, only some of which are linked to foreign or indigenous jihadists.[13] However, parts of Iraq are becoming training grounds for jihadists and areas for them to network. Ensuring that these jihadists do not dominate the current insurgency is essential for the struggle against al-Qa'ida.

Nigeria, too, faces several terrorist groups that espouse a jihadist ideology. In recent years its Muslim and Christian communities have clashed over the division of power and the imposition of Islamic law in parts of the country. Several Muslim areas have already replaced the secular criminal code with Islamic law.[14] The country's poverty, corruption, and poor governance make it a prime candidate for unrest that jihadists could use to their advantage.

Pakistan, of course, currently sponsors numerous jihadist groups active in Kashmir and hosts others, some of which oppose the military regime. As such, it is both a vital ally and part of the problem as it actively sponsors terrorist groups against India and abets Taliban activity against the U.S.-backed government of Afghanistan. Unfortunately, the situation in Pakistan may grow much worse as jihadists active in Kashmir draw closer to al-Qa'ida, which the large militant group Lashkar-e-Tayyiba appears to have done since 9/11. Moreover, with the fall of the Taliban, many al-Qa'ida operatives relocated to Pakistan's cities and to remote parts of the country that traditionally have had at best loose central government control. Given Pakistan's nuclear arsenal, the fall of the country to jihadists would be a particular nightmare for the United States.

How Has the Role of the Allies Changed?

During the Cold War, U.S. alliances focused primarily on containing Soviet power, though the interpretation of what containment meant in practice often differed considerably. After the Berlin Wall fell, strategists envisioned alliances that would serve multiple purposes. Because their goal was to ensure stability in key regions, particularly Asia, Western Europe, and the Persian Gulf, they paid most attention to industrial power states, which then equaled military power. They also attempted to limit the power of aggressors, particularly Iraq and North Korea. Key allies included the European states that formed NATO, Japan, South Korea, and pro-U.S. monarchies in the Persian Gulf, particularly Saudi Arabia. Now that the Cold War is over, the rules have changed. In the war on terrorism, weak states are more important than strong states. Less powerful states are both the locus of trouble and key actors in the fight.

Economic growth also is an important consideration. Although a robust economy is not a guarantee of freedom from an Islamist terrorist threat, a high per capita GDP and an advanced information society certainly help. None of the world's wealthiest countries faces a major insurgency. Even the strongest states in the Muslim world (Turkey, Egypt, and Indonesia) have at best a limited industrial and military base when compared with traditional major powers such as Japan, Britain, or Germany. When jihadists seek to exploit poverty and foment social unrest, much of the Muslim world is at risk.

Allied counterinsurgency capabilities are useful as well.[15] Necessary are forces that can work with local populations, train unskilled police and military units, gather intelligence, and otherwise do the gritty work of counterinsurgency. In Afghanistan, special operations forces from Australia, Canada, Denmark, New Zealand, Norway, Poland, and Turkey contributed to fighting insurgents there. Among traditional U.S. allies in Europe and Asia, however, only a few developed strong counterinsurgency capabilities with a robust training mission. Today perhaps only France, Australia, and Britain retain these skills.

After the Cold War ended, strategic locations changed. Needless to say, the Fulda Gap in Germany is not a strategic route for terrorists. Nor is the DMZ in Korea, or other post–Cold War hot spots. Rather, the area of concern has shifted to the Muslim world, including such disparate regions as parts of East and West Africa, Southeast and South Asia, and Central Asia.[16]

Old Dilemmas with New Faces

Alliances are not cost-free. During the Cold War, the United States feared that its allies would entrap the country in local conventional conflicts. Strategists worried about being associated with brutal, but anti-Communist, regimes. They tried to ensure that allies would not exploit the U.S. presence to minimize their own contributions to defense. Though the particulars vary, similar problems exist today for the war on terrorism.

States may fear that increasing ties to the United States will provoke an attack from al-Qa'ida. Bin Ladin issued just such a threat to Australia, claiming, "We warned Australia before not to join in [the war] in Afghanistan, and [against] its despicable effort to separate East Timor. Australia ignored the warning until it woke up to the sounds of explosions in Bali."[17] In April 2004, bin Ladin again tried to play on this tension, explicitly offering a "truce" to European states that refrained from what he described as hostile action in the Muslim world.

Countries have long been concerned that an alliance hostile to a potential aggressor will precipitate an attack.[18] Belgium, for example, avoided taking cooperative steps with France that would have improved both of their defensive positions vis-à-vis Germany in the years leading up to World War I. They feared that cooperation would violate its neutrality and give Berlin a pretext to attack.[19]

Allies that decide they will not be held hostage to al-Qa'ida's blackmail may still do little to eliminate the organization. They believe—and rightly so—that the United States will do the work for them. Because the United States is one of al-Qa'ida's top targets, other countries can be confident that Washington will move to quash the organization even if they do not contribute their share. Allies traditionally try to gain the most they can from one another at the least cost, a temptation that is even greater in the war on terrorism.

If association with the United States can harm allied regimes, the opposite is also true: an ally's own reprehensible record may tarnish the image of the United States and diminish public support for the U.S. counterterrorism campaign.[20] When the United States bolsters undemocratic allies with an infusion of cash or material goods, those countries are then able to resist the reforms necessary for humanitarian purposes and counterterrorism perspectives.

The day-to-day exigencies of counterterrorism exacerbate this problem. Uzbekistan, for example, is home to the Islamic Movement of Uzbekistan, which is closely linked to al-Qa'ida. In response to U.S. requests for help after September 11, the Uzbek government has offered the United States its bases as well as other assistance in the effort to crush al-Qa'ida.[21] The United States needed the government's help to crush these fighters and to gain Tashkent's assistance in identifying and stopping others who may have been active beyond Uzbekistan's borders. Because the Uzbek government was essential to that effort, the United States was forced to downplay the Karimov regime's brutality, which in itself contributes to violence in the region. To help Tashkent fight al-Qa'ida, the United States strengthened Uzbekistan's intelligence and counterinsurgency capabilities. But in the process, they gave the Karimov regime tools to crush dissent.

Some states will use the authority of the war on terrorism to bolster the legitimacy of their own particular goals. In the name of fighting terrorism, China has suppressed the Uighur community in the province of Xinjiang, generating resentment and occasional violence there.[22] Russia has tried to snuff out Chechen nationalism to prevent secession. India wants to crush the Kashmir insurgency to consolidate its control over the disputed area. In these and many other instances, the United States has condemned its ally's actions, or at least expressed discomfort. But these regimes have countered by linking their actions to the war on terrorism. Not surprisingly, U.S. denunciations of Russia's brutality in Chechnya have softened and become less frequent since 9/11.

Israel is the most problematic ally in this regard. Regardless of one's views on its dispute with the Palestinians, the constant violence of the second intifada has further inflamed Muslim opinion against the United States, Israel's most prominent supporter. Bin Ladin himself denounced Washington in his famous 1998 declaration when he claimed that various U.S. policies in the Middle East are meant "to serve the Jews' petty state."[23] Subsequent statements have echoed this theme, decrying Israel's repression of Palestinians and justifying attacks on Americans by claiming that the United States encourages Israeli brutality.[24]

If U.S. counterterrorism goals conflict with an ally's broader interests, the ally may refuse to take action, or it may do so half-heartedly. Pakistan, for example, seeks a pro-Pakistan regime in Kabul and wants to wrest Kashmir from India. While those objectives may suit Pakistan, they go directly against the U.S. aim of eliminating the remnants of the Taliban and disrupting al-Qa'ida's recruitment and logistics networks. But because al-Qa'ida's networks are interwoven with those of Kashmiri jihadists,[25] Islamabad has acted sluggishly against Kashmiri militants and has allowed the Taliban to operate below the radar screen.[26]

In contrast to conventional military allies, allies in the war on terrorism also may disagree on the means of conducting counterterrorism operations. In the past, allies would discuss different ways to combine their military power. They might have disagreed about the scope, level, and circumstances of cooperation, but they generally agreed about the means. For counterterrorism, however, allies disagree on the instruments themselves. All may agree that

Nigeria is vulnerable to insurgency, but some may call for internal reform, others for improving the security services, and still others for an aid package.

A related problem and constant fear is that an ally's local struggles will suck its friends into the vortex, creating a broader conflict that has little to do with the original purpose of the alliance. When a state becomes enmeshed in its allies' problems, it does so because it fears that a loss for an ally will disproportionately harm its own security. Thus it follows its allies down disastrous roads, even when the local conflict in question is not directly tied to its security.[27]

Today, most terrorism is local, and few groups have targeted the United States. Some militant Islamists have even criticized al-Qa'ida for focusing on the United States rather than more important local governments.[28] If the United States actively sides with a local government, the terrorists may expand their targeting to include Americans. But restraint is not always the answer. Some local jihadist groups morph on their own into anti-American groups. Kashmiri militants, for example, have recently been found fighting American forces in Iraq. Targeting them before they begin killing Americans would be ideal.

Many of the countries that the United States seeks as allies have a limited bureaucratic capacity. When a weak government cannot extend its influence, the conditions are ripe for unrest and the development of a jihadist movement.[29] The United States faces such a problem with one of its most important allies: Saudi Arabia. The Saudi government is highly personalized. Institutions are often little more than a brittle shell surrounding one individual. Decision-making is highly centralized, and the number of competent bureaucrats is low. The Ministry of Foreign Affairs, for example, revolves around Prince Saud al-Faisal; others in the Ministry cannot and will not make important decisions. Many Saudi institutions barely function. Despite having billions of dollars lavished on it over the course of several decades, and despite extensive training by American, British, and other Western forces, Saudi Arabia's military forces remain inept, even by regional standards.[30] Not surprisingly, the Saudi regime is frequently unable to respond to repeated requests for counterterrorism assistance. Lee Wolosky, a former Bush and Clinton administration staffer on the National Security Council, noted, "You have to be very careful what you ask for from the Saudis because if you have a list of more than one item you frequently don't get to the second."[31]

Another change for the United States is that it is operating primarily with countries with which it does not share close historical and immigration ties, a sharp contrast to Europe. Without these traditional links, an alliance can be difficult to sustain.[32] Although the Arab American (and Muslim) population of the United States is growing, it is a fraction of those descended from Europe, Asia, or Latin America. As a result, the relationship is not yet anchored in the strong person-to-person relationships and cultural understandings that shape other U.S. alliances.

The Curse of U.S. Help

The unpopularity of the United States has profound ramifications for U.S. counterterrorism efforts. Fearing that opposition groups will capitalize on a partnership with the United States, regimes will keep their American ties in the shadows.[33] In Pakistan, complaints have arisen even over the deployment of limited numbers of U.S. special operations forces.[34] As a result, the Musharraf government has attempted to keep the U.S. "footprint" light. Concerns over the readily observable support of the United States have some basis. A supportive regime may find itself in al-Qa'ida's crosshairs, when its neutrality would have allowed it to escape completely.

In contrast to the more visible cooperation inherent in conventional military alliances, allies' reluctance to associate publicly with the United States may be less of a problem for counterterrorism, an area where quiet cooperation is needed. Traditional alliances were formed as a visible deterrent to another state. When allies underplayed their cooperation with nations, they risked lowering their credibility. Counterterrorism alliances, however, are formed not to deter al-Qa'ida or other terrorist groups but rather to strike at them, which is better done without fanfare.

A New Alliance Architecture

The need for reconsidering the U.S. alliance structure is clear. Britain, France, Saudi Arabia, Egypt, and Turkey remain the important allies they were during the Cold War and immediate post–Cold War eras, though what we need from them has changed.

Countries important for the war on terrorism are in the Middle East, South Asia, and Africa. Because of their own experience with attacks from al-Qa'ida, Egypt, Saudi Arabia, and Turkey can offer considerable intelligence on jihadists. Saudi Arabia and Egypt in particular still face attacks from formidable terrorists. In the early 1990s, Egypt successfully beat back an Islamist insurgency. Turkey also fought Kurdish insurgents successfully, suggesting robust counterinsurgency capabilities. In different ways, all three countries have influence in the Muslim world: Turkey because of its model of successful modernization; Egypt because of its historic stature; and Saudi Arabia because of its oil wealth and links to Islamist ideologues.

Outside the Middle East, Britain and France have military forces capable of training other militaries in counterinsurgency. And both have excellent intelligence capabilities on the jihadist movement that go well beyond the activities within their borders.[35] Canada and Mexico are not essential for most aspects of the war on terrorism; nevertheless, they are vital for successful border control and thus essential for preventing terrorists from crossing U.S. borders. But neither country faces a serious problem from Islamist terrorists, and not surprisingly, their intelligence counterterrorism capabilities are limited. As a major economy, Canada can put pressure on state sponsors of terrorism, but Mexico's influence is far more limited. Nevertheless, if either country refused to cooperate with U.S. officials in policing their borders, jihadists could more easily penetrate the United States.

In contrast to Canada and Mexico, several allies in the pre–September 11 era—China, Germany, Japan, and South Korea—are less important for the struggle against al-Qa'ida. Their capabilities against al-Qa'ida are limited, particularly with regard to intelligence and influence in the Muslim world (and, indeed, China may be a negative because of its oppression of the Uighurs). Still, these states remain valuable (and several are vital) for a host of other U.S. security concerns. All four wield enough economic clout to sway potential state sponsors of terrorism.

New states have emerged as important allies, none of which were on the list before September 11: Afghanistan, Iraq, Jordan, Kenya, Mali, Nigeria, Somalia, and Yemen should be placed high on the list. Two of these, Afghanistan and Iraq, were once adversaries; Somalia was a failed state; and three—Kenya, Mali, and Yemen— were formerly of little concern. Nigeria received marginally more attention as a potential partner. Now many of these countries are at the heart of the struggle against terrorism. In particular, many face jihadist-linked violence and insurgencies, and several could plausibly succumb to the jihadists in the coming years. Most—Afghanistan, Kenya, Mali, Nigeria, and Somalia—are at the nexus where the Muslim and non-Muslim worlds meet. In almost all of these cases, alliance structures must now be built from scratch.

India, Indonesia, and Pakistan deserve particular attention, even though their pre-9/11 role in the U.S. alliance posture was limited. All three suffer from Islamist-linked unrest, and all are major players in the Muslim world. India, a predominantly Hindu country, has more Muslim citizens than do Iraq, Egypt, and Saudi Arabia combined. Indonesia is the world's largest Muslim country, and Pakistan one of its largest. All three play central roles in intelligence-gathering and counterinsurgency. The United States cooperated fitfully with all three countries during the Cold War; and in the years before September 11, improving relations with India became a priority of the Clinton and Bush administrations. But complicating our friendship with India and Pakistan is their own rivalry. These countries remain bitter enemies, and Islamabad's support for the jihadist movement is bound up in its strategy for countering India in Kashmir. Nevertheless, for counterterrorism purposes, these three countries have an importance similar to Germany during the Cold War: both are battlegrounds, and both are vital local partners who have considerable assets to offer.

Despite forging better ties, U.S. relations with these countries do not compare in closeness with that of the United States and key Cold War era allies such as Canada or Japan. The common historic and cultural ties that bound the United States and NATO members do not exist with countries such as Pakistan, Nigeria, Saudi Arabia, and Indonesia. More important, the common interests and perception of threat differ widely among the countries. Although all these countries run risks from jihadist terrorism (and the United States and Saudi Arabia share a common fear about Iran), other threats are quite different. Pakistan believes its overwhelming security menace is India, which Washington increasingly sees as an ally. Nigeria's goal is to be the preeminent force in western Africa, a goal the United States views largely with indifference. The United States also criticizes Nigeria's rampant corruption and communal violence. Pakistan is condemned for its support of Kashmiri insurgents against India, and so on. As a result of these differences, the high degree of standard operating procedures, shared decision-making arrangements, and other forms of institutionalization would be difficult to attain—a problem compounded by the limited institutional capacity of several of these states. Moreover, with the exception of Saudi Arabia, it would be surprising to see strong cooperation outside the immediate issue of striking jihadists.

Much of the war on terrorism, however, need not be institutionalized, and might even founder should this be a criterion for alliances. Many counterterrorism tasks are better accomplished in a bilateral setting. Counterinsurgency cooperation, for example, would not benefit from a large and integrated NATO-like organization, as the insurgent threat is almost invariably confined to one government. Intelligence-sharing is seldom done on a multilateral basis. Although in theory the more information pooled the better, in practice intelligence services tightly guard their sources and methods and water down the quality of what is shared as the circle of receiving countries widens.[36] In addition, much of the most important intelligence is related to law enforcement measures taken domestically, which many countries cannot share due to legal constraints. For similar reasons, the day-to-day intelligence and law enforcement efforts to take suspected terrorists off the streets are best done through overall U.S. coordination of various bilateral efforts. The more actors involved, the higher the likelihood of complicating local efforts.

For now, active state sponsorship is not a major problem with regard to al-Qa'ida, but passive sponsorship remains an issue. Because jihadist terrorists can shift bases to exploit lax controls in one country, common standards to deny terrorism fund-raising, recruitment, and other institutional necessities are necessary.[37] Here a system is needed that is quite different from that used in the Cold War. The comparison should not be to NATO, but rather to conventions used to combat money laundering. The actions demanded are far more limited than providing intelligence or military forces to hunt al-Qa'ida around the world, but the number of actors needed to fix this problem is large.

Helping weak states also requires widespread involvement, or at least the support of many wealthy states. Here the costs are far higher. The weak-state problem is one of collective action: many states have an interest in preventing a state from becoming a terrorist haven, but the sheer size of the task makes it difficult for any one outside state to take on the challenge. International institutions such as the World Bank are in theory dedicated to the problem of reconstruction, but their agendas are not linked to the challenge of counterterrorism. For this challenge, existing institutions can be redirected to focus more on countries at risk from terrorism without dramatically deviating from its mission of reconstruction. To provide this public good, the United States should work with other major powers to use their influence both to change institutions' agendas and to build their capacity for counterterrorism.

Better Relations with Europe[38]

Many Americans depict Europeans as appeasers, incapable of taking or unwilling to take forceful action, always ready to turn a blind eye to terrorists on their soil, or even to pay outrageous ransoms that go straight into the pockets of the bad guys. According to this view, even terrorist outrages such as the March 11, 2004, Madrid bombings or the July 2005 London bombings are unable to rouse the Europeans from their stupor. In the words of former U.S. deputy homeland security adviser Richard Falkenrath, "The relatively passive approach of the Spanish—and other Europeans—to the 3/11 attack on Madrid is stunning."[39]

Similarly, Europeans often seem to view the Americans as trigger-happy simpletons, engaged in a futile quest to protect against every conceivable threat, ready to bomb willy-nilly on the smallest provocation. From this perspective, Americans are losing the fight for the hearts and minds of the Islamic world even as they kill and capture specific terrorists. Even the normally diplomatic E.U. counterterrorism coordinator Gijs de Vries has asserted that the United States has relied too heavily on a military response and consistently undervalued political dimensions of counterterrorism. As a result, it unnecessarily increased the terrorists' recruitment pool and alienated many of its allies.[40]

Over time, U.S.-European strategic differences and the stereotypes they spawn will have painful policy consequences for the United States. The European continent is perhaps the heart of the struggle against terrorism. Contrary to the popular myth, neither the madrassas of Pakistan nor the slums of Cairo can churn out the shock troops of international terrorism. Rather, the graduates of the madrassa produce mostly functional illiterates who are essentially incapable of operating in the United States. On the other hand, many young and angry European Muslims are being radicalized. They are well educated; they often speak excellent English and hold passports valid for visa-free entry into the United States. Terrorism expert Marc Sageman points out that "in terms of the threat to us Americans, the threat comes from Europe."[41]

If the United States and Europe are unable to cooperate, the result will be either attacks in the United States or serious disruptions in transatlantic economic links. Commentators such as Reuel Marc Gerecht and members of Congress such as Representative James Sensenbrenner and Senator Diane Feinstein have already pointed to the possibility of suspending the Visa Waiver Program (VWP) unless European countries tighten their internal security procedures. The VWP allows about 13 million visa-free visits across the Atlantic each year. The U.S. Chamber of Commerce estimates that a suspension of the VWP would cost the U.S. economy $66 billion in tourism alone, even before taking into account the loss of business in other sectors.[42]

Rhetorically, the United States and Europe stand united in their opposition to terrorism. Governments on both sides of the Atlantic assert that counterterrorism cooperation is essential to solving the problem, and they join to condemn outrages such as the July 7, 2005, attacks in London. Day-to-day cooperation between the United States and most European countries proceeds apace and is often effective. Although officials on both sides have complaints, they are generally satisfied. The *Washington Post* reported in 2005 that the CIA's multinational counterterrorist intelligence center is located in Paris and has been a critical component of at least twelve operations, including the capture of one of al-Qa'ida's most important European operatives.[43] Indeed, during the contentious transatlantic crisis over Iraq, the practical necessity of counterterrorism cooperation helped preserve U.S. relations with Germany and France.

Sustaining effective cooperation requires an understanding of each side's interests and a respect for the strategies that follow from those interests. Viewed from that type of strategic perspective, the United States and Europe disagree on some basic issues, including the precise nature of the terrorist threat, the best methods for managing this threat, and the root causes of terrorism. It appears that neither understands nor accepts the other's positions.

In the United States and Europe, there are many internal divisions on the appropriate strategies for counterterrorism. Each European country has its own threats, each its own threat perceptions, and each its own approach to terrorism. There is no central government capable of unifying those strategies. But when compared (and contrasted) with the American approach, internal divisions in both Europe and the United States fade in significance.

These distinct approaches are not apparent in high-level strategy documents or day-to-day operations, but they can be seen in the policy disputes between the United States and Europe over counterterrorism. European officials and commentators, for example, have criticized the U.S. tendency to use the language of war, and in particular the neologism "war on terror."[44] Similarly, Americans and Europeans often disagree about what constitutes a legitimate political or charitable activity and what represents support for a terrorist group. Thus, according to former State Department counterterrorism coordinator Cofer Black, "Differing [U.S. and European] perspectives on the dividing line between legitimate political or charitable activity and support for terrorist groups similarly clouds the picture. The E.U. as a whole, for example, has been reluctant to take steps to block the assets of charities linked to Hamas and Hizballah, even though these groups engage in deadly terrorist attacks and their 'charitable' activities help draw recruits."[45] In February 2005, an E.U. official summed up this view: "This is a difficult issue because Hizballah has military operations that we deplore, but Hizballah is also a political party in Lebanon. Can a political party elected by the Lebanese people be put on a terrorist list? Would that really help deal with terrorism?"[46]

Theories abound over the cause for the dramatic differences between European and American reactions to terrorism. In truth, it boils down to this: the United States and Europe face different threats from Islamist terrorism. They have different perceptions of what that threat might be, even though they often face danger from the same source. And they have different tools in their arsenal for fighting terrorism. Not surprisingly, they also respond differently.

In April 2004, the al-Qa'ida core offered a compromise to Europe: withdraw support from U.S. policies in the Middle East and you can have a truce. The offer dramatizes the difference: the United States is the favored target, but Europe is easier to hit. Europeans immediately rejected this offer, but not simply out of solidarity with the United States.[47] They also did so because they understood that al-Qa'ida had little ability to carry out its side of the bargain and to constrain the groups that threaten Europe. Al-Qa'ida controls its own members, but not local groups such as the perpetrators of the Madrid attacks. Nonetheless, the truce offer demonstrates that Europe could, if it wished, accommodate the al-Qa'ida core. In short, Washington faces a wounded but global foe, constantly plotting to violate the sanctuary of the American homeland, whereas European states worry more about the Islamist ideology inspiring local groups.

The dangers faced from the Muslim population in Europe and from Muslims in the United States differ strikingly. The U.S. Muslim and Arab population is a small percentage of the overall population, and they are scattered throughout the country. The majority of Arab Americans are Christian, not Muslim.[48] These communities, moreover, are prospering; their average incomes are above the national average in the United States. Not surprisingly, there is little support for radicalism. Some suspected terrorists, such as the "Lackawanna Six,"[49] have even been exposed by their own communities.

The contrast with Europe could not be greater. Each European country has its own distinct mix of Arabs and Muslims. In the United Kingdom, most Muslims are from South Asia, in France most are from the Maghreb, and in Germany most come from Turkish-European Arabs. Each group in each country lives in a concentrated community. Many residents are impoverished and poorly integrated into the larger society. Youths from these communities often mingle with firebrand preachers. Many of the imams are themselves recent immigrants to Europe, and they bring old political grievances from the home country to foment unrest. Racism limits professional advancement and overall assimilation. The result is an explosive combination of social turmoil and political grievance.

The riots in France, the bombings in London and Madrid, the murder of filmmaker Theo Van Gogh in the Netherlands, and the furor over the Danish cartoons that satirized the Prophet Mohammad: all of this strife means that in a growing number of European countries the issue of Arab and Muslim integration is becoming perhaps the single largest domestic issue. The problem of Muslim unrest colors every social issue, from welfare reform to immigration to education. It has already become a far more important and more contentious issue than Hispanic integration in the United States. Dame Eliza Manningham-Butler, the director-general of Britain's Security Service, claimed in November 2006 that her officers were tracking two hundred networks and sixteen hundred individuals, a staggering figure that dwarfs the scale of the threat of jihadists on U.S. soil.[50]

The United States can pursue its counterterrorism objectives in isolation from other domestic issues, but in Europe that is simply not possible. Thus the Europeans perceive the threat in different ways. France's decision to force Muslim girls to remove their head scarves in school increased terrorists' hostility to France. France had gained some support from jihadists for its strong anti-U.S. stance during the Gulf War, but the veil issue generated tremendous hostility and was specifically mentioned by groups that kidnapped French journalists in Iraq. For France, however, the ban was part of a broader desire to uphold the principle of the separation of church and state rather than simple pandering to anti-immigrant voters. For better or for worse, these ideological and political issues trump counterterrorism.

Compared to any European country, the United States has a much broader range of interests and assets throughout the world. Not only does the United States face a global rather than domestic enemy, it also must worry about threats on targets abroad. Europe obviously has global interests and assets abroad, many of which are threatened (e.g., British targets in Istanbul), but the primary threat is either at home or against specific locations where each European country has historical or current ties: France particularly has interests in North Africa, especially Algeria, and Spain in Morocco.

The United States spends almost $500 billion annually on its military operations, which is more than twice as much as the states of the European Union combined. These raw numbers reflect a huge difference in military capability: only the United States can project power in a sustained way far from its borders. Of the European states, only the United Kingdom and France can show up without significant U.S. assistance, and they can do so only in limited numbers and for a limited period of time.

The U.S. intelligence budget alone, at about $44 billion a year according to the New York Times, is more than the entire defense budget of Germany and France and just under that of the United Kingdom.[51] Despite its well-noted weaknesses, U.S. intelligence has a far more significant presence in much of the world than the intelligence agencies of any European state. Imagery intelligence and signals intelligence are particular gaps for much of the world, as they require multibillion-dollar systems that few states other than the United States can afford. The United States also can marshal the world's intelligence services behind its counterterrorism campaign. The United States can address many of its terrorism problems by acting in cooperation with governments abroad. This involves sharing intelligence and rendering suspects to other countries, particularly in the Middle East, where "justice" systems are employed to keep them off the streets and to gain information.

This difference in power leads to divergent perspectives on the world. Much of Europe's modern history has been spent adjusting to the notion that the quarrels between peoples of faraway countries about which Europeans know nothing are not Europe's concern. The United States, in contrast, has a global perspective, in part because it can use force around the world and in part because it faces a global threat. The hard facts of geography and ability lie at the root of the United States' reliance on military power rather than any conceptual understanding of the causes of terrorism or appropriate strategies for countering it. All of the U.S. strategy documents profess that the country recognizes the need for "root cause" strategies that will win over the hearts and minds of potential terrorists, just as Europeans recognize the utility of military force in battling actual terrorists. Yet the United States' specific terrorism problem and its unmatched military capabilities lead naturally to a greater use of force.

Europeans would point out that possession of a hammer does not make the world into a nail, but from the United States' perspective, having a hammer allows you to make good use of nails.

Washington's vast military capability enables it to target terrorist sanctuaries abroad. Though clever and technologically savvy jihadists are able to exploit the Internet and take advantage of lax law enforcement to operate from Western countries, nothing beats having a sanctuary in which to openly plan, train, recruit, rest, and otherwise sustain the burden of running a major terrorist organization. The United States demonstrated the capability to destroy sanctuaries par excellence when it overthrew the Taliban regime in Afghanistan in 2001. In months, the United States was able to project force thousands of miles from its traditional allies, gaining bases and access by working with new allies in Central Asia and reinvigorating its alliance with Pakistan, something only a superpower could do with such speed and success. On arriving in Afghanistan, the United States bolstered the long-suffering domestic military opposition to the Taliban with airpower and special operations forces. Within weeks of the initial deployment, the Taliban crumbled as a government.[52]

In hindsight, the ease of this overthrow obscures the fact that for any other military force, this feat would have been impossible.

For Europe, a military effort like the U.S. overthrow of the Taliban is not an option. In the past, European powers have tried to target sanctuaries abroad, but their efforts were limited to feeble attempts at coercion or diplomatic suasion. In the 1980s, France launched a series of raids in Lebanon and even bombed Damascus after a series of Hizballah-linked attacks on French targets in Lebanon and France itself. Both efforts failed. In the 1990s, France tried to stop terrorism emerging from Algeria by pressing the Algerian government, a policy France abandoned when it realized it had little sway in Algiers. In both cases, the problem was not a lack of French will, but rather a lack of capabilities.

The contrast between the U.S. experience in Afghanistan and the French failures highlights the reason why the Europeans have made a virtue out of necessity, concentrating on fighting terrorism at home. Because their militaries are inadequate and their diplomacy weak, they rely more on using law enforcement and intelligence services to fight terrorism on their own soil rather than abroad.

Counterterrorism capability is feeble in E.U. institutions such as the European Council, Europol, and Eurojust. Coordination on counterterrorism within the European Union is almost nonexistent when it comes to actual arrests and intelligence-sharing against terrorists. Most European officials dismiss these E.U. institutions out of hand. One senior French intelligence official remarked that these "people talk but they don't act." A British official drily noted that the European Union does not do very much well, and that giving it responsibility for counterterrorism would only serve to dramatize its many weaknesses. The E.U. counterterrorism coordinator, appointed with much ceremony after the Madrid attacks in March 2004, has little power to compel cooperation. Myriad initiatives to strengthen these institutions have failed to produce major changes. One German terrorism expert cynically declared, "European counterterrorism will improve . . . after about three more attacks."[53]

Counterinsurgency Cooperation

Al-Qa'ida has many ties to local Islamist insurgencies, and countering the jihadist cause in general at times requires fighting them. Insurgencies enhance al-Qa'ida, extending its operations far beyond its own narrow location. Insurgent veterans are often at the core of the organization. Because al-Qa'ida can tap into these insurgencies for recruits, it can replenish its members as they are killed.[54] Insurgencies add legitimacy to al-Qa'ida. Muslims around the world endorse these local struggles—independence for Chechnya, opposition to Serb oppression in the Balkans, and so on—even though they might otherwise oppose al-Qa'ida's ideological agenda and its use of terrorism.

The long struggle against the Soviet Union in Afghanistan was a unifying experience for much of the al-Qa'ida leadership. Members vetted in struggles in the Balkans, Chechnya, Kashmir, and Iraq[55] also have coalesced into unified groups. Thus, fighting al-Qa'ida–linked insurgencies is a crucial task for U.S. military forces. In rare cases the United States has a central role to play in the battle, but it is important to add that whenever possible, counterinsurgency is best done by local forces.

When working with local forces, the United States should be able to speak the language and understand the culture. Armed with this knowledge, operatives can gather intelligence and avoid actions that gratuitously offend the population.[56] The United States can play a critical role in integrating intelligence; improving communications; and most important, honing the tactical skills of local forces. Still, the United States cannot expect to enter these countries as local saviors. Even with the best of intentions, foreigners can generate a nationalistic backlash among local citizens who otherwise feel little sympathy for the insurgents.[57] In Algeria, for example, the United States is working with the government against the

GSPC also known as al-Qa'ida of the Islamic Maghreb. The United States risks the possibility that the GSPC will turn against their own government to devote more resources against the United States. Significant numbers of U.S. troops destroy the legitimacy of local governments and allow the insurgents to claim that they are fighting for the people against outsiders—a damning criticism.

As the United States discovered in Iraq, many of its local allies are poorly trained and poorly motivated. In the face of enemy resistance, they often collapse. Basic training can transform a weak local force into a strong army. Novices can easily learn how to use a weapon, how to attack targets hiding in buildings, and how to coordinate small military units.

Counterinsurgency is almost invariably something done in cooperation with local allies. The most important military units will be special operations forces (SOF), which will train foreign troops to fight insurgents, liaise with local populations, help gather intelligence, and otherwise serve as the foundation for the military's broader efforts against terrorism and insurgency. The Defense Department has expanded the size of SOF since September 11 and should continue to increase the overall number.[58]

But counterinsurgency training should include more than just the allied army. It also should include police, intelligence services, and paramilitary forces. Just as it did in the Cold War, the United States can transform its mission from direct participation in jihadist conflict to direct support of local forces. During the Cold War, the United States fought Communist subversion in the developing world using its military forces to train local police. The result was a stronger police force that gave fragile political institutions time to develop.[59] This concept of "Foreign Internal Defense" (FID) can be resurrected and used once more against insurgencies.

Even when the United States finds direct intervention necessary, the locals must still assume the visible face of the fighting force, just as America is operating today in Afghanistan. To fight the Taliban, the United States has made a concerted effort to build the capacity of the Afghan security forces. The allied armies operate at the local level, working with various militias and tribal and village leaders, who are often responsible for day-to-day security for many communities.[60] This approach can be a model of how to engage today's enemy.

Direct counterinsurgency, in contrast to targeted killings or overt uses of the military, has few backers. After Vietnam, the American public was reluctant to get involved in foreign adventures, particularly those that smack of long, inconclusive struggles. And now the Iraq imbroglio has added to this reluctance. This lack of enthusiasm has at least one advantage: the United States will be forced to fight al-Qa'ida–linked insurgents by working indirectly through allied military forces, which fortunately is usually the best way to defeat them. The indirect approach also minimizes the American death toll.

The Rewards and the Perils of Intelligence Liaison

Because both al-Qa'ida and the broader jihadist movement have a presence in dozens of countries, tracking terrorists is impossible without strong liaison relationships: intelligence partnerships with other countries. Liaison services—which operate their own spies, interrogate their own detainees, and run their own wiretaps—offer the most important sources of intelligence on al-Qa'ida in particular and on jihadist groups in general. As then director of National Intelligence John Negroponte testified, "Most of al-Qa'ida's setbacks last year were the result of our allies' efforts, either independently or with our assistance," and he singled out Saudi Arabia, Australia, Canada, France, and the United Kingdom for praise.

Without local intelligence services, U.S. agencies would be helpless. That is not to criticize U.S. intelligence services. The vast majority of jihadist groups operate locally or at most regionally. Moreover, their logistical activities such as fund-raising, document forgery, and proselytizing are conducted on a local level. Local police and security forces have a keen interest in knowing the activities of potential jihadists on their own soil and can devote hundreds or thousands of people to this task. In contrast, the local CIA and FBI presence in the country may number only in the single digits. Because U.S. intelligence must derive all the necessary information from their local partners, it is essential that they maintain a strong liaison with them.

To gather this information, the U.S. services must spend more time improving the capacity of their partners than collecting information themselves (or "unilaterally," as the jargon has it). The *Washington Post* reported that the CIA runs more than two dozen "counterterrorism intelligence centers" (CTICs), where local services and the CIA work closely to monitor targets and disrupt any plots. As an inducement, the CIA will reward their collaborators with gifts ranging from SUVs to radios. They will also teach them surveillance techniques, hostage rescue, and other counterterrorism staples. In these CTICs, the CIA may provide a tip that an al-Qa'ida member is hiding locally, but the local services must take the ball from there. In addition to the CIA, the National Security Agency also is a vital partner in the CTICs and has worked to upgrade local services' ability to intercept communications—information that is then passed on to the United States.[61]

Liaison is particularly vital in remote parts of the world, be it the Afghan-Pakistani border or the wastelands of Yemen. Although such areas appear difficult to monitor, local inhabitants know them well. Strangers stand out in these tightly knit communities. The president of Mali, for example, told U.S. military officials that he could learn about radical activity in Mali's deserts because "Those regions are tribal. No one comes in without me knowing."[62]

If anything, the liaison's role is even more important once a decision is made to act. Pakistani agents, not American agents, finally apprehended Khalid Shaykh Mohammad. As one counterterrorism official told the *Washington Post* about operations in Pakistan, "the boot that went through the door was foreign."[63] Local law and local muscle are far more effective than a small number of U.S. officers breaking down a door. This is particularly so in areas such as the tribal regions of Yemen or the slums of Karachi, where U.S. officers cannot operate easily.

But liaison poses problems for counterterrorism: liaison services serve their own governments, not the people of the United States. In Qatar, where the U.S. government has an exceptionally strong relationship with the ruling Al Thani family, the government rebuffed the United States and probably informed KSM that he was about to be arrested. Despite their relationship with the United States, members of the Qatari royal family sympathized with the jihadist's cause, and the regime no doubt wanted to avoid inflaming jihadists by turning over a recognized figure.

Such rebukes remain a constant problem for the United States. Today one of the most important and problematic U.S. liaison relationships is with Pakistan's intelligence service. Much of the al-Qa'ida leadership is hiding in Pakistan, and the most important arrests so far have occurred in Pakistan, rendering Islamabad's support invaluable. Yet Pakistani intelligence sometimes stonewalls the United States. To compound the difficulties, Pakistani intelligence has ties to a broad range of jihadist groups that serve the interests of Islamabad, first by their presence in Afghanistan and second by fighting a proxy war against India in Kashmir. Not surprisingly, the government is deaf to U.S. calls to shut these groups down.

Pakistani intelligence surely hides important facts from the United States, and moles within their agencies probably pass information on to the terrorists. This problem is not limited to Pakistan. When the United States was tracking Amari Saifi through the Sahara, intelligence it gave to the government of Mali was later found in hands of Saifi's men.[64]

Recommendations for Working with Allies

Selecting new countries to align with, and deciding the type and degree of depth of new arrangements are only the beginning. For effective counterterrorism, the United States must restructure its foreign policy to make new alliances possible and to strengthen old ones. If it is to succeed in the war on terrorism, the most important thing the United States can do is identify and court new partners. Relations with India, Pakistan, and Indonesia should become top U.S. priorities. Also important are Afghanistan, Iraq, Kenya, Mali, Nigeria, Somalia, and Yemen. In only a few of these countries does the United States have embassies large enough to conduct the many tasks of diplomacy that include reaching out to all important government agencies, developing contacts among local elites, and wooing the broader population. Both the money and the personnel devoted to these countries should be increased. Secretary of State Rice's proposal to restructure State Department staffing to focus more on the developing world is a useful first step in this direction. Also vital is her proposal to increase the number of posts outside capital cities to ensure the U.S. presence in different parts of a country.[65] In Nigeria, for example, the United States needs to focus on Muslim parts of the country, to track any possible growth in jihadist ideology. This effort requires going to parts of Nigeria traditionally of little concern to U.S. diplomats.

The United States also should actively work to restart the Israeli-Palestinian peace process, which will assist the formation of alliances in the Middle East. The perception is almost universal that the United States endorses Israel's occupation of the West Bank and Gaza Strip and condones Israeli mistreatment of the Palestinians. The United States must try to combat the increasingly widespread perception that it will support Israel's position uncritically. Israel should be encouraged to accept the recommendations of the Mitchell Commission.[66]

The United States also must make clear that it will differentiate among terrorist groups. Every government has an incentive to tie their local struggle to the U.S. effort against al-Qa'ida. The United States should set a high bar for how it defines an al-Qa'ida–linked insurgency. Even areas such as Chechnya, where the jihadist presence is real but limited, should be approached with extreme caution.[67] Associating every terrorist or every Islamist cause with al-Qa'ida only adds to the movement's luster and creates new enemies for the United States.

Problems with America's European allies deserve particular scrutiny. Policymakers on both sides of the Atlantic must recognize that differences do not necessarily arise from European cowardice or American arrogance but arise from legitimate differences in the nature of the threat each country faces and its ability to deal with this threat. Until legitimate differences are accepted, current levels of cooperation are at risk because the cooperation has so little political foundation. Sudden revelations about CIA prisons in

Europe or U.S. rendition practices can threaten the United States and European capacity to cooperate in capturing terrorism suspects abroad.

With the recognition of differences comes recognition of common interests. Washington should expect European states to focus on the internal enemy. If the Europeans fail to apprehend the enemy, the radicals will kill Americans in Europe and in the United States, and then go on to innocent people in England, France, Spain, or whatever other country they choose to target. Similarly, Europeans should support the United States when the United States confronts terrorist sanctuaries in Afghanistan and Iraq (today), or if it renders terrorists to the Middle East. Acknowledgment of legitimate differences between and among countries allows for a more nuanced treatment of the threat. Algerian jihadists operating from the Maghreb and from France should be treated differently from Egyptian jihadists who are part of the al-Qa'ida internationale.

Outside of the European context, restructuring U.S. bases also is sensible.[68] Large, permanent bases may inflame nationalism in several countries, yet they offer little immediate benefit for the war on terrorism. A good first step would be to develop smaller bases that can act as jumping-off points in Eastern Europe, Central Asia, and East and West Africa.[69] When possible, these bases should be unobtrusive. The value of these bases for counterterrorism, however, is far less than the worth of the overall support of the local regime's intelligence and security apparatus. Efforts to secure military bases should defer to these concerns when necessary.

Given the vital role allies play, improved intelligence-sharing is essential for success against terrorists. But because intelligence is easily compromised, agencies generally oppose sharing sensitive information with multiple partners. Not surprisingly, the United States has moved fitfully on intelligence-sharing even though Washington has greatly expanded the number of partnerships and the volume of information exchanged. Some allies complain, however, that this sharing is a one-way street (a complaint U.S. officials also make). Russia is one country that has criticized the willingness of the United States to share useful intelligence.[70]

Information-sharing with allies reflects a Cold War counter-intelligence environment in which a highly skilled adversary sought to exploit any weakness. Al-Qa'ida, too, is skilled, but its offensive counterintelligence capabilities are a shadow of the former Soviet Union's. Perhaps more important, al-Qa'ida is likely to exploit information gained from public sources such as newspaper articles and court records. Information-sharing procedures should be loosened to reflect this different counterintelligence environment; in contrast to the past, guarding against a spy among our ranks is less important than ensuring that critical information does not leak.

To ensure the quality of the intelligence the allies provide, counterintelligence against allied security services is vital. Washington must be sure that allies are on board and that the information being passed to Washington is complete and accurate. It is vital for the United States to know if allied services are withholding information or, even worse, if they have been penetrated by al-Qa'ida.[71] A Jordanian journalist reports Saudi Arabia's past attempts to capture or kill bin Ladin may have failed because jihadist sympathizers within Pakistani intelligence tipped off bin Ladin.[72] Because the United States has limited collection capabilities of its own, it is particularly important to use caution in countries where it relies primarily on allies for intelligence.

The successful penetration of a terrorist group by a U.S.-controlled agent would be a tremendous intelligence coup and might avert attacks or even lead to the disruption of a major network. If, however, a unilateral operation on an ally's territory is detected, it would arouse anger that would jeopardize overall cooperation, which is far more important than unilateral operations. Given the current high degree of popular animosity toward the United States, the ally may respond by expelling U.S. officials, curtailing the flow of information, or even publicly criticizing the United States and disrupting cooperation on other issues. Given that allies tend to have far more operations (and more effective ones) within their own countries than the United States is capable of mounting there, the risk of unilateral operations backfiring is high. Such operations should be focused on countries where the government is providing minimal cooperation and should concentrate first on the local intelligence service, which is likely to withhold information.

The United States can bolster allied counterterrorism and counterinsurgency capabilities through programs dedicated to foreign internal security assistance. Many countries have weak security services and cannot control their own borders. In Africa and the former Soviet Union, many governments have poor and corrupt militaries and security services but must patrol vast borders.

The United States should greatly expand the scope and scale of security assistance programs. Allied intelligence and security forces are force multipliers: small U.S. investments pay huge dividends. Such programs were robust during the 1950s and 1960s, as Washington worked with local security forces against communism.[73] However, they were allowed to lapse in the latter period of the Cold War and in its aftermath. These programs increased after September 11, but they should now be massively expanded.[74]

Conclusions

Ultimate success depends not only on fostering new alliances, but also on managing them in the years to come. Such an effort may prove problematic for the United States, however; power disparities make it tempting to dismiss allies' concerns. Many of the potential compromises that must be made are unsavory, and Washington may have to countenance a range of brutal behavior that it would ordinarily condemn. The choices are not easy.

Money can smooth the path to managing an alliance. Money can work to the U.S. advantage, even more so than during the Cold War era. The vast majority of key allies are developing world nations with corrupt governments. An infusion of cash can help these regimes placate their populations and bolster economic growth. The United States can offer rewards and punishments to encourage participation and pay more of the costs of the alliance. As repugnant as it might seem to American citizens, the United States will be able to bribe local politicians to maintain the alliance.

As policymakers take on these burdens and weigh these changes, they must recognize that the United States has many interests, several of which are as important as counterterrorism. Just because Japan is not a major player in counterterrorism does not mean that Japan is no longer a vital ally. Yet if counterterrorism is the top or a leading U.S. priority, dramatic shifts are in order. Reforming U.S. foreign policy and making profound changes to the U.S. military, intelligence services, and other institutions will take money, time, and leadership. Most important, it will take a degree of consensus among the American people. Change this drastic will require decades of effort and will involve multiple administrations with different ideologies. A truly profound transformation, however, will require U.S. leaders of both parties to bridge these political shifts with a common vision.

9

The Iraq Dilemma

The career of Abu Musab al-Zarqawi, whom U.S. forces killed in June 2006, offers a fascinating but troubling glimpse into the future of the jihadist movement. Zarqawi founded and led the Monotheism and Jihad Group, which in October 2004 became the Al-Qa'ida Organization in the Land of the Two Rivers (or Al-Qa'ida of Iraq). A Jordanian by birth, Zarqawi traveled to Afghanistan in 1989 to fight the Soviets. He became truly radicalized, however, when he returned to Jordan in the 1990s to organize a jihadist cell and was quickly put in prison. In the book *Al-Zarqawi: The Second Generation of Al-Qa'ida,* Jordanian writer Fu'ad Husayn notes that jail was a formative experience for Zarqawi.[1]

Though he detested the United States, Zarqawi never fully accepted bin Ladin's focus on the far enemy. Much of Zarqawi's efforts were directed toward fomenting dissent against other Muslims. Husayn notes that the group's prison leader regularly "excommunicated everyone who failed to rule in harmony with the Islamic shari'ah." Zarqawi also viewed local regimes, particularly those near his home country of Jordan, as top targets. Although released from prison in 1999, Zarqawi quickly returned to terrorism. Al-Qa'ida helped provide start-up money for Zarqawi's organization in Jordan, which tried to bomb various hotels and tourist sites during the millennium celebrations in 2000. Zarqawi himself went to Afghanistan to escape and continue to plot attacks. After the

Taliban fell, he went to Iraq, where he correctly surmised that the Americans would strike next.

In Iraq, Zarqawi stood out from other leaders, in part because of the brutality of his tactics. Zarqawi may have personally beheaded his American hostage, Nicholas Berg, who had been working in Iraq. Al-Qa'ida leaders pushed Zarqawi to abandon this and similar tactics, unpopular even among many Islamists. Inadvertently, however, U.S. condemnations placed Zarqawi into the world's eye, which reaped dividends for him as a leader. His formerly obscure activities became front-page news and thus drew the attention of the U.S. government. Husayn claims that because of U.S. attention, "Every Arab and Muslim who wished to go to Iraq for jihad wanted to join al-Zarqawi."

Though Zarqawi worked with al-Qa'ida for many years, he did not formally join the organization until October 2004. Then he changed the group name to Al-Qa'ida of Iraq to reflect its new orientation. Zarqawi was an independent operator, and by personality did not fit in well with al-Qa'ida, which stressed teamwork. In addition, he held different views on appropriate targets, believing that local regimes were more important targets than the United States. He also saw the Shi'a as apostates and priority targets. Husayn notes that Zarqawi claimed that "Shiism had no connection with Islam whatsoever" and in September 2005 reportedly declared "all-out war" on them.[2]

Zarqawi was not an Iraqi nationalist and saw the anti-U.S. struggle as a way of achieving several frightening objectives. Zarqawi genuinely hated the United States and the West in general. Iraq, for him, was simply a theater in which he could kill with abandon. But Zarqawi also wanted to kill the Shi'a. Killing them in Iraq would prevent the success of U.S.-led reconstruction and, more importantly for him, fulfill a divine duty of killing apostates. Finally, Zarqawi saw Iraq as a launching pad for spreading the jihadist fire to Jordan, Saudi Arabia, and, of course, Israel.

For al-Qa'ida, the merger with Zarqawi proved to be a lifeline. Al-Qa'ida was essentially gaining a franchise in the hub of the global jihad at a time when the organization was weak around the world. "Al-Qa'ida's operations and military activities were intermittent,"

Husayn contends. "However, following the pledge of allegiance of Abu-Mus'ab [Zarqawi] and his group, Al-Qa'ida is there every day and every hour." Al-Qa'ida also gained access to more recruits from the "Bilad al-Sham" area (Jordan, Syria, and Palestine) that Zarqawi drew from, in contrast to its traditional links to Saudi Arabia, Yemen, and Egypt.

For Zarqawi, the merger also had many benefits. Afterward, he obtained access to both al-Qa'ida's recruiting networks and, perhaps more important, received financial and logistical assistance, particularly from the Persian Gulf. The link with al-Qa'ida also legitimated Zarqawi, allowing him to associate his cause with that of bin Ladin, a hero for many in the militant community.

Zarqawi had come under considerable fire in jihadist circles for his indiscriminate attacks on civilians, and the Shi'a in particular. Abu Muhammad al-Maqdisi, who was with Zarqawi in jail and was seen by many jihadists as a learned man, issued statements praising Zarqawi's goals but criticizing him for killing noncombatants in Iraq, noting, "It is better to leave a thousand atheists than to shed the blood of one Muslim." To make his point even clearer, he called on Zarqawi to recognize that "Mujahedin should discriminate between Shiite citizens and fighters."[3]

Several letters to Zarqawi from Ayman al-Zawahiri—bin Ladin's second-in-command—suggest the tension in the relationship. Zawahiri chastised Zarqawi for beheadings and other unpopular tactics while asking him to send money. While Zarqawi toned down some of his most horrific tactics, his followers in the most important jihadist franchise in the world are still marching to the beat of their own drummer.

Zarqawi did not live long enough to see what may prove to be one of his most enduring successes—the growth of the domestic jihadist movement among Iraqis proper. When the initial unrest began against the United States after the occupation began in 2003, almost none of the Iraqis shooting at U.S. soldiers had jihadist beliefs. Over time, however, jihadist ideas have gained influence, and today many of the Sunni insurgents in Iraq who are jihadists are native-born Iraqis. Thus both in Iraq and outside it, the invasion has made bin Ladin and the broader movement stronger.

This was not supposed to happen. Toppling Saddam Hussein's regime was to have ushered in an era of prosperity for Iraq and put Osama bin Ladin and his followers on the run. Instead, the tables have turned. Today Iraq is torn by crime, plagued by a vicious insurgency, and devoid of competent government and basic services. Although the Bush administration billed the war on Iraq as part of the effort to crush al-Qa'ida, the war reinvigorated an emasculated movement ignominiously thrust out of Afghanistan. Bin Ladin and his followers have skillfully exploited the war to bolster their claim that the United States seeks to subjugate the Muslim world, a perception that is increasingly strong throughout the Middle East and among Muslims around the world. Strife in Iraq continues without end in sight, while the human and financial costs to the United States and its allies mount. Military planners and budget analysts question the country's ability to sustain its massive presence in Iraq, let alone increase its forces to meet the daunting challenges. With each car bombing and kidnapping, critics urging the withdrawal of troops grow more and more vociferous.

Every additional day that the United States remains in Iraq is a boon for al-Qa'ida and the broader jihadist movement. On the other hand, a U.S. withdrawal that left Iraq in chaos would also be a boon for al-Qa'ida.

Both proponents and critics of the war regularly reinterpret how the success of the U.S. occupation of Iraq should be defined; each redefinition has profound implications for the broader struggle against jihadist terrorism.

How then should the United States solve this conundrum? Victory in Iraq cannot be judged entirely or even primarily in light of U.S. efforts against al-Qa'ida. Added to the mix are the importance of a stable oil-rich region, the human costs of a massive civil war, and the burden that the United States must bear in the eyes of the world for the carnage it unleashed.

But Iraq, as President Bush has declared, has indeed become a "central front" in the war on terrorism.[4] This "central front" exists in no small part because of administration policies, which have created a jihadist problem in Iraq where none existed. The problem is that outright victory appears unattainable, but defeat and withdrawal are exceptionally costly. If the United States will not pay the costs, it must come to grips with the painful reality that it should set its sights lower. A more limited strategy of drawing down U.S. forces and preparing for the spillover of the civil war in Iraq, has many shortcomings. However, it is less costly than a complete withdrawal and is far more sustainable than the current U.S. approach.

Developing a long-term Iraq policy is vital. From a counterterrorism point of view, the problem of Iraq does not go away if the United States abandons the country to strife. Indeed, in many ways it would get worse. By the end of 2006, the conflict had already generated almost 2 million refugees who could spread instability and terrorism to neighboring states. In Iraq, jihadists from around the world are learning new skills, forging new networks, and otherwise training to fight the next war as well as to defeat America and its Iraqi allies.

Iraq and the Sunni Jihadist Movement

The insurgents number at least twenty thousand—the number becomes well over a hundred thousand when various local militias are included—but they are far from a unified movement. Fighters include groups such as former regime elements, members of the Baath Party angered by the loss of their perks and privileges, foreign Sunni jihadists, domestic Sunni jihadists, Iraqi nationalists opposed to foreign occupation, and various Shi'a groups as well as common criminals. These groups are further divided by tribe and leadership divisions, as well as competition for a share of the black market.

Since the U.S. occupation of Iraq began in 2003, foreign jihadists have flocked to Iraq, making it a new center of jihad—and in the process, they have transformed the nature of the anti-U.S. Iraqi resistance. Iraq's insurgency is concentrated in the Sunni Arab parts of Iraq, though much of the rest of the country is convulsed in civil war. Their motivations are varied: some fight because they lost power and influence in the post-Saddam Iraq, while others are angered at the presence of foreign troops on Iraqi soil. Originally, only a small portion of the insurgency consisted of jihadists who took up arms in the name of God. Yet these foreign jihadists are capitalizing on, and exacerbating, the strife in Iraq. Between a thousand and two thousand foreign fighters are in Iraq, and they carry out most of the suicide bombings. Most are from Arab countries, with Saudi Arabians comprising the lion's share of those killed.

Much of the violence today in Iraq is a civil war between or among different Iraqi communities (and, frequently, within them, as all the major communities have rivalries and tribal divisions). The jihadists also are at the forefront of efforts to foment a sectarian war between Iraq's Shi'a and Sunni populations. They hate the Shi'a and also believe that spreading sectarian violence is a way to undermine the government. The jihadists have attacked Shiite shrines, pilgrims, political leaders, and other civilian targets.[5]

The United States has tried to isolate the jihadists from other parts of the Iraqi resistance in an attempt to divide the enemy. Then director of National Intelligence Negroponte testified that jihadists' brutal actions and heavy-handed style have led them to conflict with their erstwhile allies, leading some Sunni tribal and nationalist groups to reach out to the government.[6] This strategy may be too late. In a 2006 report, the International Crisis Group finds that "virtually all [Iraqi Sunni resistant groups] adhere publicly to a blend of Salafism and patriotism."[7]

Shifting the direction of an insurgency by hijacking local grievances is a classic al-Qa'ida pattern. In Afghanistan, Kashmir, Chechnya, and now Iraq, the organization has sent fighters and other forms of support to assist Muslim insurgencies that typically began for nationalistic or ethnic reasons. Over time, the salafist strand of thinking crept in and began to shape the resistance— something well under way in Iraq, which had no domestic jihadist movement before the United States invaded.

As the insurgency coalesces around Iraqi nationalism and Islamic extremism, it also has become far more sophisticated in waging the war of ideas. In 2004 and 2005, the insurgents regularly fought openly among themselves. They also used such unpopular tactics as public beheadings and attacking voters, including Sunni voters supporting candidates who were sympathetic to resistance groups.[8] Today their public information campaign is much more coherent:

they lambaste the United States and its local allies and deny sectarian violence.

The U.S. war in and occupation of Iraq have benefited al-Qa'ida in many ways. As long as the United States is in Iraq, al-Qa'ida has the best recruiting tool it could wish for. As Michael Scheuer, formerly head of the CIA's bin Ladin unit, sarcastically notes, "If Osama was a Christian—it's the Christmas present he never would have expected."[9] In the heart of the Muslim world, with more than a hundred thousand U.S. troops occupying the country for a long time, Iraq has become the focus of the media throughout the world and especially the Middle East. Arab and Muslim communities are united in their belief that the U.S. intervention is an attack on Islam and an attempt to subjugate a powerful Arab state.

Not surprisingly, Iraq is at the center of the jihadists' fundraising and recruitment efforts. A 2006 National Intelligence Estimate found that "The Iraq conflict has become the 'cause célèbre' for jihadists, breeding a deep resentment of U.S. involvement in the Muslim world and cultivating supporters for the global jihadist movement."[10] Fighting the United States is tremendously popular in radical and even mainstream Islamist circles. Equally important for al-Qa'ida, it is proof of the "far enemy" theory it promulgates: for many Muslims, the conflict overshadows the misdemeanors or even high crimes of their own governments and convinces them that the proper focus for opposition should be faraway Washington.

Within the broader salafist community, Iraq has become an enormous public relations boon to al-Qa'ida. Many salafists condemn al-Qa'ida for being excessively violent and political, and in particular condemn its willingness to declare jihad at the drop of a hat. Even shaykhs critical of al-Qa'ida, however, see the struggle in Iraq as a legitimate defensive jihad. This is true even in countries that are close allies of the United States. In November 2004, twenty-six leading Saudi clerics wrote an "open letter to the Iraqi people" calling for a defensive jihad against the United States in Iraq.[11]

Iraq has fostered a new brand of jihad. It has been transformed into a country where budding insurgents gain combat experience and forge lasting bonds that will enable them to work together in the years to come, even if they leave Iraq. Former French defense official Alexis Debat contends that jihadists seek "to turn Iraq into what Afghanistan was before autumn 2001: a public relations windfall for their ideologues, a training ground for their 'rookies,' and even a safe-haven for their leadership."[12] And Iraq is becoming just such a haven. Indeed, it is no small irony that some of those who launched attacks on U.S. and Afghan forces in Afghanistan appear to have trained in Iraq.

For now, the jihadists are focused on victory in Iraq, which they define not only as ousting the Americans but also as destroying the Iraqi regime and either murdering or subordinating Iraq's Shi'a majority. In a media description of their Iraq strategy, jihadists note that their immediate goal is to drive a wedge between the U.S. Army and its local allies. Soon afterward, they say, the American occupiers will flee with their tails between their legs, and the jihadists will make Iraq a true Islamic republic. Jihadists would then launch the second part of their plan, where Iraq would serve as a base for attacking the country's neighbors such as Jordan and Syria. With that stage of the war complete, the final war will be waged on both the United States and Israel.

Problems with Iraq beyond Counterterrorism

U.S. efforts against jihadists in Iraq are bound up in the broader campaign to bring peace and good government to Iraq. This campaign has suffered frustration after frustration and at this point appears unsustainable.

Since conventional military operations ended in May 2003, the United States and its allies have conducted direct operations against Sunni (and, less frequently, Shi'a) insurgents and militias and foreign jihadists as part of an overall program to provide security for Iraq. The U.S. strategy appears to be as follows: Once Iraq enjoys a modicum of security, the United States can pass much of the responsibility for running the country to a legitimate civilian government duly elected by the Iraqi people. While the legitimate government is being established, coalition forces are training Iraqi security forces. As these forces become larger and more capable, the United States hopes they will increasingly take responsibility for policing, counterinsurgency, and border security missions. If all goes well, in several years the United States would be able to withdraw.

The U.S. failure to achieve these goals is multidimensional: the scale of the violence is wide and growing, the government of Iraq lacks legitimacy, democracy is troubled, and jihadists are flourishing. Communal violence escalated significantly after the bombing of the "Golden Mosque" in Samarra: the long-feared civil war became manifest to all. By the fall of 2006, Iraq had plunged into a brutal civil war that was far more lethal than the anti-U.S. insurgency.

Insurgent violence was particularly concentrated in Sunni areas, but almost all of Iraq's cities have been affected by communal strife. Shi'a militias are now taking revenge on Sunnis for attacks by Sunni insurgents, even when these Sunnis had nothing to do with the fighting. Outside experts warn that currently peaceful Kurdish cities may erupt.[13] Mosul, Kirkuk, and other cities with a mix of Arabs and Kurds may suffer communal violence due to property disputes and rising ethnic tensions.

Concurrent with the insurgency in parts of Iraq are problems of a "failed state" in other regions. For decades, Iraqis had learned to turn to Saddam Hussein's regime for food, medical care, law enforcement, and other basics. When the regime collapsed, Iraqis turned to local warlords or tribal leaders. The organs of the state, never strong, declined further.[14] Civil violence further undercuts the credibility of the state.

High on the list of Iraqi concerns is crime. Crime in Iraq has soared, and U.S. government polling of Iraqis consistently shows street crime to be of much higher concern than terrorist or insurgent violence.[15] Many Iraqis are afraid to leave their homes to go to work and to send their children (particularly their daughters) to school. Stopping crime requires a government that can be trusted, a large and competent police force, and a broader criminal justice system of courts and prisons; all three are lacking in Iraq today. To fill the void, local tribal leaders, militia groups, or others who claim to offer security are assuming control.[16]

Adding to the sheer scale of these problems were the earlier, misguided U.S. attempts to solve the impasse. In the early years of the occupation, the United States focused on fighting fixed engagements rather than on day-to-day security for Iraqis. Sensible insurgents flee a fixed battle, blending into the population and reemerging only when the bulk of the force is gone. In Fallujah in April 2004, most of the senior foreign jihadists and insurgency leaders left well in advance of the U.S. military operation. Providing day-to-day security would require dispersing U.S. forces into neighborhoods where they could act as police and prevent insurgents from intimidating locals. The United States avoided this action, and much of the U.S. presence was not in regular contact with many Iraqis as they went about their ordinary lives. Civilian administrators engaged Iraqis in the "Green Zone" in Baghdad but rarely ventured outside it. Military forces, when they were not patrolling, remain largely in compounds.

An emphasis on force protection is understandable and in many senses laudable: political and military leaders are concerned about the lives of U.S. soldiers, and additional deaths might weaken domestic support for the U.S. action. Unfortunately, this short-term calculation has long-term costs. The insurgents rarely engage U.S. forces directly. Instead, they look for areas where the U.S. deployment is weak and terrorize Iraqis there. Because there is no lasting U.S. presence in most areas, locals must cooperate with insurgents or risk savage reprisals when insurgents return. Many Iraqis experience American "security" only when it zooms past in an armored column with guns pointed out the windows. Even though relatively few Iraqis want the insurgents and militia thugs to win, they can intimidate anyone who might cooperate with the United States and the Iraqi government. Also, in an attempt to protect its own forces, U.S. troops often have limited contact with local Iraqis, which in turn makes it hard to cultivate sources for intelligence.[17]

So far, U.S. efforts to train Iraq's army and police force have met with at best limited success. Insurgents recognize this weakness and focus their attacks on Iraqis who serve in the police, the army, and as translators. In other words, the insurgents pursue anyone who assists coalition forces or enables the new government to establish itself.

The government of Iraq also lacks legitimacy in the eyes of many Iraqis, particularly Sunni Arabs. Once favored by Saddam's regime, in a democracy, the Sunnis have become an ethnic minority voting bloc. Some Sunnis resent their loss in influence. Although the Sunni Arabs comprise only 20 percent of the population, they can thwart any peace Iraq might hope to enjoy. The rampant crime and communal violence demonstrate that the government cannot protect its citizens. As key ministries and portfolios are often controlled by one community or even one militia, the government is often seen as a tool for rival groups rather than as an impartial arbiter that helps all citizens equally.

The failure to deliver economic stability has further weakened the legitimacy of the United States and the interim government. Unemployment is 30 to 40 percent, and malnutrition rates have doubled since the war began.[18] Foreign capital is understandably reluctant to invest in a strife-torn and politically turbulent country. The unrealistic expectations of most Iraqis compounded these problems, as they hoped that Saddam's removal would quickly usher in an era of economic renewal despite the vast structural problems of Iraq's economy and the years of devastation that sanctions wrought under Saddam.

Although the elections represent dramatic progress over Iraq's dictatorial past, democracy's future is unclear. Major factions disagree over many core issues such as the extent of power sharing, the role of women, the proper powers of the federal government, and the pace of elections. Sunnis readily cry foul, claiming that the system is stacked against them. The new leadership has yet to tackle knotty questions related to minority rights and the degree of power sharing among Iraq's major groups (or, in the case of the Shi'a, which faction will emerge dominant)—questions that fuel much of the strife.[19] The country's pervasive insecurity has further hindered efforts to build a political system. The new regime also still depends on the United States for security, diminishing its standing among nationalist Iraqis.

The cost of this mixed record is considerable, though it is far from unsustainable. As of May 2007, more than 3,300 Americans have died, with far more wounded. Iraqi casualty figures, data for which are often limited and conflicting, are conservatively more than ten times as high, even excluding those killed in street crime.

Many estimates put the figure at well over 100,000 Iraqi deaths, and one, published in the medical journal *Lancet,* puts the number at more than 600,000. In dollars, the United States has spent several hundred billion on the war and occupation so far, with the U.S. effort in Iraq running close to $100 billion a year at current levels. This excludes the long-term but indirect costs of health care for those wounded in Iraq, lost productivity from reservists sent to Iraq, and other important but less measurable costs that put the total dollar figure at more than $1 trillion.

For the U.S. military, particularly the U.S. Army, the strain is enormous and possibly unsustainable without significant changes. To provide additional security for key events such as elections, the United States has deployed well over 100,000 troops to Iraq since the end of conventional hostilities in May 2003, with troop levels at times as high as 160,000. Military readiness for other missions has suffered, as regular forces spend much of their time deployed in Iraq rather than training for high-intensity combat. The United States has resorted to a host of methods to keep the momentum going. It has called up the individual ready reserve, requiring troops to stay deployed even after their term of service is done. It has halted individual reassignments outside of Iraq until the unit as a whole is ready to leave. Such measures and extended deployments pose challenges for recruitment and retention, particularly for the National Guard and the reserves.[20]

The strain on the force is even bigger than that suggested by simple numbers. Counterinsurgency and occupation require a different mix of troops than do conventional military operations. Armored divisions, the core of the U.S. Army, are not terribly useful for rooting out insurgents mingled among the population or for winning over local populations, though they are currently conducting such operations. Special operations forces, light infantry, military police, and civil affairs officers are often the most important forces in the field. These troops, many of whom are also required in Afghanistan or in other fronts in the struggle against al-Qa'ida, are in particularly short supply.

The cost of all this goes beyond Iraq. Diplomatically, world opinion of the United States is at its nadir. The U.S. occupation of

Iraq and ongoing counterinsurgency have fostered an image of the United States as an oppressive power bent on killing Muslims. Polls indicate opinion of the United States ranges from poor in many Western European countries to abysmal in most countries in the Muslim world.[21] Arab world satellite television stations regularly juxtapose footage of Americans fighting insurgents in cities such as Fallujah with Israeli soldiers attacking Palestinians in the West Bank and the Gaza Strip. The unpopular war and the less popular occupation have lessened trust in the United States around the world. Thus extraditions, renditions, and other tools of counterterrorism that depend on allied cooperation are much harder to employ. Lamenting the effects of this disaster on the war on terror, Scheuer declared, "America remains bin Laden's only indispensable ally."[22]

The Consequences of a U.S. Withdrawal

Given the many problems with the current U.S. approach, the case for leaving Iraq appears strong. If the United States is already failing despite its large-scale presence today, is there value in continuing these sacrifices? By withdrawing, the hemorrhaging of lives and dollars would stop—at least on the American side. The legitimacy of the new regime also might grow initially, as it would no longer be viewed as a quisling government propped up only by American power. Muslims who object to the U.S. occupation of one of the historic centers of the Muslim world also would be appeased, removing at least one source of opposition to the United States. Resources in Iraq could be used to fight bin Ladin and affiliated jihadists in Afghanistan, Pakistan, and elsewhere, while the constant irritation in the relationship between the United States and its European allies would be removed. A lasting success would require far more U.S. troops deployed for many years—and even then the situation may not improve substantially. Moreover, domestic will for staying in Iraq is diminishing. If, as I believe, victory cannot be attained, reducing the U.S. presence is justified, but it is important to factor the costs to the U.S. struggle against al-Qa'ida into this equation.

The first blow would be to U.S. credibility. Foreign jihadists would tout a pullout as a victory, contending that the United States left under fire. Already, bin Ladin has taunted the United States, declaring that it is "embroiled in the swamps of Iraq."[23] Even though their actual role in the fighting was minimal, foreign jihadists made similar claims with regard to the Soviets in Afghanistan and the United States in Somalia. Iraq is a far bigger conflict than any the United States previously waged in the Middle East. And because jihadists have played such a significant part in Iraq, they would declare, with much fanfare, that our departure was a major victory for their cause.

Bin Ladin's "success" would prove to the faithful that the United States would withdraw whenever it faces considerable resistance. Jihadists thus would be encouraged to foment unrest against other governments they oppose and against U.S. interventions, such as in Afghanistan and the Balkans. The lesson would be clear: push the United States and it will fold.[24]

Iraq itself also would suffer tremendously from a U.S. withdrawal. Iraqi government forces would find themselves outgunned, and cooperation with government opponents or wholesale defections would be likely. Already the lack of security has led local communities to turn to warlords for protection and revenge; without the presence of U.S. forces, this trend would become the dominant force. Violence, particularly in ethnically mixed areas, would grow even worse. The Kurds, who have the most organized indigenous military force in Iraq, would probably push for greater autonomy or even independence, possibly drawing Turkey into the fracas.

Jihadists will seek to foment a civil war, both because it would hasten a U.S. departure and because of their hatred for secular and Shi'a forces. They can be counted on to fuel the fire of extremism, making it difficult for moderate voices to be heard. Tens or even hundreds of thousands more Iraqis may die, and even more would become refugees.

The hopes for democracy, and possibly even for a unified Iraqi state, would dim in the absence of the security provided by the United States. The elected government would have no muscle to enforce its decrees. The warlords, not the politicians, would hold the ultimate sway. Rival factions would not trust each other to honor long-term treaties. Kurds, for example, might fear that a new government in Iraq might retract promises of a high level of autonomy once it consolidated power, leading them to reject any compromise.[25]

Iran could exploit the power vacuum left by departing U.S. troops. Already Iran has numerous intelligence and paramilitary forces in Iraq and has ties to numerous groups well beyond its close and long-standing relationship with several Shi'a leaders. Iran might even become a kingmaker in parts of Iraq, free to exploit its already strong influence. It would be an overstatement to say that Iraq would become an Iranian proxy; Iran is neither loved nor admired by most nationalist Iraqis, including most Shi'as. Nevertheless, Iranian influence would be tremendous. In a chaotic political environment, Tehran's resources and agents would be able to undermine leaders hostile to Iran and bolster those who favor Iran's interests.

If there is a bright side to the civil war, it is that the jihadist movement could be diverted. As Zarqawi's statements and deeds made clear, he was more hostile to the Shi'a, and perhaps to what he regarded as local apostate regimes, as he was to the United States. Without the presence of America, the fighters could focus on killing other Iraqis. Over time killing fellow Muslims would discredit their cause. In addition, the jihadists and the rest of the opposition in Iraq have little to unify them beyond getting rid of the United States. Infighting would almost certainly increase should U.S. troops depart.

Nor should we assume that all of Iraq would fall under the jihadists' sway. Iraq's Shi'a majority and large Kurdish population would fiercely resist the jihadists, as would many Sunni Arabs. But control of Iraq is not an all-or-nothing proposition. Even if the jihadist presence in Iraq remained limited at no more than a few thousand fighters, it would exert disproportionate influence in the absence of any alternative. Entire regions of Iraq, particularly Sunni areas such as al-Anbar Province, might be under their sway.

Beyond Iraq

This blow to U.S. credibility can be sustained, and a civil war in Iraq may be inevitable whether or not the United States remains in Iraq.

But these factors are only part of the price of withdrawal. Most worrisome, Iraq is becoming a new field of jihad, a place where radicals come to meet, train, fight, and forge bonds that last when they leave Iraq for the West or for other countries in the region. Iraq could become a new terrorist haven comparable to or perhaps exceeding Afghanistan under the Taliban. Peter Bergen, an expert on al-Qa'ida, argues that the war in Iraq may prove more valuable to the jihadist movement than the anti-Soviet struggle in Afghanistan. Although many jihadists travel to Iraq to fight now, the situation could be even worse. Right now the U.S. military presence limits the scale of the jihadist effort: there is no equivalent to the massive training camps or aboveground existence that the radicals enjoyed in Afghanistan. From a less restricted base, jihadists could organize and train to strike at U.S. or allied facilities around the world, including in the U.S. homeland.

The jihadists who would rise from Iraq's ashes would be far more capable fighters than they were when they first arrived in the land of the two rivers. Many Muslims came to Iraq to expel the United States from Muslim lands; many Iraqis took up arms for the same reason. In the course of the conflict, however, their agendas grew broader. Exposed to hardened jihadists such as Zarqawi, their ambitions and grievances went beyond Iraq, expanding their agenda to embrace one closer to that of the al-Qa'ida core.

The war served a Darwinian function for jihadist fighters. Those who survived ended up better trained, more committed, and otherwise more formidable than they had been when they began. Otherwise they would have perished. Unfortunately, the skills the jihadists picked up in Iraq are readily transferable to other theaters. They include sniper tactics, experience in urban warfare, an improved ability to avoid enemy intelligence, and use of man-portable surface-to-air missiles. Jihadists also have learned how to get through U.S. checkpoints, which are far less formidable at U.S. borders than they are in the war zone of Iraq. The ethos that glorifies suicide bombing has spread as well. The United States and its allies are more likely to face young men and women willing to kill themselves as they kill others, making targets much harder to defend. Most important, jihadists have learned how to use improvised explosive devices (IEDs), which have proven the greatest killer of U.S. forces in Iraq. Iraq-style IEDs have already shown up in other countries.

The jihadists would be particularly likely to reach out and strike Saudi Arabia, given the long, lightly patrolled border between the two countries and the jihadists' long interest in destabilizing the al-Saud family, who rule the heartland of Islam. Ties are tight: resistance groups in Iraq have at times turned to Saudi religious scholars to validate their activities.[26] Terrorism expert Reuven Paz finds that the bulk of the foreign Arabs fighting in Iraq are Saudis. As he notes, "The Iraqi experience of these mainly Saudi volunteers may create a massive group of 'Iraqi alumni' that will threaten the fragile internal situation of the desert kingdom."[27]

The turmoil in Iraq also has energized young Saudi Islamists, who see it as emblematic of broader problems facing the Muslim world. For now, many Saudi jihadists have decided to fight in Iraq, in part because doing so is a clearer "defensive jihad" than struggling with the al-Saud.[28] If the United States left, the balance could shift from Saudis helping Iraqi fighters to Iraqi fighters helping Saudis. To be clear, such a development would not be likely to lead to the collapse of the Saudi government, but even a few dozen terrorists operating from Iraq could foster civil strife, attack Saudi Arabia's oil infrastructure, and otherwise cause instability in a critical ally.

The November 9, 2005, attacks on three hotels in Amman, Jordan, that killed sixty people may be a harbinger. The attacks were carried out by Iraqis, though Zarqawi, a Jordanian, orchestrated them. Because the attackers were foreigners, Jordan's impressive security force did not have long dossiers on them, as it does with many domestic radicals. As a result, the bombers slipped through the net. European intelligence services, too, are intensely concerned about Iraq. Dozens, perhaps hundreds, of European Muslims are going to Iraq to fight. So far these individuals have not returned to Western Europe (and we can hope that many get their wish and become martyrs), but European officials believe that it is only a matter of time before they do.

The war in Iraq has several implications for the U.S. homeland. The more of the global ideology that jihadists pick up in Iraq, to say nothing of their new skills, the more likely and more able they will be to strike U.S. targets. The war and the occupation also have energized the European Muslim community, who can enter the United States easily because of their European passports. They have the skills to function in the United States, and now they have the cause.

The Next Iraq Problem

The United States also must hedge against the possibility that unrest will spread beyond Iraq. Iraq's neighbors, particularly Saudi Arabia and Jordan, are highly vulnerable. Bolstering these countries' security forces further, and helping them with border security, are obvious priorities. Even more important, the United States must be on the alert for jihadist veterans of Iraq and recognize that their tactics are likely to spread. In several analyses I coauthored with Kenneth Pollack of the Brookings Institution's Saban Center for Middle East Policy, we argue that in addition to the risk of terrorism stemming from Iraq, the United States must be prepared to confront the patterns of "spillover," by which civil wars in one state can deleteriously affect another. One set of problems involves refugees—and the Iraq conflict has already produced 2 million. Refugees can create strategic problems, serving as a ready recruiting pool for armed groups still waging the civil war and involving neighboring states in the larger struggle. Moreover, large refugee flows can overstrain the economies and even change the demographic balances of small or weak neighboring states. Neighboring populations also often become highly agitated and mobilized as a result of developments in the state in civil war. Civil war also may spur on groups in a neighboring state to demand or even fight for a reordering of the status quo in their own states. Secessionism also may spread, leading to bloody struggles for independence. These problems and the general instability of war also can impose heavy economic burdens on neighboring states. Not surprisingly, neighbors may intervene to head off these problems (or seize perceived opportunities), but in practice their interventions often backfire.

Shifting to Containment

The United States must work to reduce the scale of the Iraq war and contain the spillover from it. This involves taking steps to head off these problems and reassure neighboring states or, if necessary, threaten them to behave responsibly. Almost all the steps, however, require that the United States remain engaged in the region.[29]

In the months and years to come, the United States is likely to draw down its forces as civil war consumes Iraq. The Iraq that America leaves behind will be an utter disaster: a charnel house for Iraqis, its political systems in tatters, and its economy a basket case. The United States would also have to weather a short-term blow in prestige. Jihadists and other opponents of the United States would tout any drawdown as a victory. Initially, such a perception will be hard to deny. Not even the best public relations campaign can overcome this perception. Images of departing U.S. forces will only serve to bolster the picture of defeat.

Even as the United States reduces its forces there, it must recognize that terrorists will continue to find a home in Iraq and will use it as a base to conduct attacks outside it. All of the different militias are likely to engage in terrorist attacks of one kind or another, and some will try to ally with transnational terrorist groups to enlist their support.

Some U.S. forces should remain in and near Iraq. Many of these will be devoted to the problems of assisting refugees, preventing neighboring states from massively intervening, and otherwise trying to stop the Iraq disaster from metastasizing further. However, one of the most important tasks for the United States is to limit the ability of terrorists to use Iraq as a haven for attacks outside the country. The best way to do that will be to retain assets (particularly airpower, special operations forces, and a major intelligence and reconnaissance effort) in the vicinity to identify and strike major terrorist facilities such as training camps, bomb factories, and arms caches before they can pose a danger to other countries.

The goal is to stop Anbar Province and other parts of Iraq from becoming a jihadist center on the scale of the Taliban's Afghanistan. Iraq is already partway there, and Iraq's centrality makes it an even more ideal hub than Afghanistan in the 1980s and 1990s. Yet the jihadists there spend much of their time fighting other Sunnis and cannot train (and relax) on the same scale as they could when they enjoyed the Taliban's hospitality.

To keep the haven limited as the United States draws down forces, Washington should continue to make intelligence collection in Iraq a high priority, and whenever a terrorist facility is identified, American forces would move in quickly to destroy it. When possible, the United States would work with various factions in Iraq that share our goals regarding the local terrorist presence. This involves giving them money, training, supplies, and other assistance. However, we should be under no illusions: these fighters will not be under U.S. control, and many of these groups are also hostile to other U.S. interests in the region.

This approach is difficult, as it does not remove the U.S. military presence from the region. If such strike forces were based in Iraq's neighbors they would upset the local population and might face limits on their ability to operate in Iraq by the host governments. This was exactly the set of problems the United States encountered during the 1990s, and which led Washington to eliminate many of its military facilities in the region after the invasion of Iraq.

On the other hand, maintaining American troops in Iraq, even at reduced levels, would have negative repercussions on the terrorism threat as well. It would allow the jihadists to continue to use this as a recruiting tool, although the diminished presence of U.S. troops would make this slightly harder. The U.S. presence in Iraq, as well as in Kuwait, Qatar, Jordan, and other neighbors will continue to enrage them. It would also mean that American troops will continue to be targets of terrorist attacks, although redeploying them from Iraq's urban areas to the periphery would diminish the threat from current levels.

Beyond the military, the United States must work hard to increase the governmental capacity of neighboring states. It should assist Jordan, Kuwait, Saudi Arabia, Turkey, and other allies in managing refugee flows and ensuring that any settlements are properly policed. In addition, strengthening military and intelligence training programs for neighbors is essential so they can better manage any unrest in their countries. A diplomatic priority should be discouraging Iraq's neighbors from meddling in Iraq, particularly on behalf of the jihadists.

Finally, the United States will have to recognize the limits of what can be accomplished. Terrorism in Iraq has flourished despite the presence of up to 160,000 U.S. troops; it is absurd to expect that fewer troops could accomplish more. Over time, Iraq may become less of a recruiting cause for anti-U.S. terrorists, but in the short term the operational advantages the jihadists gain are likely to outweigh this potential loss for them. Through continued military, intelligence, and diplomatic engagement, the United States can reduce the frequency of attacks and the scale of the training and other activities, but our expectations must by necessity be modest.

Notes

Introduction

1. This book uses the term "jihadist" to refer to what French scholar Gilles Kepel describes as *"salafi jihadists."* As discussed in chapter 1, I am focusing on a subset of the Sunni Islamist community that embraces violent struggle as a solution to the Muslim world's problems. I do not focus on other groups that call themselves jihadists, be they people using the term to refer to peaceful struggles or non-Sunni groups.

1. The Faces of the Adversary

1. A thorough report that focuses on the performance of intelligence agencies is Intelligence and Security Committee, "Report into the London Terrorist Attacks on 7 July 2005," Report to Parliament, May 2006.

2. Patrick Hennessy and Melissa Kite, "Poll Reveals 40pc of Muslims Want Sharia Law in UK," *Telegraph* (London), February 19, 2006, 1; "Islamic Sharia Law," *Sunday Times* (London), February 19, 2006, 13.

3. Bergen, *Holy War, Inc.,* 35.

4. The full text of the speech is available at http://www.cnn.com/2001/US/09/20/gen.bush.transcript/.

5. The full text is available at http://www.fas.org/irp/world/para/docs/980223-fatwa.htm.

6. For an excellent review of the impact of sanctions see Amatzia Baram, "The Effect of Iraqi Sanctions: Statistical Pitfalls and Responsibility," *Middle East Journal* 54, no. 2 (Spring 2000). The text is available at http://www.mideasti.org/articles/baram.html.

7. As quoted in "Al-Zarqawi, the Second Generation of Al-Qa'ida," serialized in *Al-Quds Al-'Arabi,* June 8, 2005.

8. As quoted in Anonymous, *Through Our Enemies' Eyes,* 53. Anonymous was subsequently revealed to be Michael Scheuer, a retired U.S. government counterterrorism officer.

9. UBL Audio Message Offering Reward for Killing Kofi Annan (May 5, 2004). Global Terror Alert, http://www.globalterroralert.com/ublmsg0506.html.

10. Bergen, *Holy War, Inc.*, 226.

11. Pillar, *Terrorism and U.S. Foreign Policy*, 67–68.

12. Anonymous, *Through Our Enemies' Eyes*, 256.

13. As quoted in Anonymous, *Through Our Enemies' Eyes*, xviii.

14. Benjamin and Simon, *The Age of Sacred Terror*, 48–55. The authors note that all references to jihad in the most authoritative collections of the Prophet Mohammad's sayings portray jihad as warfare and back up their argument with a reference to the entry "Djihad," *The Encyclopedia of Islam* 2, ed. B. Lewis, Ch. Pellat, and J. Schacht (Leiden: E. J. Brill), 538–540.

15. Many Wahhabis, however, see themselves as part of the Hanbali school, while most salafists reject the schools for relying on sayings and traditions of the Prophet that are not well documented. International Crisis Group, "Indonesia Backgrounder: Why Salafism and Terrorism Mostly Don't Mix." September 13, 2004, 1. For a good review, see also Quintan Wiktorowicz, "Anatomy of the Salafi Movement," *Studies in Conflict & Terrorism* 29 (2006): 207–239.

16. Wiktorowicz, "Anatomy of the Salafi Movement," 208.

17. International Crisis Group, "Indonesia Backgrounder: Why Salafism and Terrorism Mostly Don't Mix," 1; Kepel, *War for Muslim Minds*, 86.

18. Nimrod Raphaeli, "Ayman Muhammad Rabi' Al-Zawahiri: The Making of an Arch-Terrorist," *Terrorism and Political Violence* 14, no. 4 (Winter 2002): 8.

19. As quoted in Kepel, *Jihad*, 318.

20. As quoted in Bergen, *Holy War, Inc.*, 28.

21. Benjamin and Simon, *Age of Sacred Terror*, 113.

22. Anonymous, *Through Our Enemies' Eyes*, 40; Benjamin and Simon, *Age of Sacred Terror*, 144–145.

23. Anonymous, *Through Our Enemies' Eyes*, 18.

24. G. H. McCormick and G. Owen, "Security and Coordination in a Clandestine Organization," *Mathematical and Computer Modeling* 31, 175–192.

25. David C. Rapoport, "Terrorism," in Mary Hawkesworth and Maurice Kogan, eds., *Routledge Encyclopedia of Government and Politics*, vol. 2 (London: Routledge, 1992), p. 1067, as cited in Hoffman, "The Modern Terrorist Mindset," 84.

26. As quoted in Bergen, *Holy War, Inc.*, 32.

27. In a videotaped meeting with followers in November 2001 where details of the September 11 plot were revealed, bin Ladin said, "The brothers, who conducted the operation, all they knew was that they have a martyrdom operation and we asked each of them to go to America but they didn't know anything about the operation, not even one letter. But they were trained and we did not reveal the operation to them until they are there and just before they boarded the planes. . . . Those who were trained to fly didn't know the others. One group of people did not know the other group." Source: bin Ladin videotape, December 13, 2001. Available at http:// www.pbs.org/newshour/terrorism/international/video_12–13.html.

28. Gunaratna, RAND report.

29. Bruce Hoffman, "Rethinking Terrorism and Counterterrorism since 9/11," *Studies in Conflict & Terrorism* 25 (2002): 304. Martha Crenshaw argues that in general, "Terrorists are impatient for action." "The Logic of Terrorism," in *Terrorism and Counterterrorism*, 58; Bergen, *Holy War, Inc.*, 109; and Anonymous, *Through Our Enemies' Eyes*, 21–22.

30. For a fascinating account see Lawrence Wright, "The Man behind Bin Laden," *New Yorker*, September 16, 2002. Available at http://www .newyorker.com.

31. For example, the Lebanese Hizballah, while promoting the concept of Islamic unity regardless of nationality, draws primarily on Lebanese Shiite Muslims. Similarly, the Palestinian group Hamas recruits Palestinians rather than Arab Muslims more broadly.

32. Hoffman, "Rethinking Terrorism and Counterterrorism," 308.

33. Gilles Kepel, *The War for Muslim Minds: Islam and the West*, 129.

34. In 2003, George Tenet, then director of Central Intelligence, testified that more than three thousand arrests had been made in connection with al-Qa'ida. "Worldwide Threats," Tenet testimony to U.S. Senate Select Committee on Intelligence, February 11, 2003. The CIA has not since released figures, but presumably the pace of arrests has continued.

35. National Commission on Terrorist Attacks upon the United States, "Monograph on Terrorist Financing," 28. However, approximately $10 million to $20 million of the organization's money went to supporting the Taliban government, so the organization's expenses have also fallen considerably.

36. Kepel, *War for Muslim Minds*, 144.

37. John Negroponte, "Annual Threat Assessment of the Director of National Intelligence," testimony before the Senate Select Committee on

Intelligence, February 2, 2006. Available at http://intelligence.senate.gov/0602hrg/060202/negroponte.pdf.

38. Malise Ruthven, *A Fury for God: The Islamist Attack on America*, 150.

39. As quoted in Anonymous, *Through Our Enemies' Eyes*, 6.

40. Mark Mazzetti, "Qaeda Is Seen as Restoring Leadership," *New York Times*, April 2, 2007, p. A1.

41. "Algerian Group Backs al-Qaeda," BBC News, October 23, 2003.

42. Raffi Khatchadourian, "Pursuing Terrorists in the Great Desert," *Village Voice*, January 31, 2006. Available at http://www.villagevoice.com/news/0605,khatchadourian,71993,6.html.

43. Bergen, *Holy War, Inc.*, 32.

44. A Web site that claimed to be affiliated with Chechen rebel leader Shamil Baseyev, who has taken credit for and denied responsibility for the Beslan attack, issued an e-mail message from Baseyev, where he claimed that there were thirty-three hostage takers (the Russians claim thirty-two), including twelve Chechens, nine Ingush, two Chechenki, three Russians, two Arabs, two Ossets, one Tatar, one Kabardian, and one Guran. Jill Dougherty, "Chechen 'Claims Belsan Attack'," CNN.com, September 17, 2004.

45. Translated from Russian news service Newsru.com, September 17, 2004. Available at http://www.online-translator.com/url/tran_url.asp?direction=re&autotranslate=on&transliterate=on&url=http%3A%2F%2Fwww.newsru.com%2Frussia%2F17Sep2004%2Fbasaev_print.html. Nurpashi Kulayev, twenty-four, a former sergeant in the Russian Army, was the only hostage-taker captured alive.

46. Mark Franchetti and Matthew Campbell, "How a Repressed Village Misfit Became the Butcher of Beslan," *Sunday Times* of London, September 12, 2004.

47. Statement of Thomas Wilshere before the Senate Foreign Relations Committee, December 18, 2001, 7.

48. Anonymous, *Through Our Enemies' Eyes*, xviii.

49. Pillar, *Terrorism and U.S. Foreign Policy*, 55.

50. U.S. Department of State, "Country Reports on Terrorism, 2004," April 2005, 7.

51. Benjamin and Simon, *The Next Attack*, 5.

52. Frontline: "Al Qaeda Today: The New Face of the Global Jihad," Available at http://www.pbs.org/wgbh/pages/frontline/shows/front/etc/today.html.

53. Benjamin and Simon, *The Next Attack*, 128.

54. Scheherezade Faramarzi, "Drawn to Insurgency," Associated Press, November 26, 2004.

55. Tara Pepper and Mark Hosenball, *Newsweek*, July 25, 2005.

56. Home Office, U.K., "Summary," Report on Relations with the Muslim Community, May 10, 2004, 1.

57. Pew Global Attitudes Project, "The Great Divide," 3–5.

58. Home Office, "Summary," 8.

59. Bill Powell, "Generation Jihad," *Time*, September 26, 2005.

60. Benjamin and Simon, *The Next Attack*, 52; Home Office, "Summary," 10.

61. Pew Global Attitudes Project, "The Great Divide," 25.

62. Robert Winnett and David Leppard, "Leaked No 10 Dossier Reveals Al-Qaeda's British Recruits," *Sunday Times* of London, July 10, 2005; Bill Powell, "Generation Jihad," *Time*, September 26, 2005; Benjamin and Simon, *The Next Attack*, 86.

63. Winnett and Leppard, "Leaked No 10 Dossier Reveals Al-Qaeda's British Recruits."

64. Christopher Dickey, *Newsweek*, March 21, 2005.

65. Pew Global Attitudes Project, "The Great Divide."

66. Jean Chichizola, "Madmen of Allah and Criminals Make Common Cause on Holdups," *Le Figaro*, January 3, 2006.

67. The text of the president's speech is available at http://usinfo .state.gov/usa/islam/s092001.html.

68. Benjamin and Simon, *The Next Attack*, 172–175.

69. Pew Global Attitudes Project, "View of a Changing World," 20. The document is available at http://www.pewtrusts.com/pdf/vf_pew_research _global_attitudes_0603.pdf.

70. Pew Global Attitudes Project, "America's Image Slips, but Allies Share U.S. Concerns Over Iran, Hamas," 15 Nation Pew Global Attitudes Survey, June 13, 2006, available at http://www.pewglobal.org/reports/pdf/ 252.pdf. See also Shibley Telhami, *Reflections of Hearts and Minds: Media, Opinion, and Identity in the Arab World* (Washington, D.C.: Brookings Institution Press, 2007).

71. "Faithful, but Not Fanatics," *Economist*, June 28, 2003, 50. The article contends that bin Ladin has more appeal as a symbol of rebellion by many who do not share his exact ambitions rather than as a model for revolution.

72. Benjamin and Simon, *The Age of Sacred Terror*, 213.

73. As quoted in Benjamin and Simon, ibid., 66.

74. Anonymous, *Through Our Enemies' Eyes,* 245.

75. Gunaratna, *Inside Al-Qaeda,* 10.

76. Benjamin and Simon, *The Age of Sacred Terror,* 171.

77. This may be true for those who are well within al-Qa'ida orbit. Even as late as 1995, bin Ladin's now number two, Ayman al-Zawahiri, authored a book called *The Way to Jerusalem Passes through Cairo,* a title suggesting that he thinks locally, not globally.

78. Lawrence Wright, unpublished paper written for the RAND Corporation (2006). See also Combating Terrorism Center, "Harmony and Disharmony," February 14, 2006, 47.

79. See Saad Eddin Ibrahim, "Anatomy of Egypt's Militant Islamic Groups: Methodological Note and Preliminary Findings," *International Journal of Middle East Studies* 12 (1980): 434.

80. Pew Global Attitudes Project, "The Great Divide," 3.

81. Bin Ladin himself probably held this view in the 1980s, before he came under the influence of Zawahiri and other Egyptians who had developed this doctrine of rebellion after suffering massive crackdowns under Nasser in the 1960s. Bin Ladin and al-Qa'ida now believe that various Arab and Muslim states are takfir, not society in general.

82. International Crisis Group, "Indonesia Backgrounder: Why Salafism and Terrorism Mostly Don't Mix," September 13, 2004, 4.

83. International Crisis Group, "Saudi Arabia Background: Who Are the Islamists?" September 21, 2004, 2.

84. Kepel, *Jihad,* 304.

85. Ibid., 290–320.

86. Pew Global Attitudes Project, "Support for Terror Wanes among Muslim Publics," July 14, 2005, 29. The document is available at http://pewglobal.org/reports/display.php?ReportID=248.

87. Ibid., 2.

88. Robin Wright, "Support for Bin Laden, Violence down among Muslims, Poll Says," *Washington Post,* July 15, 2005, A13.

89. Ibid.

90. International Crisis Group, "Indonesia Backgrounder," 17.

91. Jahangir Amuzegar, "Iran's Crumbling Revolution," *Foreign Affairs* 82, no. 1 (January–February 2003): 44–57; Kepel, *Jihad,* 205–322.

92. See Jeremy Shapiro and Benedicte Suzan, "The French Experience of Counterterrorism," *Survival* 45, no. 1 (Spring 2003): 67–98 for a strong argument on the counterterrorism expertise of the French intelligence services.

2. What Is Victory and How Do We Achieve It?

1. For a cogent review of these problems see Stephen D. Biddle, "American Grand Strategy after 9/11: An Assessment," 22.

2. British Home Office report on July 7, 2005, bombings, 5 (italics in original).

3. Todd Purdum, "How to Declare Victory," *New York Times*, October 14, 2001, 3.

4. Josh White and Ann Scott Tyson, "Rumsfeld Offers Strategies for Current War," *Washington Post*, February 3, 2006, A8.

5. See White House, "2006 National Strategy for Combating Terror, Fighting a Global War on Terror." Available at http://www.whitehouse.gov/nsc/nsct/2006/nsct2006.pdf.

6. Scheuer, *Imperial Hubris*, 241.

7. National Academy of Public Administration, *Transforming the FBI* (September 2005), 16.

8. Saxby Chambliss, "Counterterrorism Intelligence Capabilities and Performance Prior to 9-11," Subcommittee on Terrorism and Homeland Security House Permanent Select Committee on Intelligence, July 2002.

9. John Diamond, "It's No Secret: CIA Scouting for Recruits," *USA Today*, November 22, 2005.

10. Andrew Higgins and Christopher Cooper, "CIA-Backed Team Used Brutal Means to Break Up Terrorist Cell in Albania," *Wall Street Journal*, November 20, 2001.

11. Philip B. Heymann, *Terrorism and America: A Commonsense Strategy for a Democratic Society*, 158.

12. John Mueller, "Six Rather Unusual Propositions about Terrorism," *Terrorism and Political Violence* 17 (2005): 487–488.

13. Clark Chapman and Allan Harris, "A Skeptical Look at September 11: How We Can Defeat Terrorism by Reacting to It More Rationally," *Skeptical Inquirer* (September–October 2002).

14. See John Mueller, "The Banality of 'Ethnic War,'" *International Security* 25, no. 1 (Summer 2000): 42–70.

15. The conflict in Kashmir had many causes, but a decision by the Jammu and Kashmir Liberation Front to kidnap the daughter of a prominent politician is often seen as the "spark" that led to a massive conflagration. Similarly, the latest round of violence in Chechnya began after bombings of several apartment buildings in Russia, which Moscow claimed was done by Chechen terrorists.

16. Cathleen A. Berrick, "Efforts to Measure Effectiveness and Strengthen Security Programs," November 20, 2003, GAO-040285T, 22.

17. According to James Fallows, more than 80 percent of the entire TSA budget ($5.3 billion) in 2005 went to cover the cost of airport screening. This left less than $1 billion for all other forms of transportation, including roads, bridges, subways, ports, etc., which are more frequented by Americans than airlines. "Success without Victory," *Atlantic Monthly* (January–February 2005); DHS budget-in-brief (FY 2007) available at http://www.dhs.gov/interweb/assetlibrary/Budget_BIB-FY2007 .pdf.

18. Steve Orr, "No Change in Airport Screening," *Rochester Democrat & Chronicle,* November 27, 2004.

19. Scott Higham and Robert O'Harrow Jr., "Contracting Rush for Security Led to Waste, Abuse," *Washington Post,* May 22, 2005, A1.

20. Eric Lipton, "U.S. to Spend Billions More to Alter Security Systems," *New York Times,* May 7, 2005.

21. Kaiser Commission on Medicaid and the Uninsured, "The Costs of *Not* Covering the Uninsured" (June 2003). Available at http://www.kff.org/ uninsured/upload/Cost-of-Not-Covering-the-Uninsured-Project-Highlights .pdf.

22. Michael Isikoff and Mark Hosenball, "Wrong Priorities?" *Newsweek,* September 7, 2005 (Web edition). Available at http://www.msnbc .msn.com/id/9246373/site/newsweek/fromRL.1/.

23. "International Student Enrollment Growth Slows in 2002/2003," Institute of International Education (IIE) press release, November 3, 2003. Available at http://opendoors.iienetwork.org/?p=36523.

24. Jeremy Shapiro and Benedicte Suzan, "The French Experience of Counterterrorism," *Survival* 45, no. 1 (Spring 2003): 68.

25. Richard Falkenrath, Remarks at Brookings Institution Panel "How to Win the War on Terrorism," September 22, 2005. Available at http:// www.brookings.edu/fp/saban/events/20050922_panel1.pdf.

26. "President Addresses Nation, Discusses Iraq, War on Terror," speech at Fort Bragg, June 28, 2005. http://www.whitehouse.gov/news/ releases/2005/06/20050628–7.html. See also "President Discusses War on Terror," talk at the National Defense University, March 8, 2005.

27. As quoted in Anonymous, *Through Our Enemies' Eyes,* 111.

28. "President Discusses War on Terror at National Endowment for Democracy," speech before the National Endowment for Democracy, October 5, 2005.

29. Ted Robert Gurr, "Terrorism in Democracies: Its Social and Political Bases," in Walter Reich, ed., *Origins of Terrorism: Psychologies, Ideologies, Theologies, and States of Mind,* 87–98.

3. Tracking Down and Disrupting Terrorists

1. Terry McDermott, Josh Meyer, and Patrick McDonnell, "The Plots and Designs of Al Qaeda's Engineer," *Los Angeles Times,* December 22, 2002; 9/11 Report, 147.

2. "Verbatim Transcript of Combatant Status Review Tribunal Hearing for ISN 10024," March 14, 2007. http://www.defenselink.mil/news/transcript_ISN10024.pdf.

3. Ibid.

4. *9/11 Commission Report,* 154.

5. Don Van Natta Jr. and Desmond Butler, "How Tiny Swiss Cellphone Chips Helped Track Global Terror Web," *New York Times,* March 4, 2004, A1.

6. *9/11 Commission Report,* 145–149.

7. McDermott, Meyer, and McDonnell, "Plots and Designs."

8. James Risen and David Johnston, "Qaeda Aide Slipped Away Long before Sept. 11 Attack," *New York Times,* March 8, 2003, 12.

9. *9/11 Commission Report,* 149–150.

10. Ibid., 150.

11. McDermott, Meyer, and McDonnell, "Plots and Designs." Web version available at http://www.latimes.com/news/nationworld/nation/la-fg-khalid-arch,1,4896108.story.

12. Van Natta and Butler, "Tiny Swiss Cellphone Chips," A1.

13. Raymond Bonner and David Johnston, "Pakistanis Say Suspect Described Meeting with bin Laden," *New York Times,* March 3, 2003, 1.

14. Mackey and Miller, *The Interrogators,* 479–483.

15. Speech at Georgetown University, February 5, 2004. Transcript available at http://www.foxnews.com/story/0,2933,110545,00.html.

16. Bonner and Johnston, "Pakistanis Say Suspect," A1; Erik Eckholm and David Johnston, "Qaeda Suspect, Sound Asleep at Trail's End, Offers No Resistance," *New York Times,* March 3, 2003, A1.

17. "Letter from al-Zawahiri to al-Zarqawi," October 11, 2005. Available at http://www.dni.gov/letter_in_english.pdf.

18. Kepel, *War for Muslim Minds,* 132.

19. Michael A. Sheehan, "Walking the Terror Beat," *New York Times,* September 10, 2006, 10.

20. Van Natta and Butler, "Tiny Swiss Cellphone Chips," A1.

21. See Erik Eckholm, "Pakistanis Arrest Qaeda Figure Seen as Planner of 9/11," *New York Times,* March 2, 2003, 1, and statement by press secretary, "Detention of Khalid Shaikh Mohammed," White House, March 1, 2003. See also Erik Eckholm, "Muted Alliance: FBI Active in Pakistan, but Profile Is Low," *New York Times,* March 4, 2003, A14.

22. Peter Bergen, "The Long Hunt for Osama," *Atlantic Monthly* (October 2004). Available at http://www.theatlantic.com/doc/200410/bergen.

23. Hoffman, *Inside Terrorism,* 8 and 175–176.

24. Pillar, "Intelligence," in Ludes and Cronin, *Attacking Terrorism,* 115.

25. Ibid.; author's italics.

26. Intelligence and Security Committee, "Report into the London Terrorist Attacks on 7 July 2005," May 2006, 16.

27. Bruce Hoffman, "The Modern Terrorist Mindset," in Russell D. Howard and Reid L. Sawyer, eds., *Terrorism and Counterterrorism: Understanding the New Security Environment* (Guilford, Conn.: McGraw-Hill, 2002), 84.

28. Jaber, *Born with a Vengeance,* 117.

29. Hoffman, "The Logic of Suicide Terrorism," *Atlantic Monthly* (June 2003), 42.

30. Shulsky, *Silent Warfare,* 116–125.

31. Coll, *Ghost Wars,* 417.

32. George Tenet, "Worldwide Threat 2001: National Security in a Changing World." *Statement before the U.S. Senate Select Committee on Intelligence,* February 7, 2001.

33. Wohlstetter, *Surprise Attack,* 1–2, 111–112.

34. Ibid., 387.

35. Pillar, "Intelligence," in Ludes and Cronin, *Attacking Terrorism,* 125.

36. "Report of the Accountability Review Boards on the Embassy Bombings in Nairobi and Dar es Salaam. January 1999. Washington, D.C." Available at http://www.fas.org/irp/threat/arb/accountability_report.html.

37. Coll, *Ghost Wars,* 492.

38. See *Jihad Manual* 12, lesson 5.

39. Ibid.

40. Kassimeris, *Europe's Last Red Terrorists,* 106–151.

41. MIPT Terrorism Knowledge Base, "Group Profile: Revolutionary Organization 17 November." Available at http://www.tkb.org/Group.jsp?groupID=101.

42. Eleanor Hill, "Joint Inquiry Staff Statement," October 8, 2002.

43. As quoted in the Congressional 9/11 Inquiry, "Joint Inquiry Staff Statement: Hearings on the Intelligence Community's Response to Past Terrorist Attacks against the United States from February 1993 to September 2001," October 8, 2002, 11.

44. *Jihad Manual* 12, paragraph 9.

45. See Tareekh Osama "Osama's History," in Peter Bergen, *The Osama bin Laden I Know,* 78–82.

46. Hoffman, "The Modern Terrorist Mindset," 307.

47. *Report of the Joint Inquiry,* 387–388.

48. Fu'ad Husayn, "Al-Zarqawi: The Second Generation of Al-Qa'ida," serialized in *Al-Quds Al-'Arabi,* June 8, 2005, 3–4.

49. Renwick McLean, "20 Arrested as Spain Breaks Militant Network," *New York Times,* January 11, 2006, A12.

50. Bruce Hoffman, "All You Need Is Love," *Atlantic Monthly,* December 2001, 36.

51. http://www2.chinadaily.com.cn/english/doc/2004–04/27/content_326647.htm.

52. http://forums.officer.com/forums/showthread.php?t=31719.

53. Hoffman, "All You Need Is Love," 36–37.

54. http://www.foxnews.com/story/0,2933,51252,00.html.

55. Harmony document AFGP-2002–600048, Al-Qa'ida Bylaws, available from the Combating Terrorism Center, February 14, 2006, report.

56. Alison Jamieson, "Entry, Discipline, and Exit in the Italian Red Brigades," *Terrorism and Political Violence* 2, no. 1 (Spring 1990): 9.

57. McCormick and Owen, "Security and Coordination," 186.

58. "Substitution for the Testimony of Khalid Sheikh Mohammad," Defendant's Exhibit 941, *U.S. v. Moussaoui,* 52.

59. Dana Priest, "Foreign Network at Front of CIA's Terror Fight," *Washington Post,* November 18, A1.

60. Don Van Natta Jr., "Al Qaeda Hobbled by Latest Arrest, U.S. Says," *New York Times,* March 3, 2003, 1.

61. McDermott, Meyer, and McDonnell, "Plots and Designs." Available at http://www.latimes.com/news/nationworld/nation/la-fg-khalid-arch,1,4896108.story.

62. Mark Mazzetti, "Qaeda Is Seen as Restoring Leadership," *New York Times,* April 2, 2007, p. A1.

4. Killing Terrorists

1. Gal Luft, "The Logic of Israel's Targeted Killing," *Middle East Quarterly* X, no. 1 (Winter 2003); available at http://www.meforum.org/article/515.

2. Dan Ephron, "Most Israelis Are Combatants," *Newsweek,* July 2002.

3. The figures given are through October 2005 and come from the Israeli human rights organization B'tselem.

4. http://www.btselem.org/english/Statistics/Casualties.asp.

5. http://www2.chinadaily.com.cn/english/doc/2004–04/27/content _326647.htm.

6. David Margolick, "Terrorism: Israel's Payback Principle," *Vanity Fair* 509 (January 2003): 40–47.

7. Khaled Hroub, "Hamas after Shaykh Yasin and Rantisi," *Journal of Palestine Studies* XXXIII, no. 4 (Summer 2004): 33.

8. http://forums.officer.com/forums/showthread.php?t=31719.

9. Margolick, "Terrorism: Israel's Payback Principle," 40–47.

10. Molly Moore, "Israel's Lethal Weapon of Choice," *Washington Post,* June 29, 2003, A01.

11. Jaber, *Hezbollah,* 20–25.

12. Jones, "Israeli Counter-Insurgency Strategy," 91.

13. Margolick, "Terrorism: Israel's Payback Principle," 40–47.

14. http://www.prb.org/Template.cfm?Section=PRB&template=/Con tentManagement/ContentDisplay.cfm&ContentID=12160.

15. The attacks on Libya in 1986 and on Iraq in 1993 were in response to the regime's use of its own operatives, not a regime's support for a particular terrorist group.

16. As quoted in Griffin, *Reaping the Whirlwind,* 174.

17. Ray Takeyh, "The Rogue Who Came in from the Cold," *Foreign Affairs* 80, no. 3 (May–June 2001): 64.

18. Joseph Stanik, *El Dorado Canyon: Reagan's Undeclared War with Qaddafi* (Annapolis, Md.: Naval Institute Press, 2002), 218–229.

19. Coll, *Ghost Wars,* 409.

20. Maley, *The Afghanistan Wars,* 249.

21. Bergen, *Holy War, Inc.,* 129.

22. Burke, *Al-Qaeda,* 168; Cullison and Higgins, "Strained Alliance: Al Qaeda's Sour Days in Afghanistan"; Griffin, *Reaping the Whirlwind,* 173.

23. Coll, *Ghost Wars,* 408.

24. Mark Bowden, "The Ploy," *Atlantic Monthly* (May 2007). Available at http://www.theatlantic.com/doc/prem/200705/tracking-zarqawi.

5. Defending the Homeland without Overreacting

1. All these examples are taken from Homeland Security planning scenarios, available at http://www.globalsecurity.org/security/library/ report/2004/hsc-planning-scenarios-jul04.htm.

2. As quoted in Mueller, "Six Rather Unusual Propositions about Terrorism," *Terrorism and Political Violence* 17 (2005): 487.

3. David Cole, *Enemy Aliens* (New York: New Press, 2003), 18; italics in original.

4. David Cole, "Enemy Aliens," 955. See also Cole, *Enemy Aliens,* 58.

5. Kayyali, "The People Perceived as a Threat," 3–4.

6. Veronique de Rugy, "What Does Homeland Security Spending Buy?" American Enterprise Institute, April 1, 2005, 8–9. Part of that is spent on nonhomeland defense activities (e.g., the coast guard's efforts to enforce fishing restrictions), but other agencies spend roughly $23 billion cumulatively on homeland defense activities.

7. I would like to thank John Mueller for his thoughts on this issue.

8. Veronique de Rugy, "What Does Homeland Security Spending Buy?" American Enterprise Institute, April 1, 2005, 1.

9. James Fallows, "Success without Victory," *Atlantic Monthly* (January–February 2005), 83.

10. I would like to thank Jeremy Shapiro for pointing this out to me.

11. Nicole J. Henderson, Christopher W. Ortiz, Naomi F. Sugie, and Joel Miller, *Law Enforcement & Arab American Community Relations after September 11, 2001,"* 17–18. Available at http://www.vera.org/policerelations.

12. Testimony of Robert S. Mueller III before the U.S. Senate Committee on Intelligence, February 16, 2005.

13. Ervin, *Open Target,* 44.

14. William K. Rashbaum, "Terror Case May Offer Clues into Police Use of Informants," *New York Times,* April 24, 2006, B1.

15. Brenda Goodman, "U.S. Says 2 Georgia Men Planned a Terror Attack," *New York Times,* April 22, 2006, A12.

16. Adding Up the Ounces of Prevention," *New York Times,* September 10, 2006, 4.

17. Greg Krikorian and Solomon Moore, "Probe Elicits Disbelief at Mosque," *Los Angeles Times,* August 18, 2001, B1.

18. Testimony of Robert S. Mueller III before the U.S. Senate Committee on Intelligence, February 16, 2005.

19. "Substitution for the Testimony of Khalid Sheikh Mohammad," Defendant's Exhibit 941, *U.S. v. Moussaoui,* 35. Mohammad notes that one key operative for 9/11 was turned back at the airport because he was "too much an unsophisticated 'bedouin.'"

20. Jeremy Shapiro, "What Democratic Response to a Terrorist Attack?" Washington, D.C., 2.

21. "Substitution for the Testimony of Khalid Sheikh Mohammad," 13.

22. Director Muller noted that the transportation sector and nuclear power plants remain possible targets. Testimony of Robert S. Mueller III before the U.S. Senate Committee on Intelligence, February 16, 2005.

23. James Fallows, "Success without Victory," *Atlantic Monthly* (January–February 2005), 84.

24. Scott Sagan, "The Problem of Redundancy Problem: Why More Nuclear Security Forces May Produce Less Nuclear Security," *Risk Analysis* 24, no. 4 (2004): 935–946.

25. Ervin, *Open Target,* 34.

26. Ibid.

27. 9/11 Commission 2004, 77.

28. Benjamin and Simon 2002, 298; 9/11 Commission 2004, 358.

29. Benjamin and Simon 2002, xii–xiii.

30. 9/11 Commission 2004, 93, 265; Clarke 2004, 192.

31. Watson 2002.

32. Clarke 2004, 219; Kessler 2002, 432.

33. Benjamin and Simon 2002.

34. Statement of John Gannon to the U.S. Senate Committee on the Judiciary, May 2, 2006.

35. National Academy of Public Administration, "Transforming the FBI: Roadmap to an Effective Human Capital Program," September 2005.

36. See U.S. Department of Justice, "Federal Bureau of Investigation's Foreign Language Translation Program Follow-up," Audit Report 5–33 (July 2005), available at http://www.usdoj.gov/oig/reports/FBI/a0533/final.pdf.

37. Gannon testimony, May 2, 2006.

38. Ibid.

39. Shapiro, "What Democratic Response to a Terrorist Attack?" 7.

40. Numbers range from 2 million to 8 million. The six-million estimate comes from Zahid Bukhari, who directs the Muslims in the American Public Square project at Georgetown University. See Jim Lobe, "Muslim Support for the 'War on Terror' Plummets," Inter Press Service News Agency, October 20, 2003. Other estimates put the number of African Americans who are Muslims at close to 2 million. See Haddad and Smith, "Muslims in the United States," 220.

41. Randa Kayyali, "The People Perceived as a Threat to Security: Arab Americans since September 11," July 1, 2006. Available at http://www.migrationinformation.org/Feature/print/cfm?ID=409.

42. Benjamin and Simon, *Next Attack,* 119; Nicole J. Henderson, Christopher W. Ortiz, Naomi F. Sugie, and Joel Miller, *Law Enforcement*

and Arab American Community Relations after September 11, 2001: Engagement in a Time of Uncertainty (New York: Vera Institute of Justice, 2006), 6. Available at http://www.vera.org/policerelations.

43. Muslims in the American Public Square, "American Muslim Poll 2004," October 2004, 10.

44. Pew Global Attitudes Project, "The Great Divide," 6.

45. Muslims in the American Public Square, "American Muslim Poll," November–December 2001.

46. "MPAC Special Report: Religion and Identity of Muslim American Youth Post-London Attacks," Muslim Public Affairs Council, 2005.

47. Abdo, "Islam in America," 9–14.

48. Ibid., 13.

49. Henderson, Ortiz, Sugie, and Miller, Law Enforcement and Arab American Community Relations after September 11, 2001, 12.

50. Ibid., 17.

51. Geneive Abdo, "Islam in America: Separate but Unequal," Washington Quarterly (Autumn 2005): 7–8.

52. "MPAC Special Report: Religion and Identity."

53. Mueller, "Six Propositions," 491.

54. Michael Sivak and Michael J. Flannagan, "Flying and Driving after the September 11 Attacks," American Scientist 91 (2003): 8.

55. Sources: National Safety Council at http://www.anotherperspective .org/advoc530.html (for the drowning-in-your-bathtub figure); and others from "Robert Roy Britt, "The Odds of Dying," LiveScience.com, available at http://www.livescience.com/ forcesofnature/050106_odds_of _dying.html#table. The sources for that table are National Center for Health Statistics, CDC; American Cancer Society; National Safety Council; International Federation of Red Cross and Red Crescent Societies; World Health Organization; USGS; Clark Chapman, SwRI; David Morrison, NASA; Michael Paine, Planetary Society Australian Volunteers.

56. Brian Jenkins, Unconquerable Nation: Knowing Our Enemy, Strengthening Ourselves (Santa Monica, Calif.: RAND, 2006), 154–155.

57. The terrorism estimate is National Safety Council at http://www .anotherperspective.org/advoc530.html and http://www.cdc.gov/nchs/data/ nvsr/nvsr54/nvsr54_19.pdf.

6. Fighting Terrorism with Democracy?

1. Tamara Cofman Wittes and Sarah E. Yerkes, "What Price Freedom? Assessing the Bush Administration's Freedom Agenda," Saban

Center for Middle East Policy at the Brookings Institution, Analysis Paper no. 10 (September 2006), 10–11.

2. David Finkel, "In the End, a Painful Choice," *Washington Post,* December 20, 2005, A1.

3. Richard Clarke, "No Returns," *New York Times,* February 6, 2005, sec. 6, p. 20.

4. F. Gregory Gause III, "Can Democracy Stop Terrorism?" *Foreign Affairs* (September–October 2005): 62–76.

5. Crenshaw, "How Terrorism Declines," 86.

6. Jonathan Stevenson, "Northern Ireland: Treating Terrorists as Statesmen," *Foreign Policy* 105 (Winter 1996–1997), electronic version; Louise Richardson, "Britain and the IRA," in *Democracy and Counterterrorism: Lessons from the Past,* ed. Robert J. Art and Louise Richardson (Washington, D.C.: USIP Press, 2007), 63–104.

7. Sara Roy, "Hamas and the Transformation of Political Islam in Palestine," *Current History* (January 2003): 17.

8. *Arab Human Development Report 2003,* 19.

9. Ray Takeyh, "Let Democracy Derail Radicalism," *Baltimore Sun,* March 21, 2005.

10. Amr Hamzawy, "The Key to Arab Reform: Moderate Islamists," Policy Brief 40, Carnegie Endowment for International Peace, August 2005.

11. Graham E. Fuller, *The Future of Political Islam* (New York: Palgrave Macmillan, 2003), 14.

12. Leonard B. Weinberg and William L. Eubank, "Terrorism and Democracy: Perpetrators and Victims," *Terrorism and Political Violence* 13, no. 1 (Spring 2001): 158. To be fair, many studies are inconclusive. As F. Gregory Gause, an expert on the Middle East, contends rather blandly, "Data available do not show a strong relationship between democracy and an absence of or a reduction in terrorism." Gause, "Can Democracy Stop Terrorism?"

13. James D. Fearon and David D. Laitin, "Ethnicity, Insurgency, and Civil War," *American Political Science Review* 97, no. 1 (February 2003): 75–90.

14. Fernando Reinares, "Democratic Regimes, Internal Security Policy, and the Threat of Terrorism," *Australian Journal of Politics and History* 44, no. 3 (1998): 367.

15. Raphael Israeli, "Western Democracies and Islamic Fundamentalist Violence."

16. Peter Bergen and Swati Pandey, "The Madrassa Scapegoat," *Washington Quarterly* 29, no. 2 (Spring 2006): 118.

17. John Gieve, letter to Sir Andrew Turnbull accompanying the report "Relations with the Muslim Community," Home Office, May 10, 2005, para. 3.

18. Rajiv Chandrasekaran and Peter Finn, "U.S. behind Secret Transfer," *Washington Post,* March 11, 2002, A1; Andrew Higgins and Christopher Cooper, "Cloak and Dagger: A CIA-Backed Team Used Brutal Means to Crack Terror Cell," *Wall Street Journal,* November 20, 2001, A1.

19. Dana Priest, "CIA's Assurances on Transferred Suspects Doubted," *Washington Post,* March 17, 2005, A1.

20. Abdelwahab El-Affendi, "The Conquest of Muslim Hearts and Minds? Perspectives on U.S. Reform and Public Diplomacy Strategies," Saban Center for Middle East Policy at the Brookings Institution, working paper, Washington, D.C., September 2005, v.

21. Gause, "Can Democracy Stop Terrorism?"

22. *Arab Human Development Report, 2003,* 19.

23. Fuller, *Future of Political Islam,* 38–40.

24. Ibid., 29.

25. I would like to thank Tamara Cofman Wittes for raising this argument with me.

26. Fuller, *Future of Political Islam,* 139.

27. Wilkinson, *Terrorism versus Democracy,* 86; Stevenson, "Northern Ireland."

28. Wilkinson, *Terrorism versus Democracy,* 90.

29. Ibid.

30. Ibid., 88.

31. David Finkel, "U.S. Ideals Meet Reality in Yemen," *Washington Post,* December 18, 2005, A1.

32. Ibid.; David Finkel, "A Struggle for Peace in a Place where Fighting Never Ends," *Washington Post,* December 19, 2005, A1; David Finkel, "In the End, a Painful Choice," *Washington Post,* December 20, 2005, A1.

7. The War of Ideas

1. Alice Kendrick and Jami A. Fullerton, "Advertising as Public Diplomacy: Attitude Change among International Audiences," *Journal of Advertising Research* 44, no. 3 (September 2004): 297–311.

2. Abdelwahab El-Affendi, "The Conquest of Muslim Hearts and Minds? Perspectives on U.S. Reform and Public Diplomacy Strategies," Saban Center for Middle East Policy at the Brookings Institution, working

paper, Washington, D.C., September 2005, 3. Despite focus groups showing that the ads had some value, in practice the hullabaloo about them
led most viewers to see them as propaganda rather than as an accurate
portrayal of the way Muslims in the United States really live. For one
interesting study of the effect of the advertisements on focus groups,
see Alice Kendrick and Jami A. Fullerton, "Advertising as Public Diplomacy: Attitude Change among International Audiences," *Journal of Advertising Research* (September 2004): 305.

3. Richard Holbrooke, "Get the Message Out," *Washington Post,*
October 28, 2001, B7.

4. Bergen, *The Osama bin Laden I Know,* 32.

5. *Al Jihad* 1 (December 28, 1984). As cited in *The Early Years of Al-
Qaeda* (Santa Monica, Calif.: RAND, forthcoming).

6. Hassan M. Fattah, "Good Jihad, Bad Jihad: Struggle for Arab
Minds," *New York Times,* October 27, 2005. Available at http://www
.nytimes.com/2005/10/27/international/middleeast/27ramadan.html.

7. Daniel Benjamin and Steven Simon report in *The Next Attack,* 78,
that there were forty-four hundred jihadist Web sites.

8. See http://www.kavkazcenter.com/eng/ebook.html. I would like to
thank Charles King for bringing this to my attention.

9. Rebecca Givner-Forbes and Ned Moran, "The Internet Jihad
Date = 2006 Organization/Company." Terrorism Research Center, November 21, 2006.

10. International Crisis Group, "In Their Own Words," 15.

11. Givner-Forbes and Moran, "The Internet Jihad Date = 2006."

12. Marc Sageman, *Understanding Terror Networks* (Philadelphia:
University of Pennsylvania Press, 2004), 101–110.

13. See Hoffman, *Inside Terrorism,* 1–44, for a review of terrorism's
historical uses.

14. "Commander of Khobar Terrorist Squad Tells the Story of
the Operation," Middle East Media Research Institute, no. 731, June
15, 2004.

15. Peter Bergen and Swati Pandey, "The Madrassa Scapegoat,"
Washington Quarterly 29, no. 2 (Spring 2006): 117–125.

16. Terrorism is far more likely to be supported by those who believe
that Islam is threatened. C. Christine Fair and Bryan Shepherd, "Who
Supports Terrorism? Evidence from Fourteen Muslim Countries," *Studies
in Conflict and Terrorism* 29 (2006): 51–74.

17. "Dr. Rice Addresses War on Terror," remarks by National
Security Adviser Condoleezza Rice, U.S. Institute of Peace, August 19, 2004.

18. Ibid.

19. William Rugh in Garfinkle, ed., *A Practical Guide to Winning the War on Terrorism*, 157.

20. Daoud Kuttab and Ellen Laipson, ibid., 166.

21. Alan Cooperman, "Ministers Asked to Curb Remarks about Islam," *Washington Post*, May 8, 2003. Available at http://www.washingtonpost .com/ac2/wp-dyn?pagename=article&contentId=A27619–2003May7&not Found=true.

22. Abdelwahab El-Affendi, "The Conquest of Muslim Hearts and Minds? Perspectives on U.S. Reform and Public Diplomacy Strategies," Saban Center for Middle East Policy at the Brookings Institution, working paper, Washington, D.C., September 2005, 3, 7–8.

23. Reuel Marc Gerecht, "Selling Out Moderate Islam," *Weekly Standard*, February 20, 2006.

24. "Arab TV Discusses Terrorism in Saudi Arabia," Middle East Media Research Institute no. 752, July 23, 2004.

25. International Crisis Group, "In Their Own Words," 10.

26. Stephen Johnson, Helle C. Dale, and Patrick Cronin, "Strengthening U.S. Public Diplomacy Requires Organization, Coordination, and Strategy," Heritage Foundation Backgrounder, August 5, 2005, ii.

27. Stephen Johnson and Helle Dale, "How to Reinvigorate U.S. Public Diplomacy," Heritage Foundation Backgrounder, April 23, 2003, 3.

28. Pew Global Attitudes Project, "Support for Terror Wanes among Muslim Publics," July 14, 2005.

29. Richard Beeston, "Greek Government Is Accused of Collusion," *Times* of London, June 9, 2000.

30. Statement published in full by *Guardian*, June 10, 2000, 2.

31. Henry Schuster, "Poll of Saudis Shows Wide Support for bin Laden's Views," CNN.com. Available at http://www.cnn.com/2004/ WORLD/meast/06/08/poll.binladen.

32. Hassan M. Fattah, "Good Jihad, Bad Jihad: Struggle for Arab Minds," *New York Times*, October 27, 2005. Available at http://www .nytimes.com/2005/10/27/international/middleeast/27ramadan.html.

33. "Saudi Columnist: Terrorists Mistreat Their Wives and Children," Middle East Media Research Institute, July 15, 2005.

34. Y. Admon, "Anti-Soccer Fatwas Led Saudi Soccer Players to Join the Jihad in Iraq," Middle East Media Research Institute, October 7, 2005.

35. U.S. Department of Defense, Office of the Under Secretary for Acquisition, Technology, and Logistics, *Report of the Defense Science Board Task Force on Managed Information Dissemination*, October

2001, 1. See also the 2003 report of a government advisory group chaired by former ambassador Edward P. Djerejian, which found that U.S. public diplomacy "has become outmoded, lacking both strategic direction and resources." Report of the Advisory Group on Public Diplomacy for the Arab and Muslim World, "Changing Minds, Winning Peace: A New Strategic Direction for U.S. Public Diplomacy in the Arab and Muslim World," October 1, 2003, 8.

8. Diplomacy

1. National Commission on Terrorist Attacks upon the United States, *The 9/11 Commission Report* (New York: W. W. Norton, 2004), 379.

2. In a speech at Georgetown University on January 18, 2006, Secretary of State Condoleezza Rice called for "transformational diplomacy" and restructuring the State Department to focus less on old concerns and more on countries relevant to counterterrorism as well as other emerging issues. See "Transformational Diplomacy" at http://www.state.gov/secretary/rm/2006/59306.htm.

3. Peter Baker, "Old Enemies Enlist in U.S. Terror War," *Washington Post*, January 1, 2004, A18.

4. Paul R. Pillar, "Counterterrorism after Al-Qa'ida," *Washington Quarterly* 27, no. 3 (Summer 2004): 106.

5. Barry Posen, "The Struggle against Terrorism," 43; Jennifer Sims, "Foreign Intelligence Liaison—Devils, Deals, and Details." Allies, however, may exaggerate al-Qa'ida's links to local groups, leading to skewed U.S. assessments of the danger if there is no information to vet the liaison information. For example, the United States may have exaggerated al-Qa'ida's links to al-Ittihaad al-Islamiyya in Somalia due to information fed to Washington by the Ethiopian government. "Somalia," *The Economist Intelligence Unit: Country Profile 2004* (London: Economist Intelligence Unit, 2004), available at http://www.eui.com.

6. Former director of Central Intelligence George Tenet singled out Saudi Arabia, Jordan, Morocco, Egypt, Algeria, the UAE, Oman, and Pakistan for praise in his testimony on the worldwide threat in 2004. George Tenet, "The Worldwide Threat 2004: Challenges in a Changing Global Context," testimony of Director of Central Intelligence before the Senate Armed Services Committee, March 9, 2004. See also Fair, "India and Pakistan," 18.

7. Craig Whitlock, "French Push Limits in Fight on Terrorism," *Washington Post*, November 1, 2004, A1.

8. Daniel Byman, "Confronting Passive Sponsors of Terrorism," Saban Center Analysis Paper no. 4 (Washington, D.C.: Brookings Institution, 2005), 31.

9. James Dobbins et al., *America's Role in Nation-Building: From Germany to Iraq* (Santa Monica, Calif.: RAND, 2003), 149–166.

10. James D. Fearon and David D. Laitin, "Neotrusteeship and the Problem of Weak States," *International Security* 28, no. 4 (Spring 2004): 9.

11. Jeremy Shapiro and Benedicte Suzan, "The French Experience of Counter-terrorism," *Survival* 45, no. 1 (Spring 2003): 81.

12. Zachary Abuza, *Militant Islam in Southeast Asia: Crucible of Terror* (Boulder, Colo.: Lynne Rienner, 2003), 121–188.

13. Despite the length of the insurgency, both the number and motives of the various insurgent groups in Iraq remain confusing. See Eric Schmitt and Thom Shanker, "U.S. Pushes Upward Its Estimate of Rebels in Iraq," *New York Times,* October 22, 2004, A1.

14. "Faithful, but Not Fanatics," *Economist,* June 28, 2003, 50.

15. Posen, for example, calls for reorienting several light conventional units toward the counterterrorist mission. Posen, "The Struggle against Terrorism," 4–48.

16. For example, then secretary of State Colin Powell declared that Central Asia is now of "strategic importance to U.S. foreign policy initiatives." Secretary of State Colin L. Powell, statement to the House of Representatives Committee on International Relations, February 12, 2003. Available at http://wwwc.house.gov/international_relations/108/powe0212.htm.

17. "Bin Ladin's Message," November 12, 2002. Available at http://news.bbc.co.uk/2/hi/middle_east/2455845.stm.

18. Snyder, *Alliance Politics,* 145.

19. David Stevenson, *Cataclysm: The First World War as Political Tragedy* (New York: Basic Books, 2004), 40.

20. Jusuf Wanandi, "A Global Coalition against International Terrorism," *International Security* 26, no. 4 (Spring 2002): 187.

21. This was formalized as a strategic partnership with Uzbekistan in March 2002. See http://www.state.gov/r/pa/prs/ps/202/8736.htm.

22. "The Great Leap West," *Economist,* August 28, 2004, 38.

23. World Islamic Front statement, February 23, 1998. Available at http://www.fas.org/irp/world/para/docs/980223-fatwa.htm.

24. See in particular bin ladin's "Letter to America," November 24, 2002. Available at http://observer.guardian.co.uk/worldview/story/0,11581,845725,00.html.

25. Fair, "India and Pakistan," 9.

26. Anonymous, *Imperial Hubris: Why the West is Losing the War on Terror* (Washington, D.C.: Brassey's, 2004), 54–55.

27. Thomas J. Christensen and Jack Snyder, "Chain Gangs and Passed Bucks: Predicting Alliance Patterns in Multipolarity," *International Organization* 44, no. 2 (Spring 1990): 139.

28. Rohan Gunaratna, *Inside Al-Qa'ida* (New York: Columbia University Press, 2002), 10.

29. James D. Fearon and David D. Laitin, "Ethnicity, Insurgency, and Civil War," *American Political Science Review* 97, no. 1 (February 2003): 12.

30. Kenneth Pollack, *Arabs at War* (Lincoln: University of Nebraska Press, 2002), 425–446.

31. Don Van Natta Jr. and Timothy O'Brien, "Saudis Promising Action on Terror," *New York Times*, September 13, 2003, A1.

32. Walt, "Why Alliances Endure or Collapse," 161.

33. Fortunately, intelligence-sharing is often somewhat independent of the strength of the overall bilateral relationship. See also Sims, "Foreign Intelligence Liaison—Devils, Deals, and Details."

34. Fair, "India and Pakistan," 30–32.

35. See Shapiro and Suzan, "The French Experience of Counterterrorism Experience"; Terence Taylor, "United Kingdom," in *Combating Terrorism: Strategies of Ten Countries*, ed. Yonah Alexander (Ann Arbor: University of Michigan Press, 2002), 196; International Crisis Group, *Saudi Arabia Backgrounder: Who Are the Islamists?* September 21, 2004; Gilles Kepel, *Jihad: The Trail of Political Islam* (Cambridge, Mass.: Harvard University Press, 2002), 205–298.

36. Pillar, *Terrorism and U.S. Foreign Policy*, 75–76.

37. For a list of recommendations on this issue, see Byman, "Confronting Passive Sponsors of Terrorism," 29–33.

38. This section draws on an essay I coauthored with Jeremy Shapiro. Many of the ideas in it were originally his and appear in our piece "Where You Stand Depends on Where You Get Hit: Explaining U.S. and European Differences in Counterterrorism," *Washington Quarterly* (Fall 2006): 33–50.

39. Richard Falkenrath, "Europe's Dangerous Complacency," *Financial Times* of London, July 7, 2004, 17.

40. See Charles M. Sennott, "Europe's Terror Fight Quiet, Unrelenting," *Boston Globe*, September 26, 2004, A1.

41. The Saban Center for Middle East Policy symposium, "How to Win the War against Terrorism," Brookings Institution, Washington, D.C., September 22, 2005, available at http://www.brookings.edu/fp/saban/

events/20050922.htm. Peter Bergen and Swati Pandey, "The Madrassa Scapegoat," *Washington Quarterly* 29, no. 2 (Spring 2006): 117–125.

42. John Letzing, "Cross-Border Security: The Visa Loophole," *PBS Frontline: Al-Qa'ida'. New Front,* January 25, 2005, available at http://www .pbs.org/wgbh/pages/frontline/shows/front/special/visa.html.

43. Dana Priest, "Foreign Network at Front of CIA's Terror Fight; Joint Facilities in Two Dozen Countries Account for Bulk of Agency's Post-9/11 Successes," *Washington Post,* November 18, 2005, A1; Dana Priest, "Help from France Key in Covert Operations; Paris's 'Alliance Base' Targets Terrorists," *Washington Post,* July 3, 2005, A1.

44. For examples of these views, see the interviews in Richard A. Clarke and Barry McCaffrey, *NATO's Role in Confronting International Terrorism,* Atlantic Council policy paper, June 2004, 7.

45. Cofer Black, "European Cooperation with the United States in the Global War on Terrorism," testimony before the Senate Foreign Relations Committee, Subcommittee on European Affairs, March 31, 2004.

46. Steven Weisman, "Allies Resisting as U.S. Pushes Terror Label for Hezbollah," *New York Times,* February 17, 2005, 1.

47. See Richard Bernstein, "Tape, Probably bin Laden's, Offers 'Truce' to Europe," *New York Times,* April 16, 2004, 3.

48. See Ihsan Bagby, Paul M. Perl, and Bryan T. Froehle, *The Mosque in America: A National Portrait,* a report from the Mosque Study Project, Council on American-Islamic Relations, Washington, D.C., April 26, 2001. Genieve Abdo, "Islam in America: Separate but Unequal," *Washington Quarterly* 28, no. 4 (Autumn 2005): 7–17.

49. See Mathew Purdy and Lowell Bergman, "Where the Trail Led: Inside the Lackawanna Terror Case," *New York Times,* October 12, 2003, A1.

50. Eliza Manningham-Butler, "The International Terrorist Threat to the UK," available at http://www.mi5.gov.uk/output/Page568.html#.

51. Scott Shane, "Official Reveals Budget for U.S. Intelligence," *New York Times,* November 8, 2005. Available at http://www.nytimes.com/2005/ 11/08/politics/08budget.html.

52. See Stephen Biddle, "Afghanistan and the Future of Warfare," *Foreign Affairs* 82, no. 2 (March–April 2003): 31–46. Available at http:// www.foreignaffairs.org/20030301faessay10337/stephen-biddle/afghanistan-and-the-future-of-warfare.html.

53. Author's interview with German journalist specializing in counterterrorism, May 2005.

54. The ability to recruit and replace lost cadre is vital for successful terrorist organizations. Kim Cragin and Sara A. Daly, *The Dynamic*

Terrorist Threat: An Assessment of Group Motivations and Capabilities in a Changing World (Santa Monica, Calif.: RAND, 2003), 34–36.

55. National Commission on Terrorist Attacks upon the United States, *The 9/11 Commission Report* (New York: W. W. Norton, 2004), 47–70, and Marc Sageman, *Understanding Terror Networks* (Philadelphia: University of Pennsylvania Press, 2004).

56. U.S. Army, "Counterinsurgency Operations," FMI 3–07.22 (October 2004), sec. 1–10.

57. For a discussion on the nationalistic backlash that outside occupiers face, see David Edelstein, "Occupational Hazards: Why Military Occupations Succeed or Fail," *International Security* 29, no. 1 (Summer 2004): 49–91, and Bard E. O'Neill, *Insurgency and Terrorism: Inside Modern Revolutionary Warfare* (Dulles, Va.: Brassey's, 1990), 137.

58. For a review of recent changes, see Andrew Feickert, "U.S. Special Operations Forces (SOF): Background and Issues for Congress," Congressional Research Service, September 28, 2004. In addition to expanding SOF's size, in 2003 the Defense Department has made Special Operations Command a "supported" command—that is, empowered to do independent action and planning.

59. In the Cold War, however, the U.S. military paid far more attention to external security—training militaries to fight other conventional military forces—than it did to helping paramilitary or other internal security forces. William Rosenau, *U.S. Internal Security Assistance to South Vietnam: Insurgency, Subversion, and Public Order* (New York: Routledge, 2005), 25, 77.

60. U.S. Government Accountability Office, "Afghanistan Security: Efforts to Establish Army and Police Have Made Progress, but Future Plans Need to Be Better Defined," June 2005, 1. Lieutenant General David Barno briefing, "Combined Forces Command—Afghanistan," March 15, 2006, 7.

61. Dana Priest, "Foreign Network at Front of CIA's Terror Fight," *Washington Post*, November 18, 2005, A1.

62. Raffi Khatchadourian, "Pursuing Terrorists in the Great Desert," January 31, 2006. Available at http://www.villagevoice.com/news/0605,khatchadourian,71993,6.html.

63. Priest, "Foreign Network at Front of CIA's Terror Fight," A1.

64. Khatchadourian, "Pursuing Terrorists in the Great Desert."

65. See Rice, "Transformational Diplomacy."

66. Walt, "Beyond bin Laden," 72.

67. For a review of Russia's brutal and often ineffective approach to the Chechen conflict, see Mark Kramer, "The Perils of Counterinsurgency:

Russia's War in Chechnya," *International Security* 29, no. 3 (Winter 2004–2005): 5–63.

68. Ron Hutcheson and Jonathan S. Landay, "Bush Plan Would Close Military Bases Overseas," *Detroit Free Press,* August 17, 2004. Available at http://www.freep.com/news/nw/troops17e_20040817.htm.

69. "Pentagon Expands Middle East Outposts," Associated Press, September 23, 2004. Available at http://www.military.com/NewsContent/0,13319,FL_outposts_092304,00.html.

70. "FSB Says CIA Holding Back in the War on Terror," *Moscow Times,* April 24, 2002, 4. I would like to thank Nora Bensahel for bringing this point to my attention.

71. Al-Qa'ida, of course, has probably penetrated some governments. Anonymous, *Through Our Enemies' Eyes,* 24. The level of this penetration is nowhere near the masterful level of the Soviet Union.

72. Fu'ad Husayn, *Al-Zarqawi: The Second Generation of Al-Qa'ida,* serialized in *Al-Quds Al-'Arabi,* June 8, 2005.

73. For a review, see William Rosenau, "The Eisenhower Administration, U.S. Foreign Internal Security Assistance, and the Struggle for the Developing World, 1954–1961," *Low Intensity Conflict and Law Enforcement* 10, no. 3 (Autumn 2001): 1–32.

74. Already U.S. special operations forces are in West Africa, Central Asia, and other remote locations to train local soldiers against groups linked to al-Qa'ida. The State Department also has antiterrorism assistance (ATA) programs to help train foreign law enforcement and security officers with regard to counterterrorism, and since September 11 this training has focused on many countries in the Arab world, South Asia, and Central Asia, among other key areas. Craig S. Smith, "U.S. Training African Forces to Uproot Terrorists," *New York Times,* May 11, 2004, A1.; U.S. Department of State, *Patterns of Global Terrorism 2003* (Washington, D.C., 2004), 147–148.

9. The Iraq Dilemma

1. Fu'ad Husayn, *Al-Zarqawi: The Second Generation of Al-Qa'ida,* serialized in *Al-Quds Al-'Arabi,* June 8, 2005. Zarqawi, as with many jihadists, had a Shakespearean quality to him: he was a thug full of hate, yet capable of admirable love. He loved his mother, with his compatriots noting that in prison he "used to count the minutes until his mother's visit." He wrote plaintively, "God knows, I wish for nothing more than I wish to be with you, my most beloved mother."

2. http://english.aljazeera.net/NR/exeres/407AAE91-AF72-45D7-83E9-486063C0E5EA.htm.

3. Husayn, *Al-Zarqawi,* June 8, 2005.

4. http://www.whitehouse.gov/news/releases/2003/09/20030907–1.html.

5. Rueven Paz, "Arab Volunteers Killed in Iraq: An Analysis," Project for the Research of Islamist Movements Occasional Papers 3, no. 1 (March 2005).

6. Negroponte, "Annual Threat Briefing," February 2, 2006, testimony before the Senate Select Committee on Intelligence.

7. International Crisis Group, "In Their Own Words: Reading the Iraqi Insurgency," Middle East Report 50, February 15, 2006, i.

8. Ibid., 9.

9. "Bin Ladin Expert Steps Forward," *60 Minutes,* November 14, 2004; available at http://www.cbsnews.com/stories/2004/11/12/60minutes/main655407.shtml.

10. Director of National Intelligence, "Declassified Key Judgments of the National Intelligence Estimate "Trends in Global Terrorism: Implications for the United States" (April 2006). Available at http://www.dni.gov/press_releases/Declassified_NIE_Key_Judgments.pdf.

11. Toby Craig Jones, "The Clerics, the Sahwa, and the Saudi State," *Strategic Insights* 4, no. 3 (March 2005). Electronic version.

12. Alexis Debat, "Vivisecting the Jihad," *National Interest* 76 (Summer 2004): 22.

13. Barton and Crocker, "Progress or Peril?" 86.

14. I would like to thank Ken Pollack for bringing this issue to my attention.

15. Brookings Institution, "The Iraq Index." Available at http://www.brookings.edu/iraqindex.

16. Barton and Crocker, "Progress or Peril?" 22 and 79.

17. Scott Wilson, "Fear Hamstrings Quest for Intelligence in N. Iraq," *Washington Post,* December 11, 2004, A19.

18. "Malnutrition Rising among Iraq's Children," Associated Press, November 22, 2004. Brookings Institution, "The Iraq Index," downloaded on November 18, 2004.

19. Changing the system to increase Sunni rights, however, might anger Iraq's majority Shi'a population. Many Shi'a leaders favor democracy because they believe majority rule will lead to their community's dominance. This has led to concerns among Sunnis but also among Kurds, who worry that they will lose the high degree of autonomy that they have enjoyed for years.

20. Eric Schmitt, "Guard Reports Serious Drop in Enlistment," *New York Times,* December 17, 2004; Krepinevich, "The Thin Green Line," 5–7; Michael E. O'Hanlon, "A Matter of Force—and Fairness," *Washington Post,* October 1, 2004. For a good overview of the many problems, see On Point, "Military Overstretch," September 30, 2004; audio available at http://www.onpointradio.org/shows/2004/09/20040930_ a_main.asp.

21. Pew Charitable Trust, "A Year after Iraq War Mistrust of America in Europe Ever Higher, Muslim Anger Persists," March 16, 2004.

22. Anonymous, *Imperial Hubris* (Dulles, Va.: Brassey's, 2004), xiii.

23. "Bin Laden Statement," http://english.aljazeera.net/NR/exeres/79C6AF22-98FB-4A1C-B21F-2BC36E87F61F.htm.

24. The jihadists' conspiratorial worldview is already making much of its "victory" so far in Iraq. Their discourse contends that the United States entered Iraq to pillage its oil reserves, and they claim that the United States has lost $20 trillion due to their actions—an absurd claim, but one that appears to be accepted by many. Benjamin and Simon, *The Next Attack*, 38.

25. James D. Fearon, "Commitment Problems and the Spread of Ethnic Conflict," in David A. Lake and Donald Rothschild, eds., *The International Spread of Ethnic Conflict: Fear, Diffusion, and Escalation* (Princeton, N.J.: Princeton University Press, 1998), 107–126.

26. International Crisis Group, "In Their Own Words," 10.

27. Rueven Paz, "Arab Volunteers Killed in Iraq: An Analysis," Project for the Research of Islamist Movements Occasional Papers, 3, no. 1 (March 2005): 6.

28. International Crisis Group, "In Their Own Words," 12.

29. Daniel Byman and Kenneth Pollack, *Things Fall Apart* (Washington, D.C.: Brookings, 2007).

Bibliography

Abdo, Genieve. "Islam in America: Separate but Unequal." *Washington Quarterly* 28, no. 4 (Autumn 2005): 7–17.

Abuza, Zachary. *Militant Islam in Southeast Asia: Crucible of Terror.* Boulder, Colo.: Lynne Rienner, 2003, 121–188.

"Adding Up the Ounces of Prevention." *New York Times,* September 10, 2006, A4.

Admon, Y. "Anti-Soccer Fatwas Led Saudi Soccer Players to Join the Jihad in Iraq." Middle East Media Research Institute, October 7, 2005.

"Algerian Group Backs al-Qaeda." BBC News, October 23, 2003. http://news.bbc.co.uk/1/hi/world/africa/3207363.stm.

Amuzegar, Jahangir. "Iran's Crumbling Revolution." *Foreign Affairs* 82, no. 1 (January/February 2003): 44–57.

Anonymous [Michael Scheuer]. *Imperial Hubris: Why the West Is Losing the War on Terror.* Washington, D.C.: Brassey's, 2004.

———. *Through Our Enemies' Eyes.* Washington, D.C.: Potomac Books, 2003.

"Arab TV Discusses Terrorism in Saudi Arabia." Middle East Media Research Institute Special Dispatch Series 752, July 23, 2004.

Art, Robert J. *A Grand Strategy for America.* Ithaca, N.Y.: Cornell University Press, 2004.

Bagby, Ihsan, Paul M. Perl, and Bryan T. Froehle. "The Mosque in America: A National Portrait: A Report from the Mosque Study Project." Washington, D.C.: Council on American-Islamic Relations, April 26, 2001.

Baker, Peter. "Old Enemies Enlist in U.S. Terror War." *Washington Post,* January 2004, A18.

Baram, Amatzia. "The Effect of Iraqi Sanctions: Statistical Pitfalls and Responsibility." *Middle East Journal* 54, no. 2 (Spring 2000): 197–223.

Barton, Frederick, and Bathsheba Crocker. "Progress or Peril? Measuring Iraq's Reconstruction." Washington, D.C.: Center for Strategic and International Studies, September 1, 2004.

Beeston, Richard. "Greek Government Is Accused of Collusion." *Times* of London, June 9, 2000.

Benjamin, Daniel, and Steven Simon. *The Age of Sacred Terror.* New York: Random House, 2002.

———. *The Next Attack: The Failure of the War on Terror and a Strategy for Getting It Right.* New York: Owl Books, 2005.

Bensahel, Nora. "The Counterterror Coalitions: Cooperation with Europe, NATO, and the European Union." Santa Monica, Calif.: RAND, 2003.

Bergen, Peter. *Holy War, Inc. Inside the Secret World of Osama bin Laden.* New York: Free Press, 2002.

———. *The Osama bin Laden I Know: An Oral History of al Qaeda's Leader.* New York: Free Press, 2006.

Bergen, Peter, and Swati Pandey. "The Madrassa Scapegoat." *Washington Quarterly* 29, no. 2 (Spring 2006): 118.

Bernstein, Richard. "Tape, Probably bin Laden's, Offers 'Truce' to Europe." *New York Times,* April 16, 2004, A3.

Berrick, Cathleen A. "Aviation Security: Efforts to Measure Effectiveness and Strengthen Security Programs." Testimony before U.S. House of Representatives Committee on Government Reform, November 20, 2003.

Biddle, Stephen. "Afghanistan and the Future of Warfare." *Foreign Affairs* 82, no. 2 (March–April 2003): 31–46. http://www.foreignaffairs .org/20030301faessay10337/stephen-biddle/afghanistan-and-the-future-of-warfare.htm.

———. "American Grand Strategy after 9/11: An Assessment." Carlisle, Pa.: U.S. Army War College, April 2005.

"Bin Ladin Expert Steps Forward." *60 Minutes,* November 14, 2004. http://www.cbsnews.com/stories/2004/11/12/60minutes/main655407 .shtml.

"Bin Ladin Statement." http://english.aljazeera.net/NR/exeres/ 79C6AF22-98FB-4A1C-B21F-2BC36E87F61F.htm.

"Bin Ladin's 'Letter to America.'" *Guardian,* November 24, 2002. http://observer.guardian.co.uk/worldview/story/0,11581,845725,00 .html.

"Bin Ladin's Message." BBC News, November 12, 2002. http://news .bbc.co.uk/2/hi/middle_east/2455845.stm.

Black, Cofer. "European Cooperation with the United States in the Global War on Terrorism." Testimony before the Senate Foreign Relations Committee, Subcommittee on European Affairs, March 31, 2004.

Bonner, Raymond, and David Johnston. "Pakistanis Say Suspect Described Recent Meeting with Bin Laden." *New York Times,* March 6, 2003, A1.

Britt, Robert Roy. "The Odds of Dying." LiveScience.com, January 6, 2005.   http://www.livescience.com/forcesofnature/050106_odds_of _dying.html#table.

Brookings Institution. "The Iraq Index," November 18, 2004. Available at www.brookings.edu/iraqindex.

B'Tselem: The Israeli Information Center for Human Rights in the Occupied Territories. "Statistics." http://www.btselem.org/english/ Statistics/Casualties.asp.

Burke, Jason. *Al-Qaeda: The True Story of Radical Islam.* New York: Penguin, 2004.

Byman, Daniel. "Confronting Passive Sponsors of Terrorism." Saban Center Analysis Paper 4. Washington, D.C.: Brookings, 2005.

Byman, Daniel, and Kenneth Pollack. *Things Fall Apart.* Washington, D.C.: Brookings, 2007.

Centers for Disease Control. "Deaths: Preliminary Data for 2004." *National Vital Statistics Report* 54, no. 19 (June 28, 2006). http:// www.cdc.gov/nchs/data/nvsr/nvsr54/nvsr54_19.pdf.

Chambliss, Saxby. "Counterterrorism Intelligence Capabilities and Performance Prior to 9-11," Subcommittee on Terrorism and Homeland Security House Permanent Select Committee on Intelligence, July 2002.

Chandrasekaran, Rajiv, and Peter Finn. "U.S. behind Secret Transfer." *Washington Post,* March 11, 2002, A1.

Chapman, Clark, and Allan Harris. "A Skeptical Look at September 11: How We Can Defeat Terrorism by Reacting to It More Rationally." *Skeptical Inquirer* (September–October 2002).

Chichizola, Jean. "Madmen of Allah and Criminals Make Common Cause on Holdups." *Le Figaro,* January 13, 2006.

Christensen, Thomas J., and Jack Snyder. "Chain Gangs and Passed Bucks: Predicting Alliance Patterns in Multipolarity." *International Organization* 44, no. 2 (Spring 1990): 139.

Clarke, Richard. *Against All Enemies: Inside America's War on Terror.* New York: Free Press, 2004.

————. "No Returns." *New York Times,* February 6, 2005.

Clarke, Richard A., and Barry McCaffrey. "NATO's Role in Confronting International Terrorism." Atlantic Council Policy Paper, June 2004, 7.

CNN. "Transcript of President Bush's Address to a Joint Session of Congress on Thursday Night, September 20, 2001," September 21, 2001. http://www.cnn.com/2001/US/09/20/gen.bush.transcript/.

Cole, David. "Enemy Aliens." *Stanford Law Review* 54 (May 2002): 955.

Cole, David. *Enemy Aliens.* New York: New Press, 2003.

Coll, Steve. *Ghost Wars: The Secret History of the CIA, Afghanistan, and bin Laden, from the Soviet Invasion to September 10, 2001.* New York: Penguin, 2004.

Combating Terrorism Center at West Point. "Harmony and Disharmony: Exploiting Al-Qa'ida's Organizational Vulnerabilities," February 14, 2006. http://www.ctc.usma.edu/aq_challenges.asp.

"Command of Khobar Terrorist Squad Tells the Story of the Operation." Middle East Media Research Institute Special Dispatch Series 731, June 15, 2004.

Congressional 9/11 Inquiry. "Joint Inquiry Staff Statement: Hearings on the Intelligence Community's Response to Past Terrorist Attacks against the United States from February 1993 to September 2001," October 8, 2002, 11.

Cooperman, Alan. "Ministers Asked to Curb Remarks about Islam," *Washington Post,* May 8, 2003, A03. http://www.washingtonpost .com/ac2/wpdyn?pagename=article&contentId=A27619–2003May7 &notFound=true.

Cordesman, Anthony. *Iran's Military Forces in Transition: Conventional Threats and Weapons of Mass Destruction.* Westport, Conn.: Praeger, 1999.

Cragin, Kim, and Sara A. Daly. *The Dynamic Terrorist Threat: An Assessment of Group Motivations and Capabilities in a Changing World.* Santa Monica, Calif.: RAND, 2003, 34–36.

Crenshaw, Martha. "How Terrorism Declines." *Terrorism and Political Violence* 3, no. 1 (Spring 1991): 69–87.

Cronin, Audrey Kurth, and James M. Ludes, eds. *Attacking Terrorism: Elements of a Grand Strategy.* Washington, D.C.: Georgetown University Press, 2004.

Cullison, Alan, and Andrew Higgins. "Strained Alliance: Al Qaeda's Sour Days in Afghanistan." *Wall Street Journal,* August 2, 2002.

Debat, Alexis. "Vivisecting the Jihad." *National Interest* (Summer 2004): 22.

Department of Homeland Security. "DHS Budget-in-brief (FY 2007)." http://www.dhs.gov/interweb/assetlibrary/Budget_BIB-FY2007.pdf.

de Rugy, Veronique. "What Does Homeland Security Spending Buy?" Washington, D.C.: American Enterprise Institute, April 1, 2005.

Diamond, John. "It's No Secret: CIA Scouting for Recruits." *USA Today*, November 22, 2005.

Dickey, Christopher. "Jihad Express." *Newsweek*, March 21, 2005, 34–36.

Dobbins, James, et al. *America's Role in Nation-Building: From Germany to Iraq*. Santa Monica, Calif.: RAND, 2003.

Doran, Michael Scott. "Somebody Else's Civil War." *Foreign Affairs* 81, no. 1 (January–February 2002): 22–42.

Dougherty, Jill. "Chechen 'Claims Belsan Attack.'" CNN.com, September 17, 2004.

"Dr. Rice Addresses War on Terror." Remarks by National Security Adviser Condoleezza Rice, U.S. Institute of Peace, August 19, 2004.

Eckholm, Erik. "Muted Alliance: FBI Active in Pakistan, but Profile Is Low." *New York Times*, March 4, 2003, A14.

———. "Pakistanis Arrest Qaeda Figure Seen as Planner of 9/11." *New York Times*, March 2, 2003, A1.

Eckholm, Erik, and David Johnston. "Qaeda Suspect, Sound Asleep at Trail's End, Offers No Resistance." *New York Times*, March 3, 2003, A1.

Economist Intelligence Unit. "Somalia." Country Profile, 2004.

Edelstein, David. "Occupational Hazards: Why Military Occupations Succeed or Fail." *International Security* 29, no. 1 (Summer 2004): 49–91.

El-Affendi, Abdelwahab. "The Conquest of Muslim Hearts and Minds? Perspectives on U.S. Reform and Public Diplomacy Strategies." Working paper, Saban Center for Middle East Policy, Brookings Institution, September 2005.

Ephron, Dan. "Most Israelis Are Combatants." *Newsweek*, July 2002.

Ervin, Clark Kent. *Open Target: Where America Is Vulnerable to Attack*. New York: Palgrave Macmillan, 2006.

Fair, C. Christine. "Militant Recruitment in Pakistan: Implications for Al-Qa'ida and Other Organizations." *Studies in Conflict and Terrorism* 27, no. 6 (November/December 2004): 8.

Fair, C. Christine, and Bryan Shepherd. "Who Supports Terrorism? Evidence from Fourteen Muslim Countries." *Studies in Conflict and Terrorism* 29, no. 1 (January/February 2006): 51–74.

"Faithful, but Not Fanatics." *Economist,* June 28, 2003, 50.

Falkenrath, Richard. "Europe's Dangerous Complacency." *Financial Times* of London, July 7, 2004, 17.

———. Remarks at Brookings Institution Panel "How to Win the War on Terrorism," September 22, 2005. http://www.brookings.edu/fp/saban/events/20050922_panel1.pdf.

Fallows, James. "Success without Victory." *Atlantic Monthly* (January–February 2005).

Faramarzi, Scheherezade. "Drawn to Insurgency." Associated Press, November 26, 2004.

Fattah, Hassan M. "Good Jihad, Bad Jihad: Struggle for Arab Minds." *New York Times,* October 27, 2005.

Fearon, James D. "Commitment Problems and the Spread of Ethnic Conflict." In David A. Lake and Donald Rothschild, eds., *The International Spread of Ethnic Conflict: Fear, Diffusion, and Escalation.* Princeton, N.J.: Princeton University Press, 1998.

Fearon, James D., and David D. Laitin. "Ethnicity, Insurgency, and Civil War." *American Political Science Review* 97, no. 1 (February 2003): 75–90.

———. "Neotrusteeship and the Problem of Weak States." *International Security* 28, no. 4 (Spring 2004): 9.

Feickert, Andrew. "U.S. Special Operations Forces (SOF): Background and Issues for Congress." Congressional Research Service, September 28, 2004.

Finkel, David. "In the End, a Painful Choice." *Washington Post,* December 20, 2005, A1.

———. "A Struggle for Peace in a Place where Fighting Never Ends." *Washington Post,* December 19, 2005, A1.

———. "U.S. Ideals Meet Reality in Yemen." *Washington Post,* December 18, 2005, A1.

FoxNews.com. "Documents: Saudis Paid Bombers' Families," April 26, 2002. http://www.foxnews.com/story/0,2933,51252,00.html.

Franchetti, Mark, and Matthew Campbell. "How a Repressed Village Misfit Became the Butcher of Beslan." *Sunday Times* of London, September 12, 2004.

Frontline: Al Qaeda's New Front. "Al Qaeda Today: The New Face of the Global Jihad," January 25, 2005. Telvick, Marlena. http://www.pbs.org/wgbh/pages/frontline/shows/front/etc/today.html.

"FSB Says CIA Holding Back in the War on Terror." *Moscow Times*, April 24, 2002.

Fuller, Graham E. *The Future of Political Islam*. New York: Palgrave Macmillan, 2006.

Garfinkle, Adam, ed. *A Practical Guide to Winning the War on Terrorism*. Stanford, Calif.: Hoover Institution Press, 2004. http://www.hoover.org/publications/books/3009071.html.

Gause, F. Gregory III. "Can Democracy Stop Terrorism?" *Foreign Affairs* (September–October 2005): 62–76.

Gerecht, Reuel Marc. "Selling Out Moderate Islam." *Weekly Standard*, February 20, 2006, 24–29.

Gerges, Fawaz. "Osama Must Be Laughing." *Age*, March 28, 2003. http://www.theage.com.au/articles/2003/03/27/1048653802724.html.

Gieve, John. Letter to Sir Andrew Turnbull accompanying report "Relations with the Muslim Community." London: U.K. Home Office, May 10, 2005, para. 3.

Global Terror Alert. Osama Bin Laden Audio Message Offering Reward for Killing Kofi Annan (May 5, 2004). http://www.globalterroralert.com/ublmsg0506.html.

Goodman, Brenda. "U.S. Says 2 Georgia Men Planned a Terror Attack" *New York Times*, April 22, 2006.

"The Great Leap West." *Economist*, August 28, 2004, 38.

Griffin, Michael. *Reaping the Whirlwind: The Taliban Movement in Afghanistan*. London: Pluto Press, 2001.

Gunaratna, Rohan. "Al Qaeda: Its Organizational Strengths and Weaknesses with a Special Focus on the pre-1996 Phases." Paper prepared for February 1, 2006, meeting at the RAND Corporation in Washington, D.C.

———. *Inside Al-Qa'ida*. New York: Columbia University Press, 2002.

Gurr, Ted Robert. "Terrorism in Democracies: Its Social and Political Bases." In Walter Reich, ed., *Origins of Terrorism: Psychologies, Ideologies, Theologies, and States of Mind*. New York: Cambridge University Press, 1990, 87–98.

Haddad, Yvonne Yazbeck, and Jane I. Smith. *Muslim Communities in North America*. Albany: State University of New York Press, 1994.

Hamzawy, Amr. "The Key to Arab Reform: Moderate Islamists." Carnegie Endowment for International Peace Policy Brief 40 (August 2005).

Hearn, Dana Leigh. "The Palestinian Territories: Signs of Change Amidst Ongoing Suffering." Population Reference Bureau. http://www.prb .org/Template.cfm?Section=PRB&template=/ContentManagement /ContentDisplay.cfm&ContentID=12160.

Henderson, Nicole J., Christopher W. Ortiz, Naomi F. Sugie, and Joel Miller. *Law Enforcement & Arab American Community Relations after September 11, 2001: Engagement in a Time of Uncertainty.* New York: Vera Institute of Justice, 2006. http://www.vera.org/ policerelations.

Hennessy, Patrick, and Melissa Kite. "Poll Reveals 40pc of Muslims Want Sharia Law in UK." *Telegraph* of London, February 19, 2006, 1.

Hewer, C T R., ed. *Understanding Islam: An Introduction.* Minneapolis: Fortress Press, 2006.

Heymann, Philip B. *Terrorism and America: A Commonsense Strategy for a Democratic Society.* Cambridge, Mass.: MIT Press, 2000.

Higgins, Andrew, and Christopher Cooper. "Cloak and Dagger: A CIA-Backed Team Used Brutal Means to Crack Terror Cell." *Wall Street Journal,* November 20, 2001, A1.

Higham, Scott, and Robert O'Harrow Jr. "Contracting Rush for Security Led to Waste, Abuse." *Washington Post,* May 22, 2005, A1.

Hill, Eleanor. "Joint Inquiry Staff Statement." Statement before the Joint 9/11 Committee of the House Permanent Select Committee on Intelligence and the Senate Select Committee on Intelligence, October 8, 2002.

Hoffman, Bruce. "All You Need Is Love," *Atlantic Monthly,* December 2001, 30–41.

———. *Inside Terrorism.* New York: Columbia University Press, 1999.

———. "The Logic of Suicide Terrorism." *Atlantic,* June 2003.

———. "Rethinking Terrorism and Counterterrorism Since 9/11." *Studies in Conflict & Terrorism* 25 (2002): 304.

Holbrooke, Richard. "Get the Message Out." *Washington Post,* October 28, 2001, B7.

Home Office, U.K. "Summary." Report on Relations with the Muslim Community, May 10, 2004, 1.

Homeland security planning scenarios, available at http://www.global security.org/security/ops/.

Howard, Russell D., and Reid L. Sawyer, eds. *Terrorism and Counter-terrorism: Understanding the New Security Environment.* Guilford, Conn.: McGraw-Hill, 2002.

Hroub, Khaled. "Hamas after Shaykh Yasin and Rantisi." *Journal of Palestine Studies* 33, no. 4 (Summer 2004): 33.

Husayn, Fu'ad. "Al-Zarqawi: The Second Generation of Al-Qa'ida." *Al-Quds Al-'Arabi,* June 8, 2005.

Hutcheson, Ron, and Jonathan S. Landay. "Bush Plan Would Close Military Bases Overseas." *Detroit Free Press,* August 17, 2004. http://www.freep.com/news/nw/troops17e_20040817.htm.

Ibrahim, Saad Eddin. "Anatomy of Egypt's Militant Islamic Groups: Methodological Note and Preliminary Findings." *International Journal of Middle East Studies* 12 (1980): 434.

Intelligence and Security Committee. "Report into the London Terrorist Attacks on 7 July 2005," May 2006, 16.

International Crisis Group. "In Their Own Words: Reading the Iraqi Insurgency." *Middle East Report* 50 (February 15, 2006): i.

———. "Indonesia Backgrounder: Why Salafism and Terrorism Mostly Don't Mix." *Asia Report* 83, September 13, 2004, 1.

———. "Saudi Arabia Backgrounder: Who Are the Islamists?" *Middle East Report* 31, September 21, 2004, 2.

"International Student Enrollment Growth Slows in 2002/2003." Institute of International Education (IIE) press release, November 3, 2003. http://opendoors.iienetwork.org/?p=36523.

Isikoff, Michael, and Mark Hosenball. "Wrong Priorities?" *Newsweek,* September 7, 2005. Available at http://www.msnbc.msn.com/id/9246373/site/newsweek/fromRL.1/.

"Islamic Sharia Law." *Sunday Times* of London, February 19, 2006, 13.

"Israel Identifies New Hamas Leader." *China Daily,* April 27, 2004. http://www2.chinadaily.com.cn/english/doc/2004–04/27/content _326647.htm.

Israeli, Raphael. "Western Democracies and Islamic Fundamentalist Violence." *Journal of Terrorism and Political Violence* (January 2001): 160–173.

Jaber, Hala. *Hezbollah: Born with a Vengeance.* New York: Columbia University Press, 1997.

Jamieson, Alison. "Entry, Discipline, and Exit in the Italian Red Brigades," *Terrorism and Political Violence* 2, no. 1 (Spring 1990): 9.

Johnson, Stephen, and Helle Dale. "How to Reinvigorate U.S. Public Diplomacy." Heritage Foundation backgrounder, April 23, 2003.

Johnson, Stephen, Helle C. Dale, and Patrick Cronin. "Strengthening U.S. Public Diplomacy Requires Organization, Coordination, and Strategy." Heritage Foundation backgrounder, August 5, 2005.

Jones, Clive. "Israeli Counter-Insurgency Strategy and the War in South Lebanon 1985–1997." *Small Wars & Insurgencies* 8 (Winter 1997): 82–108.

Jones, Toby Craig. "The Clerics, the Sahwa, and the Saudi State." *Strategic Insights* 4, no. 3 (March 2005). Electronic version.

Kaiser Commission on Medicaid and the Uninsured. "The Costs of Not Covering the Uninsured." June 2003. http://www.kff.org/uninsured/upload/Cost-of-Not-Covering-the-Uninsured-Project-Highlights.pdf.

Kassimeris, George. *Europe's Last Red Terrorists.* London: C. Hurst, 2000.

Kayyali, Randa. "The People Perceived as a Threat to Security: Arab Americans since September 11." Migration Information Source, July 1, 2006. Available at http://www.migrationinformation.org/Feature/print/cfm?ID=409.

Kendrick, Alice, and Jami A. Fullerton. "Advertising as Public Diplomacy: Attitude Change among International Audiences." *Journal of Advertising Research* (September 2004): 297–311.

Kepel, Gilles. *Jihad: The Trail of Political Islam.* Cambridge, Mass.: Harvard University Press, 2002.

———. *The War for Muslim Minds: Islam and the West.* Cambridge, Mass.: Harvard University Press, 2004.

Khatchadourian, Raffi. "Pursuing Terrorists in the Great Desert." *Village Voice,* January 31, 2006.

Kramer, Mark. "The Perils of Counterinsurgency: Russia's War in Chechnya." *International Security* 29, no. 3 (Winter 2004–2005): 5–63.

Krepinevich, Andrew. "The Thin Green Line." Center for Strategic and Budgetary Assessments (August 14, 2004), 11.

Krikorian, Greg, and Solomon Moore. "Probe Elicits Disbelief at Mosque." *Los Angeles Times,* August 18, 2001, B1.

"Letter from al-Zawahiri to al-Zarqawi." October 11, 2005. http://www.dni.gov/letter_in_english.pdf.

Letzing, John. "Cross-Border Security: The Visa Loophole." Frontline: Al-Qa'ida's New Front, January 25, 2005. http://www.pbs.org/wgbh/pages/frontline/shows/front/special/visa.html.

Lieutenant General David Barno Briefing. "Combined Forces Command—Afghanistan," March 15, 2006, 7.

Lipton, Eric. "U.S. to Spend Billions More to Alter Security Systems." *New York Times*, May 7, 2005.

Lobe, Jim. "Muslim Support for the 'War on Terror' Plummets." Inter Press Service News Agency, October 20, 2003.

Luft, Gal. "The Logic of Israel's Targeted Killing." *Middle East Quarterly* 10, no. 1 (Winter 2003). http://www.meforum.org/article/515.

Mackey, Chris, and Greg Miller. *The Interrogators*. Boston: Little, Brown, 2004.

Maley, William. *The Afghanistan Wars*. New York: Palgrave Macmillan, 2002.

"Malnutrition Rising among Iraq's Children." Associated Press, November 22, 2004.

Manningham-Butler, Eliza. "The International Terrorist Threat to the U.K." Speech given at Queen Mary's College, November 9, 2006. Text available at http://www.mi5.gov.uk/output/Page568.html#.

Margolick, David. "Terrorism: Israel's Payback Principle." *Vanity Fair*, January 1, 2003.

McCormick, G. H., and G. Owen. "Security and Coordination in a Clandestine Organization." *Mathematical and Computer Modeling* 31: 175–192.

McDermott, Terry, Josh Meyer, and Patrick McDonnell. "The Plots and Designs of Al Qaeda's Engineer." *Los Angeles Times*, December 22, 2002. Available at http://www.latimes.com/news/nation world/nation/la-fg-khalid-arch,1,4896108.story.

McLean, Renwick. "20 Arrested as Spain Breaks Militant Network." *New York Times*, January 11, 2006, A12.

Memorial Institute for the Preservation of Terrorism (MIPT) Terrorism Knowledge Base. "Group Profile: Revolutionary Organization 17 November." http://www.tkb.org/Group.jsp?groupID=101.

Moore, Molly. "Israel's Lethal Weapon of Choice." *Washington Post*, June 29, 2003.

"MPAC Special Report: Religion & Identity of Muslim American Youth Post-London Attacks." Muslim Public Affairs Council, 2005.

Mueller, John. "The Banality of 'Ethnic War.'" *International Security* 25, no. 1 (Summer 2000): 42–70.

———. "Six Rather Unusual Propositions about Terrorism." *Terrorism and Political Violence* 17 (2005): 487.

Mueller, Robert S. III. Testimony before U.S. Senate Committee on Intelligence, February 16, 2005.

National Academy of Public Administration. "Transforming the FBI: Roadmap to an Effective Human Capital Program," September 2005.

National Commission on Terrorist Attacks upon the United States. "Monograph on Terrorist Financing," 28.

———. *The 9/11 Commission Report*. New York: W. W. Norton, 2004.

Negroponte, John. "Annual Threat Assessment of the Director of National Intelligence." Testimony before the U.S. Senate Select Committee on Intelligence, February 2, 2006. http://intelligence .senate.gov/0602hrg/060202/negroponte.pdf.

O'Hanlon, Michael E. "A Matter of Force—and Fairness." *Washington Post*, October 1, 2004.

O'Neill, Bard E. *Insurgency and Terrorism: Inside Modern Revolutionary Warfare*. Dulles, Va.: Brassey's, 1990.

On Point. "Military Overstretch." September 30, 2004. http://www .onpointradio.org/shows/2004/09/20040930_a_main.asp.

Online NewsHour. "Bin Laden Video Tape," December 13, 2001. http:// www.pbs.org/newshour/terrorism/international/video_12-13 .html.

Orr, Steve. "No Change in Airport Screening." *Rochester Democrat & Chronicle*, November 27, 2004.

Overy, R. J. *The Origins of the Second World War*. New York: Longman, 1998.

Paz, Reuven. "Arab Volunteers Killed in Iraq: An Analysis." Project for the Research of Islamist Movements Occasional Papers 3, no. 1 (March 2005).

"Pentagon Expands Middle East Outposts." Associated Press, September 23, 2004. http://www.military.com/NewsContent/0,13319,FL_out posts_092304,00.html.

Pepper, Tara, and Mark Hosenball. "A Deadly Puzzle." *Newsweek*, July 25, 2005.

Pew Charitable Trust. "A Year after Iraq War Mistrust of America in Europe Ever Higher, Muslim Anger Persists," March 16, 2004.

Pew Global Attitudes Project. "The Great Divide: How Westerners and Muslims View Each Other," June 22, 2006.

———. "Support for Terror Wanes among Muslim Publics." July 14, 2005. http://pewglobal.org/reports/display.php=ReportID=248.

———. "View of a Changing World." June 2003. http://www.pewtrusts .com/pdf/vf_pew_research_global_attitudes_0603.pdf.

Pew Research Center for the People and the Press. "Additional Findings and Analysis." http://people-press.org/reports/display.php3 ?PageID=796.

———. "A Year after Iraq War Mistrust of America in Europe Ever Higher, Muslim Anger Persists." March 16, 2004. http://people -press.org/reports/display.php3?ReportID=206.

Pierre, Andrew J. *Coalitions: Building and Maintenance.* Washington, D.C.: Georgetown University Press, 2002.

Pillar, Paul R. "Counterterrorism after Al-Qa'ida." *Washington Quarterly* 27, no. 3 (Summer 2004): 106.

———. *Terrorism and U.S. Foreign Policy.* Washington, D.C.: Brookings, 2004.

Police Forums and Law Enforcement Forums. "Israeli Targeted Killings in War on Terror." http://forums.officer.com/forums/showthread .php?t=31719.

Pollack, Kenneth. *Arabs at War.* Lincoln: University of Nebraska Press, 2002.

Posen, Barry R. "Exit Strategy." *Boston Review* (January–February 2006). Available at http://bostonreview.net/BR31.1/posen.html.

———. "The Struggle against Terrorism: Grand Strategy, Strategy, and Tactics." *International Security* 26, no. 3 (Winter 2001): 39–55.

Powell, Bill. "Generation Jihad." *Time,* September 26, 2005.

Priest, Dana. "CIA's Assurances on Transferred Suspects Doubted." *Washington Post,* March 17, 2005, A1.

———. "Foreign Network at Front of CIA's Terror Fight: Joint Facilities in Two Dozen Countries Account for Bulk of Agency's Post-9/11 Successes." *Washington Post,* November 18, 2005, A1.

———. "Help from France Key in Covert Operations: Paris's 'Alliance Base' Targets Terrorists." *Washington Post,* July 3, 2005, A1.

Priest, Dana, and Barton Gellman. "U.S. Decries Abuse but Defends Interrogations." *Washington Post,* December 26, 2002, A1.

Priest, Dana, and Joe Stephens. "Secret World of U.S. Interrogation." *Washington Post,* May 11, 2004, A1.

Project MAPS: Muslims in the American Public Square. "American Muslim Poll," November–December 2001. Poll available at http:// www.projectmaps.com.

Purdum, Todd. "How to Declare Victory." *New York Times,* October 14, 2001, 3.

Purdy, Matthew, and Lowell Bergman. "Where the Trail Led: Inside the Lackawanna Terror Case." *New York Times,* October 12, 2003: A1.

Raphaeli, Nimrod. "Ayman Muhammad Rabi' Al-Zawahiri: The Making of an Arch-Terrorist." *Terrorism and Political Violence* 14, no. 4 (Winter 2002): 8.

Rapoport, David C. "Terrorism." In Mary Hawkesworth and Maurice Kogan, eds., *Routledge Encyclopedia of Government and Politics.* Vol. 2. London: Routledge, 1992.

Rashbaum, William K. "Terror Case May Offer Clues into Police Use of Informants." *New York Times,* April 24, 2006, B1.

Reinares, Fernando. "Democratic Regimes, Internal Security Policy, and the Threat of Terrorism." *Australian Journal of Politics and History* 44, no. 3 (1998): 367.

Report of the Accountability Review Boards on the Embassy Bombings in Nairobi and Dar es Salaam. January 1999.

Report of the Advisory Group on Public Diplomacy for the Arab and Muslim World. "Changing Minds, Winning Peace: A New Strategic Direction for U.S. Public Diplomacy in the Arab and Muslim World." October 1, 2003, 8.

Risen, James, and David Johnston. "Qaeda Aide Slipped Away Long before Sept. 11 Attack." *New York Times,* March 8, 2003, A12.

Rosenau, William. "The Eisenhower Administration, U.S. Foreign Internal Security Assistance, and the Struggle for the Developing World, 1954–1961." *Low Intensity Conflict & Law Enforcement* 10, no. 3 (Autumn 2001): 1–32.

Roy, Sara. "Hamas and the Transformation of Political Islam in Palestine." *Current History* (January 2003): 17.

Ruthven, Malise. *A Fury for God: The Islamist Attack on America.* New York: Granta Books, 2002.

Saban Center for Middle East Policy Symposium. "How to Win the War against Terrorism." Washington, D.C.: Brookings Institution, September 22, 2005. http://www.brookings.edu/fp/saban/events/20050922.htm.

Sagan, Scott. "The Problem of Redundancy Problem: Why More Nuclear Security Forces May Produce Less Nuclear Security." *Risk Analysis* 24, no. 4 (2004): 935–946.

Sageman, Marc. *Understanding Terror Networks.* Philadelphia: University of Pennsylvania Press, 2004.

"Saudi Columnist: Terrorists Mistreat Their Wives and Children." Middle East Media Research Institute Special Dispatch Series 935, July 15, 2005.

Scheuer, Michael. *Imperial Hubris: Why the West Is Losing the War on Terror.* Washington, D.C.: Potomac Books, 2004.

Schmitt, Eric. "Guard Reports Serious Drop in Enlistment." *New York Times,* December 17, 2004, A32.

Schmitt, Eric, and Thom Shanker. "U.S. Pushes upward Its Estimate of Rebels in Iraq." *New York Times,* October 22, 2004, A1.

Schuster, Henry. "Poll of Saudis Shows Wide Support for bin Laden's Views." CNN.com. http://www.cnn.com/2004/WORLD/meast/06/08/poll.binladen.

Secretary of State Colin L. Powell. Statement to the House of Representatives Committee on International Relations, February 12, 2003. http://wwwc.house.gov/international_relations/108/powe0212.htm.

Secretary of State Condoleezza Rice. "Transformational Diplomacy." Speech at Georgetown University, Washington, D.C., January 18, 2006. http://www.state.gov/secretary/rm/2006/59306.htm.

Sennott, Charles M. "Europe's Terror Fight Quiet, Unrelenting." *Boston Globe,* September 26, 2004, A1.

Shane, Scott. "Official Reveals Budget for U.S. Intelligence." *New York Times,* November 8, 2005, A18.

Shapiro, Jeremy. "What Democratic Response to a Terrorist Attack?" Washington, D.C. (unpublished paper, 2006): 2.

Shapiro, Jeremy, and Daniel Byman. "Bridging the Transatlantic Counterterrorism Gap." *Washington Quarterly* (Autumn 2006): 33–50.

Shapiro, Jeremy, and Benedicte Suzan. "The French Experience of Counter-terrorism." *Survival* 45, no. 1 (Spring 2003): 81.

Sheehan, Michael A. "Walking the Terror Beat." *New York Times,* September 10, 2006, A10.

Shulsky, Abram, and Gary Schmitt. *Silent Warfare: Understanding the World of Intelligence.* Washington, D.C.: Potomac Books, 2002.

Sims, Jennifer. "Foreign Intelligence Liaison—Devils, Deals, and Details." *International Journal of Intelligence and Counterintelligence* 19, no. 2 (Summer 2006): 195–217.

Sivak, Michael, and Michael J. Flannagan. "Flying and Driving after the September 11 Attacks." *American Scientist* 91 (2003): 8.

Smith, Craig S. "U.S. Training African Forces to Uproot Terrorists." *New York Times,* May 11, 2004, A1.

Snyder, Glenn H. *Alliance Politics.* Ithaca, N.Y.: Cornell University Press, 1997.

Stevenson, David. *Cataclysm: The First World War as Political Tragedy.* New York: Basic Books, 2004.

Stevenson, Jonathan. "Northern Ireland: Treating Terrorists as Statesmen." *Foreign Policy* 105 (Winter 1996–1997). Electronic version.

"Substitution for the Testimony of Khalid Sheikh Mohammed." Defendant's Exhibit 941, *U.S. v. Moussaoui,* p. 52. Text available at http://en.wikisource.org/wiki/Substitution_for_the_Testimony_of_KSM.

Takeyh, Ray. "Let Democracy Derail Radicalism." *Baltimore Sun,* March 21, 2005.

Taylor, Terence. "United Kingdom." In Yonah Alexander, ed., *Combating Terrorism: Strategies of Ten Countries.* Ann Arbor: University of Michigan Press, 2002, 196.

Tenet, George. "Worldwide Threat 2001: National Security in a Changing World." Testimony before U.S. Senate Select Committee on Intelligence, February 7, 2001.

———. "Worldwide Threats." Testimony before U.S. Senate Select Committee on Intelligence, February 11, 2003.

———. "The Worldwide Threat 2004: Challenges in a Changing Global Context." Testimony before the U.S. Senate Armed Services Committee, March 9, 2004.

U.S. Army. "Counterinsurgency Operations." FMI 3-07.22 (October 2004), secs. 1–10.

U.S. Department of Defense, Office of the Under Secretary for Acquisition, Technology, and Logistics. Report of the Defense Science Board Task Force on Managed Information Dissemination. October 2001, 1.

U.S. Department of Justice. "Federal Bureau of Investigation's Foreign Language Translation Program Follow-up." Audit Report 5-33, July 2005. http://www.usdoj.gov/oig/reports/FBI/a0533/final.pdf.

U.S. Department of State. "Country Reports on Terrorism, 2004," April 2005, 7.

———. *Patterns of Global Terrorism 2003,* April 2004, 147–148.

U.S. Government Accountability Office. "Afghanistan Security: Efforts to Establish Army and Police Have Made Progress, but Future Plans Need to Be Better Defined," June 2005, 1.

United Nations. "Arab Human Development Report 2003: Building a Knowledge Society," 2003.

Van Natta, Don Jr. "Al Qaeda Hobbled by Latest Arrest, U.S. Says." *New York Times,* March 3, 2003, A1.

Van Natta, Don Jr., and Desmond Butler. "How Tiny Swiss Cellphone Chips Helped Track Global Terror Web." *New York Times,* March 4, 2004, A1.

Van Natta, Don Jr., and Timothy O'Brien. "Saudis Promising Action on Terror." *New York Times,* September 13, 2003, A1.

Walt, Stephen M. "Beyond bin Laden: Reshaping U.S. Foreign Policy." *International Security* 26, no. 3 (Winter 2001): 56–78.

———. "Why Alliances Endure or Collapse." *Survival* 39, no. 1 (Spring 1997): 156–179.

Wanandi, Jusuf. "A Global Coalition against International Terrorism." *International Security* 26, no. 4 (Spring 2002): 187.

Weinberg, Leonard B., and William L. Eubank. "Terrorism and Democracy: Perpetrators and Victims." *Terrorism and Political Violence* 13, no. 1 (Spring 2001): 158.

Weisman, Steven. "Allies Resisting as U.S. Pushes Terror Label for Hezbollah." *New York Times*, February 17, 2005, A1.

———. "2006 National Strategy for Combating Terror, Fighting a Global War on Terror." http://www.whitehouse.gov/nsc/nsct/2006/nsct2006.pdf.

———. "President Addresses Nation, Discusses Iraq, War on Terror." President George W. Bush, speech at Fort Bragg, June 28, 2005. http://www.whitehouse.gov/news/releases/2005/06/20050628-7.html.

———. "President Discusses War on Terror." President George W. Bush, speech at National Defense University, March 8, 2005. http://www.whitehouse.gov/news/releases/2005/03/20050308-3.html.

———. "President Discusses War on Terror at National Endowment for Democracy." President George W. Bush, speech before National Endowment for Democracy, October 5, 2005. http://www.whitehouse.gov/news/releases/2005/10/20051006-3.html.

White House. "Detention of Khalid Shaikh Mohammed." Statement by Press Secretary, March 1, 2003.

White, Josh, and Ann Scott Tyson. "Rumsfeld Offers Strategies for Current War." *Washington Post*, February 3, 2006, A8.

Whitlock, Craig. "French Push Limits in Fight on Terrorism." *Washington Post*, November 1, 2004, A1.

Wiktorowicz, Quintan. "Anatomy of the Salafi Movement." *Studies in Conflict & Terrorism* 29 (2006): 207–239.

Wilkinson, Paul. *Terrorism versus Democracy.* New York: Routledge, 2006.

Wilshere, Thomas. Statement before U.S. Senate Foreign Relations Committee, December 18, 2001, 7.

Wilson, Scott. "Fear Hamstrings Quest for Intelligence in N. Iraq." *Washington Post*, December 11, 2004, A19.

Winnett, Robert, and David Leppard. "Leaked No 10 Dossier Reveals Al-Qaeda's British Recruits." *Sunday Times* of London, July 10, 2005.

World Islamic Front Statement, February 23, 1998. http://www.fas.org/
irp/world/para/docs/980223-fatwa.htm.

Wright, Lawrence. Unpublished paper. 2006.

———. "The Man behind Bin Laden." *New Yorker,* September 16,
2002, 56. http://www.newyorker.com.

Wright, Robin. "Support for Bin Laden, Violence Down among
Muslims, Poll Says." *Washington Post,* July 15, 2005, A13.

Index